D1285162

ACKNOWLEDGEMENTS

Hot Lead All Reviews Special published May 2020

Edited by Justin Marriott
thepaperbackfanatic@sky.com

Proofread by Jim O'Brien

Cover design by Bill Cunningham

Special thanks to Steve Myall for scans

Contributors full list on page 161 - 167

Dedicated to Paul Bishop, who lit the fuse

To the memory of George G Gilman - as I was finishing this publication I was informed of the death of Terry Harknett, who wrote westerns as George Gilman. This publication wouldn't exist had it not been for Terry. Terry had actually died in January 2019, but this was not widely known as he was a widower with no children and living in a care home. I think anyone who has read a western paperback published after the debut of Terry's Edge series in the early 70s, has somehow been touched by his influence.

FOREWORD

I grew up in the west. Well, West Philadelphia anyway.

But, in the world of my imagination, I rode the range with my trusty rifle on my loyal cayuse. I wasn't alone. When I was a kid, we were awash in westerns on television, at the movies and in the toy aisle. Every kid had a cowboy hat and a six-shooter. Every single one, pardner. You had to stand in line to ride the horse in front of the drug store. And John Wayne was the paragon of manly virtue to us all.

Yet, my bona fides as a buckaroo went deeper than that. My dad grew up in the west too. Okay, it was West Virginia. But he was surrounded by cowboys too when he was a young 'un. Guys like Bob Steele and William Boyd. These inspired him to practice with a lariat and he wound up actually learning from a performing roper how to toss a lasso with accuracy and perform complex tricks. He was skilled enough to be sent by his Army Air Force unit to the home of an English lord who wished to meet a real American cowboy. This furlough to spend time with nobility earned my dad the nickname "Duke" which stuck with him all his life.

In addition to throwing a mean lasso, Dad was also a self-taught gunsmith and specialized in making replacement parts for vintage weapons. My dad could tool new parts indistinguishable from the originals or refurbish an existing part. I lost count of how many times I saw him sweating a new firing pin in place.

He was much sought after by hardcore collectors who needed new hammers, springs or triggers made for their valuable museum pieces. That meant I got to see and handle actual period Colts, Winchesters, Henrys and Remingtons in my dad's workshop and out on the shooting range. Unknown to him, I used to stand on my parents' bed and practice fast draws and spins with his matched pair of Bisley Colts. At least I thought ahead to stand on a soft surface in case I dropped one. You might think a ten-year-old playing Johnny Ringo with a pair of loaded .44s on an unstable surface could have turned into an Afterschool Special. I guess someone up there liked me.

More influential than any of these things was the collection of western books my dad had down in the basement. There was a complete collection of Zane Grey in hardcover along with piles of paperbacks that I would root through when I wasn't sneaking peeks at his Playboys. He always had a paperback in the car or on the nightstand and would pick up a stack at the news agency before we went on vacations. The garish covers of tough hombres stalking down dusty streets, badass outlaws blazing away while clutching some babe in a torn blouse, cavalry troopers hunkered down behind their arrow-studded dead horse were irresistible draws to me.

Authors like Clifton Adams, Ernest Haycox, Luke Short, Giles A. Lutz and, of course Louis L'Amour and loads more than I can remember. Dad would try a new author and, if the new guy met the standard, he'd pick up a bunch more. Once I was old enough, I started in on the collection myself and found my own favourites. We both liked Gordon D. Shirreffs quite a lot as well as Clair Huffaker. We both grew tired of L'Amour after a while and we both gave the Piccadilly westerns a try, not knowing their provenance, but they really didn't catch on with us.

And it was these novels that really solidified and refined my appreciation of the western genre. I became fascinated with the language of the west. By virtue of the details that were included in these stories, I was drawn into the lives of the characters in a way that movies and television could never do. These authors worked hard to make the men, women, animals and locales come to life in their stories while creating the purest form of escapist fiction. While the fictional west is pure fantasy for the most part, the authentic details are important to making these stories work. Terminology and the uses of saddlery, weapons, wagons, mining, wrangling and hunting all need to be written with a degree of authority.

Like most urban cowboys, this was the stuff, the tools, I would need if I ever wanted to write in my favourite genre. Sure, I wrote a bunch of western comics books. But comics are broad. They're pastiches. I only needed enough research to fake it and hope my artist knew how to draw a horse or a Stetson. You'd be surprised how few artists can draw a convincing hat.

But to write western prose I was up against a lot of guys who'd actually done the stuff they write about and been to the places where they set their stories. The only working cowboy I ever met was an English guy who lived on a Wyoming ranch during a gap year. As mentioned above, I had first-hand experience with the weapons of the west. And I did own and ride and maintain a quarter horse for a few years. But, for the rest, I had to rely on the knowledge learned, gleaned, absorbed and, yeah, lifted from the hundreds of western paperbacks borrowed from my father's basement hoard.

And, like anyone else reading this, as well as the writers of the review here, I still haunt dusty old used bookstores looking either for books I've never read or to re-acquaint myself with an old friend. And, like you, I'll be devouring this book from cover-to-cover to read the words of other western writers, looking to learn from their critiques as well as learning about titles I may never have read.

Chuck Dixon
West Florida
11/11/2019

INTRODUCTION

Welcome to the first All Reviews Special of **Hot Lead**, which contains reviews of 215+ western books and comics from 1927 right up to the modern day.

When I first embarked upon this special, I had a vision of a publication that would be eclectic, irreverent yet informative, and showcased a diversity of voices. Thanks to the enthusiasm, knowledge and craft of the reviewers, I am confident the final product goes a long way to delivering that vision. They have all contributed their time for no financial reward, so please join me in thanking them for their efforts.

However, I didn't have any vision as to how I would structure the publication, other than I wanted it to be something that readers could pick up at any time and dip in and out of at will, rather than a traditional book that needed to be read cover to cover in page order. I held romantic visions of producing a trusted companion for the discerning western reader, a volume that would become dog-eared and tattered due to being regularly pulled down from a shelf in search of a new recommendation for a new book or author.

But as the reviews piled up, it became obvious to me that their diversity tracked the entire history of the western in paperback, and that by running the reviews in order of their subject's original publication, they formed a much larger and chronological patchwork of the western genre's development. So although this zine was never intended to be a history of the genre, it has by default gone some way to becoming one.

I have included reviews of some more outré examples of the genre – there are four reviews involving dinosaurs – due to my own sense of mischief but also as a riposte to close-minded readers who dismiss the western without appreciating its wonderful diversity and eternal themes.

I haven't counted up, but I imagine that the positive reviews in these pages hugely outnumber the negative ones. I discussed this with one of the contributors and his well-made response was that he wanted to showcase some of the best examples of the genre and chose accordingly. And generally speaking, that was a feeling that shone though in most of the multiple contributor's words, an enthusiasm for the genre and the opportunity to share it.

This is currently a one-off but I know that I have enjoyed working on it immensely and I think enough of the contributors feel the same way to make it very possible to turn this into a yearly event. Please let us know through your reviews on Amazon and Good Reads and comments on Social Media and maybe we'll saddle up and ride out again in 2021 (I managed to hold off on the clichés 'til the final line...).

Justin Marriott
West England
25/4/2020

CONTENTS

22

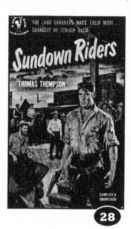

28

31

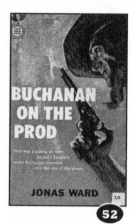

52

1980- 1989

1990+

THE PIONEERS

Paul Bishop on his top ten western authors.

The pioneers whose trail-blazing works both define and transcend the genre.

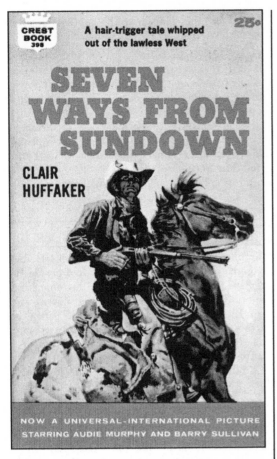

CREST
BOOK
398

A hair-trigger tale whipped
out of the lawless West

25¢

SEVEN
WAYS FROM
SUNDOWN

CLAIR
HUFFAKER

NOW A UNIVERSAL-INTERNATIONAL PICTURE
STARRING AUDIE MURPHY AND BARRY SULLIVAN

As Huffaker found success as a screenwriter in Hollywood, often adapting his own books for film or TV episodes, his home in Los Angeles became a gathering place for actors, stuntmen, directors and writers, all of whom could regularly be found there shooting pool, playing poker and exchanging tall tales.

The words of Huffaker's daughter, Samantha Kirkeby, perhaps best explain the emotional impact of his most popular western novel, **The Cowboy and the Cossack**, 'As I stumbled into middle age, my father's ability to touch people was opened up to me in a dramatic and unexpected way. I found myself reading reviews from readers all over the world. Families in Russia who considered their page worn copy of **The Cowboy and the Cossack** a family treasure. A wife who read the book aloud to her husband when he was ill and bedridden.

An American soldier who brought me to tears when I read how **The Cowboy and the Cossack** was his favourite novel, and the very first thing he put into his backpack each time he left for duty. For over a decade, he carried the ragged paperback copy of **The Cowboy and the Cossack** he bought in a used book store to dozens of countries, reading and rereading it, passing it among his fellow soldiers to give them strength and inspiration, until the pages were frayed and worn.' **Paul Bishop**

CLAIR HUFFAKER

Clair Huffaker was a legendary Western novelist and screenwriter. His screenplays include **The Comancheros, Hellfighters,** and **The War Wagon**, which starred John Wayne. Huffaker's first novel, **Flaming Lance**, became the basis for the Elvis Presley film, **Flaming Star**. Huffaker also wrote for numerous TV Westerns, including **Bonanza, The Rifleman, The Virginian, Rawhide** and **Lawman**. He started his own film production company in 1969.

By the time Huffaker joined the Navy during World War II, he was an experienced cowboy, a champion boxer and a part-time smuggler. After the war, he attended Princeton and Columbia universities and the Sorbonne in Paris. He worked in Chicago as an assistant editor for **Time** magazine before turning to writing western fiction. In his fifties, Huffaker wrote a memoir titled **One Time I Saw Morning Come Home** in which he tries to come to grips with the fact his parents were just teenagers when they had him.

BEN HAAS

During the course of his career, Ben Haas wrote over one hundred novels under his own name, a dozen pseudonyms (including John Benteen) and a handful of publishers' house names. The uniting factor of this vast output was the highly readable, sheer storytelling force he brought to every page. Beginning his career writing paperback original westerns, Haas quickly developed the spare, fast-paced, muscular prose for which he became known. When Tower Books publisher Harry Shorten asked Haas to create an original western series, Haas responded by assaulting his typewriter and letting loose the taciturn, granite-hard Neal Fargo in a series of neo-westerns now considered classics of the genre.

Born Benjamin Leopold Haas in Charlotte, North Carolina in 1926, Haas stated he inherited his love of books during the depression when his father who would bid on hundreds of books at unclaimed freight auctions. After serving in the Philippines as an Army sergeant, Haas returned home taking on whatever work he

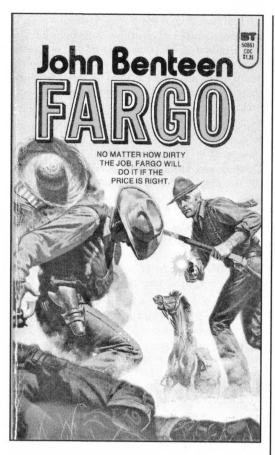

John Benteen

FARGO

NO MATTER HOW DIRTY THE JOB, FARGO WILL DO IT IF THE PRICE IS RIGHT.

could find to support his family while pursuing his dream to be a writer. In 1961, he submitted a manuscript to Beacon Books. It was accepted, with a request for more, and Haas became a full-time writer for the rest of his life. He wrote every day and every night, attempting to keep a regular output of at least 5,000 words a day. His son Joel later recalled, 'My Mom learned to go to sleep to the sound of a typewriter.'

Under the pseudonym John Benteen—named after one of Custer's cavalry officers—Haas wrote (or co-wrote with his son, Joel) twenty of the twenty-three **Fargo** adventures. The other three books (**Sierra Silver**, **Dynamite Fever** and **Gringo Guns**) are attributed to John W Hardin—a pseudonym taken from a real-life outlaw. While there are various provably incorrect theories, fiction scholar Lynn Munroe—the last word on all things related to Benteen/Haas—believes the man behind the mask of John W Hardin was most likely Norman Rubington, a prolific hack writer who also wrote an entry in Benteen's also-popular **Sundance** series. Common consensus is Haas based Fargo on the character portrayed by Lee Marvin in the 1966 movie **The Professionals**, which was based on the novel **A**

Mule for the Marquesa** by another popular western wordslinger, Frank O'Rourke.

Haas aspired to being a writer of significant books. He took to banging out paperback original genre fiction as a way to support his efforts to break into the mainstream. While he did get a number of more serious books published, they never attained the kind of success he was seeking. However, his highly regarded legacy prevails, as his paperback originals, especially both his **Fargo** and **Sundance** series, remain popular and sought after by collectors today. **Paul Bishop**

FRANK O'ROURKE

Frank O'Rourke was a prolific, versatile and popular writer of novels, westerns and mysteries. Early in his career, he specialized in young adult sports fiction, and wrote numerous short stories for the pulp magazines. During his career he wrote over sixty novels. In fact, he wrote as many as three books a year, forcing him to adapt a number of pseudonyms, including Patrick O'Malley, Frank O'Malley, and Kevin Connor.

Considered a master of the western caper, O'Rourke specialized in writing about groups of hard men hired to do impossible jobs on both sides of the law. A prime example of his talent is his novel **A Mule for the Marquesa**, which underwent a title change to **The Professionals** when it moved from page to screen. Movie tie-in versions and subsequent reprints all retained the punchier title. **The Professionals** begins as a straightforward Western actioner but packs a kick by the time the last page is turned. A group of Mexican revolutionaries have kidnapped Angelina Grant, the fiery Mexican wife of American cattle baron Augustus Grant. The arrogant, very rich, Grant recruits a band of five larger-than-life soldiers of fortune – led by ex-cavalryman turned arms dealer Henry Fardan – to cross the desert and rescue his wife. Each man is a hardened expert in logistics, combat, explosives or improvisation. The caper – five men against a hundred – is ingenious, exciting and vividly told.

A number of O'Rourke's other books, including **The Bravados** and **The Great Bank Robbery**, also made their way onto the silver screen. His Westerns **Concannon**, **Gun Hand** and **The Big Fifty** all received high praise – which O'Rourke was wont to eschew. Intensely independent, he rejected personal publicity claiming, 'I've always felt it was the writer's job to write the books and the publisher's to sell them. I believe in personal

privacy.' Of his traditional Westerns, **Warbonnet Law** contains his strongest character, range detective John McMahon. His most memorable character, however, is Andres '**Shotgun**' Arau who battles his way through the 1910 Mexican revolution in **The Shotgun Man**. His companions are a beautiful woman, a .97 shotgun, and a hidden fortune with killers on its trail. **Paul Bishop**

LOUIS L'AMOUR

Arguably the most popular western writer of all time, Louis L'Amour (1908-1988) is certainly the best-known western author outside of the western genre. He is quoted as having said, 'I write my books to be read aloud and I think of myself in that oral tradition.' There have been over three hundred million L'Amour books sold to date, with almost all of his westerns (which L'Amour preferred to call frontier stories) still in print today. He is the only novelist in history to

receive both the Presidential Medal of Freedom award and the Congressional Gold Medal.

At fifteen years old, he left school full of plans to work and travel. He also changed his surname from LaMoore to L'Amour, which was its original form. Referring to what followed as his yondering years, L'Amour's travels provided him with a vast experience, which he would later incorporate into his writings. He was an elephant handler in a circus, a fruit picker, a gold prospector, a longshoreman, a lumberjack and a miner. He skinned cattle in Texas, lived with bandits in Tibet and served on an East African schooner. He also boxed professionally – winning fifty-one out of fifty-nine matches. His extensive reading was as adventurous and varied as his travel and jobs as he sought out and collected rare books.

Having 'wanted to write from the time I could walk', L'Amour returned to his family home in the late 1930s to pursue his literary endeavours. However, after only small successes, WWII interrupted his plans and L'Amour was off to serve his country becoming an army tank officer in the transportation corps in 1942. After

earning an honourable discharge in 1946, L'Amour moved to Los Angeles where he battered relentlessly at the keys of his typewriter.

Success was an elusive maiden, but L'Amour refused to give up. He published numerous short stories, finding most of his sales in the western pulps. Eventually, he got a break when Clarence Mulford handpicked him to carry on the adventures of Mulford's famous character, Hopalong Cassidy. Needing the money, L'Amour accepted the work-for-hire contracts offered by Mulford's publisher, Bantam, eventually writing four Hopalong adventures under the pseudonym Tex Burns. Due to the work-for-hire nature of the contracts, it was 1991 before L'Amour was given public credit for writing the books.

In 1953, **Hondo,** L'Amour's first novel, was published by Fawcett Books. It was an instant bestseller, with John Wayne buying the movie rights and starring in the film. The success of **Hondo** wasn't lost on Bantam (who had published L'Amour's Hopalong tales). When Western stalwart Luke Short, who was under contract to Bantam for two books a year, could no longer keep up with the demand, Bantam desperately needed someone to fill the void. They turned to L'Amour to pick up the slack – and a legend was born, with L'Amour increasing the original contract for two books to three, a pace he maintained until the very end of his life. **Paul Bishop**

OWEN WISTER

Owen Wister's iconic novel **The Virginian** is often touted as the first true western. Originally published in 1902, **The Virginian** legitimized the western genre as literature and opened the **West of The Imagination** to the likes of Zane Grey, Louis L'Amour and every other western wordslinger who slapped typewriter or keyboard leather.

Born into a wealthy Eastern family, Wister was an unlikely champion for the western. He attended boarding schools in New England and Switzerland and went on to graduate from Harvard in 1882. After experiencing health issues, he spent the summer of 1885 in Wyoming. After recovering and returning to Harvard to graduate from Law school, he became part of a legal practice in Philadelphia for two years but continued to spend his summers in the West. When two of his western sketches were enthusiastically acceptance by **Harper's,** he left the law behind to devote himself to a literary career.

Drawing on the works he wrote for **Harper's,** Wister began to pull together other stories from his experiences into a book-length narrative. He created an unusual structure for the episodic nature of the chronicle by varying the titled chapters from third-person omniscient narration following the actions of key characters to the first-person narration of an unnamed tenderfoot. Coupled with Wister's personal vision of chivalric behaviour applied to the frontier, the result reads more like a cross between Sir Walter Scott and Jane Austen than the traditional western as we know it today.

However, **The Virginian** still managed to establish the cowboy as a folk hero as it follows the story of a hardened, unnamed, cowboy who nevertheless follows a credo of chivalry and honour in the uncivilized wilderness. This development of character exemplified the stoicism and principles leading to the romanticized public view of the West and its importance to the American cultural identity.

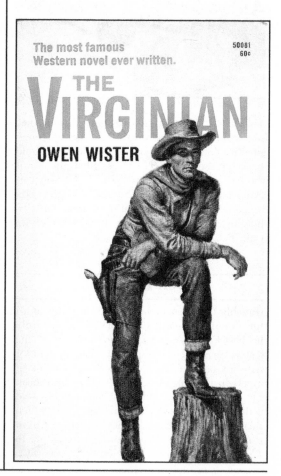

The most famous Western novel ever written.

50081
60c

THE VIRGINIAN

OWEN WISTER

The Virginian became an immediate best seller and made Wister a wealthy man well beyond his family's fortunes. **Paul Bishop**

Although none of his later work achieved that level of success, he continued to write short stories for magazines and to publish them in collections. **Members of the Family** came out in 1911, and **When West Was West** appeared in 1928. Each of these books has a story that may interest modern readers. 'The Gift Horse', in **Members of the Family**, takes place in the Wind River country, again with the tenderfoot narrator who is learning the ways of the country. 'At the Sign of the Last Chance', in **When West Was West**, again features the tenderfoot narrator, this time in later life when he meets up with some old cowboy pals who are seeing the end of an era. This was Wister's last western story, published ten years before his death.

Wister wrote many other books, notably a biography of Ulysses S Grant, a biography of George Washington, a novel set in South Carolina and an account of his lifelong friendship with Theodore Roosevelt. A bibliography published in 1958 in a book of his western journals and letters credits Wister for writing twenty-two books of fiction, history, political essays, biography, verse and drama. For people interested in Wyoming literature and history, however, his western fiction is most important.

And **The Virginian** has stayed popular since it was published. Wister himself wrote a stage adaptation of the novel in 1903, and the play toured for ten years. In the first century of its existence, the book sold more than two million copies, spawned five movies and a long-running 1960s TV series. **Paul Bishop**

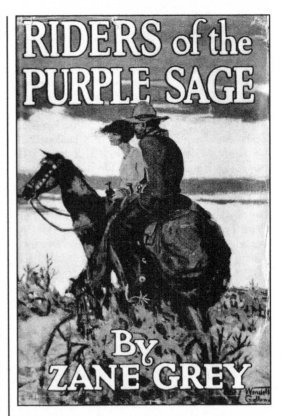

ZANE GREY

Before there were westerns, there was the western, a novel called **Riders of the Purple Sage** by Zane Grey, which is often credited for truly kick-starting the western as a genre. It is the story of Jane Withersteen, a Utah rancher whose livelihood is threatened by a proposed marriage she does not want, until a lone cowboy named Lassiter comes to town.

Born Pearl Zane Gray on January 31, 1872, in Zanesville, Ohio – a town founded by his mother's family – famed western novelist Zane Grey was an athlete and outdoorsman from an early age, with his main interests being fishing and baseball. He attended the University of Pennsylvania on a baseball scholarship, graduating with a degree in dentistry in 1896. He played minor-league baseball for a short period for a team in West Virginia. He started a dentistry practice in New York City, where he met the woman who would become his wife, Lina Roth, who got him to focus more on his writing. He would, however, periodically take fishing trips to the upper Delaware River in Lackawaxen in Pike County, Pennsylvania. In 1902 he became a published author by selling a story about fishing. Three years later he and Lisa married and moved to a farm in Lackawaxen.

Grey began to take an interest in the West after accompanying a friend to Arizona on a trapping expedition to capture mountain lions. He published his first western novel, **Spirit of the Border**, in 1906, and it quickly became a bestseller. In 1912 he published what is probably his best-known western novel, **Riders of the Purple Sage**, which was also a big seller. Aiming to get his books made into films, he formed his own motion-picture production company, which he later sold to Paramount Pictures executive Jesse Lasky. Paramount would produce a large number of westerns based on Grey's novels.

Unlike many successful authors, Grey didn't content himself with simply churning out more novels. He travelled all over the world and involved himself in a variety of endeavours, from working a mining claim on Oregon's Rogue River to fishing for sharks in New Zealand and writing books – both fiction and non-fiction – about his adventures. He had a special affinity for New Zealand and wrote many best-selling books about his fishing experiences there, which helped to make the country a mecca for deep-sea sport fishermen. Grey himself held many world records for catching big-game fish.

He died in 1939 and is buried at the Union Cemetery in Lackawaxen, Pennsylvania. The city is also the location of the Zane Grey Museum, which is administered by the National Park Service. **Paul Bishop**

LUKE SHORT

Frederick Dilley Glidden, aka Luke Short, was a prolific writer of western stories. Between 1934 and 1941, he sold twenty novels and more than a hundred short stories to the top western pulps of the day. When Glidden found publishing success as Luke Short, his wife thought she

would try writing fiction. Using a woman's point of view (an anomaly for the pulps), she began selling stories on a regular basis to **Rangeland Romances** for many years. Not to be left out of what was now a family cottage industry, Glidden's brother, Jonathan, began writing and selling western stories under the pen name Peter Dawson – a pseudonym based on his favourite brand of whisky. Peter Dawson would later become a house name owned by the publishing company. It would be used as a pseudonym by many different authors for the next two decades.

After World War II – where he served with the Office of Strategic Services (the precursor to the CIA) –Short hit a writing wall. He tried writing screenplays, but these were met with constant rejection. In response, he left writing behind and founded a mining company, but this endeavour quickly failed.

Furthermore, and much to Short's consternation, he became aware that his original stories were being plagiarized by others. This meant he was missing out on much needed compensation. He tried to rectify the situation but didn't have the financial means to support drawn-out civil prosecution. Instead, he changed his writing focus in an attempt to break out of the western genre but couldn't get a literary foothold elsewhere.

Finally, he secured a lucrative contract to produce two titles a year for Bantam Books and began to find a wider audience. His popular novel **Hardcase** is the perfect example of his pulse-pounding style of storytelling. Luke Short's best book provides a master-class in creating vibrant characters who embody the courage, toughness and loyalty of American frontiersmen. As a founding member of the Western Writers of America, Short often offered help and advice to many younger writers, including Brian Garfield – who would go on to become a best-selling Western (**Relentless**) and thriller (**Death Wish**) writer. Short's advice to Garfield is still relevant today and applicable to any genre – 'Take out all the western trappings. Your story should depend on characters and behaviour. If it still works after you get rid of the clichés, it's a story.'

However, despite the success Short was experiencing with Bantam, his early failures still preyed on him. A rapidly cascading mental deterioration dragged Short down into severe depression, which had a direct effect on curtailing his output. Short began repeatedly failing to meet extended and extended deadlines, eventually forcing Bantam to use a ghost-writer to complete Short's contract. Notwithstanding, the popularity of the original books Short wrote for Bantam, the ghost-written efforts didn't generate similar sales.

Bantam saw other publishers' western authors were continuing to be strong sellers. Wanting to retrieve their share of the paperback market, Bantam sought out Louis L'Amour—whose recently published first novel **Hondo**, had become a bestseller. Offering him the chance to take over from Short and deliver two paperback originals per year, was the break for which L'Amour had been waiting. It was an event heralding the start of a lifelong relationship. A more than prolific writer, L'Amour extended the two book a year contract into three books a year, a pace he maintained for the rest of his lauded career. **Paul Bishop**

FRANK GRUBER

Frank Gruber (February 2, 1904 – December 9, 1969) wrote short stories at such a rapid-fire pace he became known as one of the 'Kings of Pulp Fiction'. When the pulps died, Gruber made a quick transition to the burgeoning market of paperback originals writing dozens of novels – most of them westerns – for a hungry audience, along with many scripts for movies and television.

Born in Elmer, Minnesota, Gruber served his time in the army before looking to hone his literary skills. He took on jobs as a trade journal editor and correspondence schoolteacher before his first stories began to sell to the pulps. Married to Lois Mahood and with a young son, Gruber wrote furiously to keep his family above the poverty level. In doing so, he created many popular characters in his stories, including the rascal Johnny Fletcher and his sidekick, strongman Sam Gragg, and the better known **Simon Lash** series.

However, it was in the western genre where Gruber made his lasting mark. Many of his dozens of western stories and novels were snapped up for the movies. Seeing another potential source of writing income, Gruber successfully turned his talents into writing original screenplays for low budget westerns. A writing chameleon, Gruber would change directions again moving seamlessly into writing teleplays during the early years of television. All told, he cranked out over two hundred episodes (mostly all westerns) for a wide variety of shows. He would go on to create the series **Tales of Wells**

1198
BANTAM BOOKS
25¢

A STIRRING NOVEL OF THE 7th CAVALRY— AND ONE MAN'S FIGHT FOR REVENGE

BROKEN LANCE

Frank Gruber

COMPLETE AND UNABRIDGED

Fargo (1957), **The Texan** (1958), and **Shotgun Slade** (1959).

Gruber is also known for establishing a list of the seven basic plots of the western genre. He claimed good writers used strong dialogue and plot development to build these basic plots into believable stories

The Union Pacific Story: Centred around the construction of a railroad, a telegraph line or some other type of modern technology or transportation. Wagon train stories fall into this category.

The Ranch Story: Plots involving threats to the ranch from rustlers or large landowners attempting to force out the proper owners.

The Empire Story: Tales involving building a ranch empire or an oil empire from scratch—a classic rags-to-riches plot.

The Revenge Story: The plot often involves an elaborate chase and pursuit by a wronged individual, but it may also include elements of the classic mystery story.

The Cavalry & Indian Story: Taming the wilderness for white settlers.

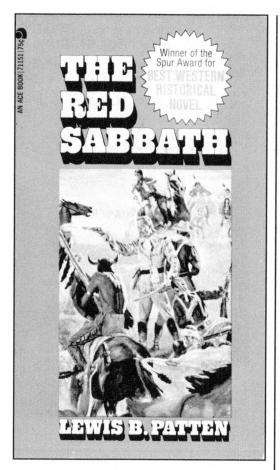

An Ace Book [71151] 75¢

Winner of the Spur Award for BEST WESTERN HISTORICAL NOVEL

THE RED SABBATH

LEWIS B. PATTEN

The Outlaw Story: Outlaw gangs dominate the action.

The Marshal Story: The lawman and his challenges drive the plot. **Paul Bishop**

LEWIS B PATTEN

The author of over one hundred westerns (in thirty years), Lewis Byford Patten was born in Denver, Colorado. He served in the US Navy, 1933-37. After, he worked professionally for the Colorado Department of Revenue, and as a rancher. He began writing full-time in 1949. Aside from his given name, Patten also wrote under the pseudonyms Lewis Ford, Lee Leighton and Joseph Wayne. He used the last two names when writing in collaboration with another prolific western writer, Wayne D Overholser. For his efforts, Patten received a Spur Award for Best Historical Novel for **The Red Sabbath** in 1968, and another Spur Award for Best Novel for **A Killing in Kiowa** in 1972.

While diverse in plotting, there is one theme running throughout Patten's many books – justice. While this plays out clearly in most of his works, **Lynching at Broken Butte** is surprisingly subtle in its handling of justice. In westerns, justice is most often delivered from the barrel of a gun – usually wielded by a loner in search of revenge, or a man who finds the spine to stand up to whatever villainy is in play. However, when the citizens of the small town of Broken Butte lynch two innocent men, they fall prey to their own guilt and begin to destroy themselves from the inside. Violence ensues and **Lynching at Broken Butte** becomes a study of justice served at the hands of the offenders themselves.

In 1971, a loose adaptation based on one of Patten's novels became the spaghetti western, **Don't Turn the Other Cheek!** (originally **Viva la Muerte...Tua!**). As many of the films in this western sub-genre were, the movie is a comedic romp with a stellar cast – Franco Nero, Eli Wallach, Lynn Redgrave. Set during the Mexican revolution, the story involves a Russian con man named Dmitri Vassilovich Orlowsky who is looking for the other half of a treasure map, which is tattooed on the buttock of imprisoned Mexican convict Max Lozoya. Young Irish reporter Mary O'Donnell wants to break the legendary El Salvador out of prison – hoping to motivate the Mexican people against the corrupt system and get a good news story. Knowing El Salvador is long dead, Orlowsky creates a ruse, convincing Mary the imprisoned Lozoya is El Salvador. Once free from prison, Lozoya wears the El Salvador name loosely, but trouble brews when he actually starts to care. All in all, the movie drifted far away from the novel's original content.

Throughout his books, Patten showed a disdain for Indian fighters and military officers – including Custer, who comes in for a drubbing in the Spur-winning **The Red Sabbath**. On the other hand, Patten's marshals and sheriffs are competent and willing to confront injustice or prejudice – usually against the plains Indians, with whom Patten clearly sympathized. **Paul Bishop**

ALAN LE MAY

Alan Le May's novel, **The Searchers**, has remained in the public consciousness since its publication in 1954 because of the seminal film for which it was the basis. However, beyond the gushing plaudits for the movie version of **The**

Searchers, the novel is an American masterpiece. Prior to writing the novel for which he is best remembered, Le May wrote many short stories, but found the pay minimal, even when published by top pulps like **Adventure** or slicks such as **Collier's**.

Believing there would be better money to be made in Hollywood, Le May turned his talents to becoming a journeyman screenwriter of B-westerns. While filming in the Texas panhandle, he was told the story of Cynthia Ann Parker, a nine-year-old girl abducted by Comanches from her prairie home in Texas. Spending years among the Comanche, Cynthia eventually married Chief Peta Nocona, with whom she raised three children – Prairie Flower, Pecos and Quanah. Her uncle, James Parker, spent years searching for her until she was finally found during a cavalry raid on her Comanche village in 1860. Things, however, did not turn out well, as after twenty-four years Cynthia did not want to leave the Comanches and her second family.

After having toiled in relative obscurity, producing forgettable novels and scripts, the undistinguished writer, was struck by literary lightening. Fascinated by the impact the kidnapping of the young girl during an Indian raid might have on her family, Le May began to research and write the story that would become his crowning achievement, **The Searchers**.

Based on the true story, the plot of **The Searchers** is deceptively simple – a quest to rescue Debbie, a young girl kidnapped by the Comanches who slaughtered her family during a raid on settlers in the Texas panhandle. However, beneath this unassuming premise lurk much darker, dangerous and vaguely psychosexual themes. John Ford's film version of **The Searchers** (1956) is considered one of the best westerns of all time. Cementing the film's reputation is a subtle, layered, career-making performance from John Wayne, which resonates even today. With its overtones of racism and hatred, it is much more complicated than any straightforward oater.

Continuing to write, Le May would later turn the premise of **The Searchers** on its head **in The Unforgiven** – a tale in which a child thought to be white was stolen as a baby during a retaliatory raid by white ranchers on a Kiowa village. **The Unforgiven** went on to become a successful – but troubled – film directed by John Huston and starring Burt Lancaster.

Le May also wrote the original source novel for the film **Along Came Jones** (1945) and a score of other screenplays – including High Lonesome (1950) – novels, and short stories. However, he never again reached the literary inspiration or success of **The Searchers**.   Paul Bishop

"These people had a kind of courage that may be the finest gift of man: the courage of those who simply keep on, and on, doing the next thing, far beyond all reasonable endurance, seldom thinking of themselves as martyred, and never thinking of themselves as brave. . . ."

1920- 1959

The dawn of the western paperback.

Future legends such as Frank Gruber, Luke Short and Max Brand make their way from the pulps to the new format of the paperback.

A new breed of paperback authors emerge with the likes of Donald Hamilton, Harry Whittington and Elmore Leonard, and a pioneering publisher in the form of Gold Medal.

The comic books join the posse, with a Scottish cowboy and by taking on Hitler.

THE WAR CHIEF
Edgar Rice Burroughs
1927

"It became its own story and I was fully absorbed in its complexities ..."

Edgar Rice Burroughs has created some of the finest adventuring heroes in all of literature, including household names like Tarzan, John Carter, David Innes and more. But many readers are surprised to learn ERB also wrote several fine westerns, including the 'Apache novels', which consist of only two books. As a young man, Burroughs enlisted in the 7th Cavalry and saw active service in southern Arizona, so he had some first-hand experience with the setting of the Apache Indians. First published in 1927, **The War Chief** is the first of the two books and is centred around the character Shoz-Dijiji or 'The Black Bear'.

The novel opens swiftly with a pioneer family getting ambushed and slaughtered by a band of Apaches. All, that is, except for a young baby boy who doesn't even cry when dangled by the ankle for all to see. Go-yat-thlay, the leader of the band of Apaches (and who will go down in history as 'Geronimo') thinks the young babe is unusually brave so decides to raise him as his adopted son. The first half of the book is a coming of age story as young Shoz-Dijiji learns the ways of the Apache, including hunting and tracking skills, extreme patience, religious beliefs and especially their hatred for the Pindah-lickoyee ('White Eyes'). He grows to young adulthood, becomes an accepted warrior and eventually War Chief, still operating under the ultimate leadership of Geronimo. A central theme of the book revolves around the Apache way of bringing maximum fierceness through mutilation of their foes even after death and the purposeful slaughter of women and children, all for the purpose of becoming so feared that the white men will leave. Shoz-Dijiji however sees no honour in doing this, choosing to define bravery by his actions against enemies that can fight back. The resulting strife combined with his white origins lead to all sorts of misadventure.

The novel is written in Burroughs's unmistakable style and includes quite a few of his typical plot devices. In fact, for the first couple of chapters I thought I was reading 'Tarzan among the Apaches' with very similar origin stories, (including earning his name by killing a black bear at the age of 10). Just substitute Apaches for the Great Apes. But soon, it became its own story and I was fully absorbed in its complexities. Reading through the various skirmishes from the Apache point-of-view was absolutely riveting.

Burroughs, I think was ahead of his time when it comes to describing the plight of these indigenous peoples and how both sides reacted to the other. Being written in the 1920s it is, of course, not entirely politically correct by today's standards. But if readers can adjust to complex names like Nakay-do-klunni, Be-don-ko-he and Chi-e-a-hen, this one is worth reading.

Benjamin Thomas

DESTRY RIDES AGAIN
Max Brand
1930

"Immensely satisfying fun and filled with plenty of very memorable characters..."

If your mental images of **Destry Rides Again** are of Jimmy Stewart whittling, or Marlene Dietrich seeing what the boys in the backroom are having – well, I can't blame you, because it's a great film. But the greatest piece of fiction in the film is that it claims to be based on a Max Brand novel of the same name.

It isn't, not even remotely. Brand's Destry is a cocky, boastful fighter whose greatest pleasure in life is beating people up to prove he's better than they are. Not surprisingly, several of his victims want revenge, and they get it by being on a biased jury that sends Destry to jail for ten years for a crime he didn't commit. Destry swears to get even, and when he's released from jail, there are twelve rather worried men who decide that their best move is to get Destry before he can get them. Their plans go a bit awry, however.

What this book is is a lovely, well-crafted tale of revenge. Destry moves through the opposition like a lion on the prowl, aided by a young, hero-worshipping boy and his long-time girlfriend (sometimes). It's violent, and it's rather loaded with the N-word (well, it was written in 1930, so it's hardly PC). But it is immensely satisfying fun and filled with plenty of very memorable characters. And Destry, despite himself, starts to grow up and understand that he's brought a lot of this on himself.

Time for more Max Brand!

John Peel

★ ★ ★ ★ ★

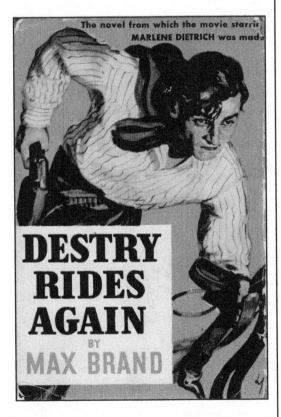

THE HORROR FROM THE MOUND
Robert E Howard
Weird Tales May 1932

"Defilers of Indian burial grounds usually get their just desserts ..."

Already a prominent contributor to pulp magazines, and revered for his creation of Hyperborean warrior Conan the Cimmerian in particular, by the early 1930s Texas-born Robert E Howard was devoting an increasing amount of time and energy to writing westerns for magazines such as **Argosy** and **Cowboy Stories**. Unsurprisingly given his background in weird publishing and his fascination with the history of the old southwest, Howard on occasion combined the two enthusiasms into excursions into 'weird western' territory. **The Horror from the Mound** from 1932 was one of his earliest exercises in the genre and still stands up as one of the best.

Howard's seminal tale opens with former cowboy and now-struggling Texas farmer Steve Brill quizzically contemplating the Indian burial mound that sits on the edge of his failing property. Brill has clocked that his Mexican neighbour Juan Lopez avoids the mound at all costs and, despite Lopez's desperate warnings, the ex-cowboy determines to break into it – simply out of curiosity at first, but also in the hope of striking the gold that would alleviate his tricky financial situation.

Like many a tale by Howard's friend H P Lovecraft, **The Horror from the Mound** begins as (to ruin a title borrowed from another great purveyor of the form, M R James) 'a warning to the archaeologically curious'. Defilers of Indian burial grounds usually get their just desserts and in Brill's case his nemesis is a 16th century Spanish vampire, Don Santiago de Valdez, imprisoned within the tomb by Lopez's ancestor.

Not a long story, **The Horror from the Mound** nevertheless manages to evoke drought-ridden Texas very effectively. Brill's Anglo-Saxon condescension for the Mexican Lopez may now seems crude and archaic, but as Brill is presented as being entirely unwise to tamper with the grave in the first place (and, in any event, very nearly pays with his life for his curiosity), Howard's ethnic stereotyping comes across as satirical more than anything.

Jim O'Brien

★ ★ ★ ☆ ☆

MONTANA RIDES!
Evan Evans (Max Brand)
1933

"Plenty of satisfying gunplay and all the standard Western tropes are covered..."

I dug this novel out of a pile of vintage Penguin Books. Their edition was published in 1957 and was a lone venture into the Western genre. What possessed them to choose this book? I needed to know.

The story follows the adventures of our hero, Montana, also known as The Montana Kid, The Mexican Kid or simply The Kid. He approaches a rich rancher family and poses as their long-lost son with an aim to deceive and rob them. However, he becomes so fond of them, particularly the beautiful daughter, that he can no longer go through with the deception.

He goes in search of their real son whereupon they both get into adventures in bandit-ridden Mexico. There's plenty of satisfying gunplay and all the standard Western tropes are covered, including romance. Bearing in mind the time this book was written, I shouldn't have been surprised about the way black characters are treated within. However, I did find a couple of bits a little distasteful for today's standards and I can't help but wonder if this is why the book has slipped into obscurity?

Evan Evans was a pseudonym for noted genre writer Max Brand. The book was popular enough to produce a sequel, **Montana Rides Again**, published in 1934. Brand himself became a correspondent in the Second World War and was killed in Italy.

Jules Burt

★★★☆☆

DESPERATE DAN
Dudley D Watkins
The Dandy, 1937 onwards

"There are sheriffs and saloons, cowboys and horses but there are also London buses and red pillar boxes..."

When Scottish publisher D C Thomson launched their new humour title **The Dandy** in 1937, the comic featured from its very first issue the exploits and adventures of the unfeasibly strong and lantern-jawed Desperate Dan, resident of Cactusville, USA, consumer of vast cow pies and all 'round gentle giant hero. In fact, Dan's western hometown wasn't explicitly named until 1940 and he hadn't actually tucked into a cow pie until the year before that but, even then, the strip was still in its infancy, only winding up when **The Dandy** itself did in 2012. Based on those dates, I'd imagine that Desperate Dan can possibly lay claim to being one of the longest running of all comedy cowboy strips, a feat made all the more amazing by the fact that just one man was responsible for every Desperate Dan storyline between 1937 and 1965 – the humour strip genius that was Dudley D Watkins. The wild west of Watkins' imagination is a strange place, to be sure: there are sheriffs and saloons, cowboys and horses, but there are also London

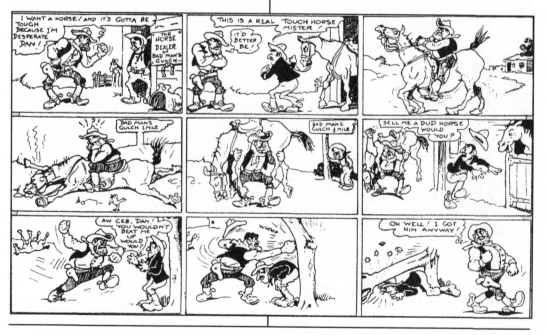

buses and red pillar boxes, British bobbies on the beat and a Mayor who would not have looked out of place in D C Thomson's home town of Dundee. The gags are solid stuff though in any episode: Dan uses his great strength to solve all manner of problems and generally gets to stuff his face with some gargantuan meal as a reward for his endeavours – and use a succession of blowtorches, lathes and other pieces of heavy plant to keep his unruly stubble in check. Check out Bud Neill's excellent **Lobey Dosser** for another humorous Scottish western comic, but Desperate Dan is still Top Sheriff in my book.

Jim O'Brien

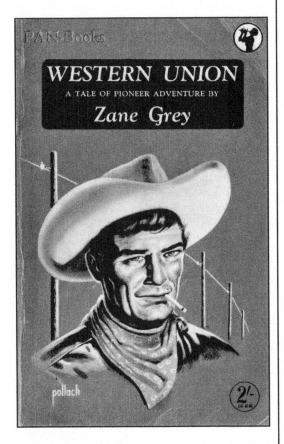

WESTERN UNION
Zane Grey
1939

"Accurately describes the old west and the oncoming and relentless march of modern technology..."

Browsing through my Pan Books collection recently, I spotted this early Zane Grey novel and decided to give it a try. Set in 1861, the story revolves around the extension of the Western Union telegraph line across the American continent that would eventually oust The Pony Express.

Our main protagonist, Cameron, with the help of three experienced pioneers, joins the telegraph workers as they set upon this epic task of joining the 'little piece of iron' from one side of America to the other. There is of course a love interest in the form of an exotic dancer who joins them part way across the journey.

Along the way, they encounter and overcome various toughs and Indians, a prairie-fire and floods. Extreme weather conditions are also superbly depicted. You actually feel cold when the characters do! One of the most exciting parts is when they, along with other cowboys, try to calm the stampede of a herd of buffalo. This is achieved by placing two wagons in their path and setting them on fire in an attempt to split the herd.

This novel accurately describes the old west and the oncoming and relentless march of modern technology on an otherwise untouched part of America. From Nebraska to Wyoming the wire is built, one telegraph pole at a time.

I found Grey's writing had an almost addictive quality with my only criticism coming from how some of the accents are represented on the actual page. The characters are likeable and you want them to succeed. Published the year of Grey's death, in 1939, it's a little dated but still entertaining and recommended.

Jules Burt

HARDCASE
Luke Short
1941

"The plot is a complex whirlwind of intriguing characters but at times it gets a little too complicated..."

Frederick Dilley Glidden chose the pen name of Luke Short, not to be confused with the gunfighter of the same name. He studied journalism, become a trapper in Canada, and worked as an archaeologist's assistant in New Mexico. But it was after reading Western pulp magazines and trying to escape unemployment that he began to write Western fiction. **Hardcase** was first published in 1941 and has that pulp western vibe to it.

WITH MAP ON BACK COVER

A DELL WESTERN

Dave Coyle is an outlaw. The sort of outlaw that thumbs his nose at the law, that can escape any jail he's thrown in, and generally is able to strut about with confidence that his skills are superior to anybody who might disagree with him. But he's loyal to his friends and his actions are mostly honourable. So, when pretty Carol McFee asks for his help in saving her father from having his ranch suckered out from under him with a fake bill-of-sale, Coyle steps in to assist.

Hardcase is certainly a western novel but it has many hallmarks of other genres, especially hard-boiled crime. Coyle is an interesting character, a man not afraid to act outside the law to right a wrong. He's hardheaded but smart. The novel certainly is titled appropriately. The plot is a complex whirlwind of intriguing characters but at times it gets a little too complicated to follow easily. However, the very nature of the power structure in the town, including the sheriff and his deputy, was well thought out and provided lots of intrigue, double-crosses, and several fun fight scenes. It's not a flawless novel to be sure, with some parts that wandered around a little bit, but ultimately it pulled me right along.

Benjamin Thomas

TRAIL TOWN
Ernest Haycox
1945

"As many abstract ideas bouncing around as there are characters…"

A seminal western novel for me, **Trail Town** is a reflective novel with more thematic layers than most. River Bend is a cattle town in flux. The day of the free-range cowboy is drawing to a close, and the future beckons with scores of new homesteaders. Day-marshal Dan Mitchell, an individualist in a community forcing him to take sides, represents balance between the merchants of Willow Street and the trail boss drovers and saloonkeepers of Race Street. He's in love with Sherry Green, fiancé of District Attorney Ford Green, but Mitchell's also a paternal figure for Rita, a soiled dove working for Big Annie on Race.

The book's deliberate pace pays off when things start popping. First, loudmouth trail boss Cap Ryker runs headlong into Mitchell and finds out the lawman won't budge. Then bad guy Jett Younger, a pal of saloonkeeper Charlie Fair, kills a man while stealing his cattle. He flees to the nearby mountain range while Ford Green and the men of River Bend task world-weary yokel Sheriff Bravo with bringing him in. Mitchell recognizes the set up for what it is and volunteers to help Bravo. With his friend Tom Leathers. It's action, but action due to a steady build-up of suspenseful machinations—it's action with lasting consequences for Mitchell, Sherry Gault, and all of River Bend.

Trail Town is important to me because of its intelligent narrative and well-crafted plot. There's as many abstract ideas bouncing around as there are characters, but Haycox guides everything with a firm and steady hand. Reportedly based on historical Abilene town marshal Tom Smith, a real sense of a town moving inevitably through history also pervades the book, just one of the themes I've mentioned. Read it straight for the action or read it for the history and social paradigm it presents, either way, **Trail Town** is a masterpiece.

Richard Prosch

SHANE
Jack Schaefer
1946

"It's slow-paced, wordy and nothing much happens for most of its short length…"

According to Mark Twain, 'A classic is something that everybody wants to have read and nobody wants to read.' I decided to test that theory with an acknowledged Western classic: **Shane**, which put author Jack Schaefer on the best-seller list. As pretty much everyone knows, it's the story of a young boy and his relationship with a gunman who is trying to go cold turkey and eventually fails due to a local rancher who's greedy for other people's land.

It certainly has a lot of signs of its classic status: it's slow-paced, wordy and nothing much happens for most of its short length (117 pages). People emote a lot and say all sorts of profound things. At least, I think they're profound; it rather depends on your expectations. And when something finally happens in the story, it's over with pretty quickly, leaving me, at least, feeling like the story is rather empty.

The copy I bought was second-hand, and had apparently been given as a class assignment, because the youngster who owned it had scribbled crib notes inside both covers – most of which are highly inaccurate. The climax, he claims, is 'when Shane and Mr Starrett cut the tree stump', for example, when that's actually pretty much the start of the story. His last note is unfinished: 'Not a lot of' ... I think he died of boredom before completing it. Despite the fact that the narrator is a child, this is not a book to excite kids.

Oh, and if you like the film, be aware that like most Hollywood films, it's not a close relative of the novel. Third or fourth cousins at best.

John Peel

★ ★ ★ ★ ☆

DALLAS
Will F Jenkins
1950

"I discovered was that his western writing is even better than his SF writing ..."

Will F Jenkins is best known these days for his wonderfully pulp science fiction stories, written under his pseudonym 'Murray Leinster'. He's always been a favourite of mine, so when I learned he was actually Jenkins and that Jenkins was actually best known for his westerns – how could I resist hunting at least one down to compare it? The one I found was his novelization of the 1950 Gary Cooper movie **Dallas** (nothing to do with J.R. Ewing!).

What I discovered was that his western writing is even better than his SF writing. **Dallas** is set just after the end of the Civil War, and the main character is unreformed rebel Blayde Hollister. He's hunting the three brothers that murdered his family while he was off at war, and they're in – you guessed it – Dallas. There are some terrific secondary characters, including a US Marshal who is a deadly shot – to everything but what he's aiming at – and Wild Bill Hickok. Any fans of **Deadwood** out there will easily recognize Jenkins' Hickok as essentially the same as the TV one (half a century earlier!), with brilliantly flowery prose and equally flowery attitudes.

The book is an absolute delight, as Blayde discovers that not all Yankees are bad, and not all Rebels are good – and that he still has something to live for after resigning himself to a lost cause. And I've discovered that I'm going to have to do a little hunting of my own... for more Will F Jenkins western novels...

John Peel

★ ★ ★ ★ ☆

A Truly Great Novel Of The Old Southwest

126

GOLD MEDAL BOOK

DALLAS
WILL F. JENKINS

From the Warner Bros. production, DALLAS starring Gary Cooper, Ruth Roman and Steve Cochran

THE TRAIL
Logan Stewart (Les Savage Jr)
1951

"In no other western have I ever found such a strong sense that the writer had ridden on a cattle drive…"

Either under his own name or his pseudonym, Les Savage Jr penned seven full novels for Gold Medal in the early '50s, along with a posthumous collaboration with Dudley Dean. Sadly, Savage died before he was 35. I'd never read a word by him before and didn't know what to expect, but I found myself in good hands. A polished writer with a honed gift for tension and a good grasp of character and human nature, Savage managed to bring even minor characters to life in this novel.

The Trail's lead character is a talented cook going by the name of Marrs, haunted by something in his past we don't learn the truth of for many pages. Believing himself pursued by an old enemy, he takes on as a trail cook for a troubled outfit run by Paul and Gail Butler and their angry ramrod, Bob Slaughter. Paul Butler's a weak and sickly man, leaving Gail the true manager of the outfit, on whom Slaughter has designs. Gail's uninterested though, partly out of loyalty to her husband, and partly because she doesn't much like Slaughter's brutal leadership style. Marrs, of course, proves to be much more than a talented cook, and his mastery of cattle driving skills wins over both the men and Gail, and angers Slaughter.

Add to this tension a gambling syndicate that wants to ensure the cattle arrive at fading Abilene rather than Dodge, some Choctaw Indians and some jayhawkers, and you get some great battle sequences, both with gunfights and fists.

Though a fairly standard story in some ways, Savage manages some surprises, and the sense of verisimilitude is impressive. In no other western have I ever found such a strong sense that the writer had ridden on a cattle drive: Savage brings every moment on the trail to life, from the way the chuck wagon is operated and the cattle behave down to the way some of the men argue about how to lasso and what equipment is best in which situation. The scenes featuring conversation with the Choctaw Indians had a "you are there" quality as well. A touch of old-fashioned melodrama in some of the scenes between Gail and Marrs brought the story down a little for me, but the most realistic depiction of a cattle drive and its hazards (and everyday practices) I've ever read counted in its favour. Recommended.

Howard Andrew Jones

★ ★ ★ ★ ☆

UTAH HELL GUNS
Steve Frazee
1951

"Enough mystery to keep me guessing until the end …"

On the outs with his Union-loving family since leaving home to fight for the South, young Reno Keegan is on his way to Utah, answering his dad's call for help, unsure what he'll find. Old Liash Keegan, foreman at a tough-as-nails railroad construction camp, is bed ridden, shot through by an unknown assailant for unknown reasons.

Was he attacked by a disgruntled worker? Or was it the competing road-grade outfit run by Penrose Capps? Or does someone else hope to end the old man's progress on the west-moving grade? When young Reno narrowly misses his own date with a bullet, the son sets out to find an answer and, hopefully, regain his father's trust at the same time.

In everything I've read by Steve Frazee, the father-son relationship is featured one way or t'other. He also seems to have a lot of personal expertise at construction work and the daily relationships between men toiling together under a hot sun. I enjoyed the technical details of building and grading a rail bed, none of which came across overly pedantic. There wasn't an over-abundance of action in the story, but enough mystery to keep me guessing until the end.

Richard Prosch

★ ★ ☆ ☆ ☆

SUNDOWN RIDERS
Thomas Thompson
1951

"Fine if you just want a straightforward battle of good versus evil …"

Thomas Thompson is probably best known (if he's known at all) for his work on **Bonanza** and other TV series, but he started his career writing westerns in the Fifties. **Sundown Riders** is from 1950 and it's an oddity. For one thing, there isn't anyone in it that rides into (or even out of) the sundown. I guess they couldn't think of a more apt title. It's the story of a couple of villains who are trying to steal land by fomenting war with the Modocs – who are happy to oblige by attacking various farmhouses and such. Hero Rod Buckley just wants to graze his cattle in peace, but we all know how that's going to work out, right? His life is complicated by being in love and being more used to talking to cows than women.

The plot is straightforward, though Thompson manages to keep it bubbling along, and the characters are standard fare. There's the Evil Villain who's a coward at heart; the Noble Heroine who appears to be in love with the Evil Villain but is secretly in love with Noble Hero; there's a weedy character who's married to a Modoc wife and helps Noble Hero. There's the Senator who is (for once) a good guy, but who doesn't understand his daughter; and there's the Army versus the Indians. It's a decent enough book – no surprises, though, but fine if you just want a straightforward battle of good versus evil. A perfect prelude to the simplistic plots of **Bonanza**, in fact.

John Peel

★ ★ ★ ☆ ☆

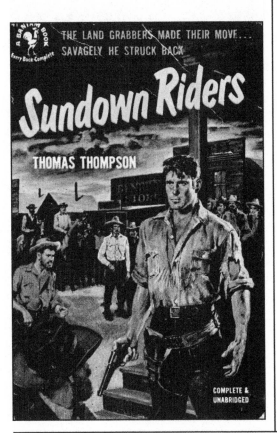

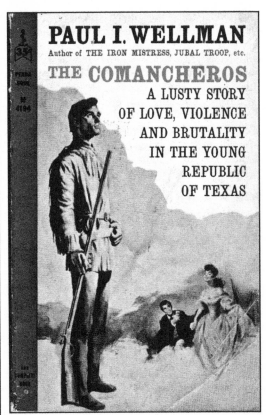

THE COMANCHEROS
Paul I Wellman
1952

"A whirling adventure peopled with well-drawn characters and with surprises and satisfying moments of action..."

Gambler Paul Regret is a man about town in New Orleans – until he shoots a judge's son in an affair of honour. Knowing what will happen if he stays, he runs, to the ends of the earth. Texas. And there he is sworn in as a Texas Ranger by Sam Houston himself, and is assigned the most dangerous mission possible: find the Comancheros. Whites who deal with the Comanches and encourage their attacks, massacres and thefts for their own profit, the Comancheros are without honour, decency or mercy. They must be stopped, whatever the cost. There's a girl, of course, and romance amidst the brutality. She's an actress and a flirt with a bevy of admirers, yet she's captured Regret's heart – something he had never expected anyone to manage. But Regret must change from a foppish gambler into a fighting man if he is to survive. This is great fun, a whirling adventure peopled with well-drawn characters and with surprises and satisfying moments of action. This brilliant tale was to later be filmed (director Michael Curtiz's final movie). The barebones of the story survived, but the rest of it was changed almost completely. And the virtually new story is, if anything, better than the novel. The reason for that is because the script was the work of Clair Huffaker – a name you'll be very familiar with from elsewhere in these reviews. Taking Wellman's ideas, he didn't simply run with them – he galloped. Regret becomes the second banana, because the star is John Wayne...

John Peel

★ ★ ★ ★ ★

WEST OF ABILENE
Vingie Roe
1952

Vingie Row was born in 1879, raised in Oklahoma territory and settled in Northern California ca. 1907. Shortly thereafter she began writing novels. She wrote until her death in 1957, with her most popular novels **The Maid of the Whispering Hills** and **Tharon of Lost Valley**, both readily available.

Working my way through a stack of vintage paperbacks, I was ambivalent when I saw Roe's **West of Abilene** up next in the pile. I was happy to finally get the chance to read something by Roe, unhappy at the condition of my Pocket Books copy and what looked like a troublesome read—the spine was obviously damaged, the pages dry and brittle. Undaunted, I began and got fifty pages in before the back half of the book dropped out, giving me not one volume to read, but three coverless pamphlets (with the promise of more if I wasn't careful).

Too far into the story to put off the conclusion, I opted not to track down a new copy, but persevered to the end. By the time I was rifling through those pages, Roe had increased the tension to such an extent I didn't wonder the back part of the book was literally springing apart. Honestly, reading **West of Abilene** could not have been better with a pristine edition smelling of fresh ink.

It starts out with a familiar setup. A trail town is under the thumb of a local cattle baron, the swaggering, arrogant, Big Red Kinkaid, whose only virtue is his daughter, the lovely Copper Ann. Naturally when Johnny Velantry comes to town and bests the big man in front of everyone, trouble follows. But Velantry is there because of Kinkaid and, as the tale unfolds, the secret past that ties the two men together becomes darkly

apparent. As revenge tales go, it's a little slow moving and melodramatic, but Roe manages to give her otherwise cliché characters some unique attributes that kept me reading. Her understanding of trail town economics and mob mentality also helped the action ring true. I was glued to the story, even as the story itself came unglued.

Richard Prosch

★ ★ ☆ ☆ ☆

.44
H A De Rosso
1953

"None have as successfully married the feel of a noir detective novel with the old west..."

.44 is a tight noir western that deserves to be better known and widely read. It hooks from the opening, when reluctant gunslinger Dan Harland's hired to kill Lancaster, a man who deliberately lets Harland shoot him. Confused and curious, the already sour Harland decides to investigate the whys and the wherefores. He knows his target could have killed him if he'd wished and wonders why he was spared.

I hesitate to give further details for fear of spoiling the mystery and the dark events uncovered during Harland's investigation. Matters are complicated by the arrival of a lawman seeking money from a missing train robbery, Lancaster's two unsavoury associates, Lancaster's beautiful widow, and a man who's clearly lying when he tries to convince Harland he's the true client. I've read plenty of westerns with mystery elements at this point, but none have as successfully married the feel of a noir detective novel with the old west.

This book is bleak and powerful and, once read, unlikely to be forgotten. Highly recommended.

Howard Andrew Jones

QUANTRELL'S RAIDERS
Frank Gruber
1953

"The action is bloody and brutal, and even more horrifying because it is factual ..."

Frank Gruber, one of the most prolific pulp writers of all time, is also famous for saying there are only seven different plots for westerns. One of those is the 'Outlaw story' in which outlaw gangs dominate the action. This book, although heavily influenced by historical events, is just such a story.

The novel opens in 1861 with new West Point graduate, Second Lieutenant Doniphan 'Donny' Fletcher on his way home to Kentucky to await his first posting. While Donny's loyalties lie with the Union, most of his family, hometown friends, and an especially attractive young lady next door are slaveholders and either pro-South or just trying to remain neutral. But no sooner does he arrive when trouble between Jayhawkers and Bushwhackers boils over onto his home turf, forcing Donny to kill a couple of Union guerrilla fighters in self-defence. Under arrest and about to face a firing squad, Donny manages to escape, but has nowhere to run. He wants revenge and the answer, at least for now resides in becoming a guerrilla fighter himself, ultimately joining up with William Quantrill and 'Bloody' Bill Anderson.

This novel is historical fiction disguised as a western. The story of Quantrill's Raiders (I'm not sure why it's spelled 'Quantrell' throughout the book) and how it became known as the breeding ground for outlaws after the Civil War's conclusion, including such luminaries as Cole Younger, Jesse and Frank James, and others is an

exciting one. The action, particularly in the second half of the book is bloody and brutal, and even more horrifying because it is factual. These men are outlaws at their worst. The scenes involving the massacre of Lawrence, Kansas are especially disturbing as some 450 guerrilla fighters swoop in and murder numerous innocent non-combatants including women and children.

The character of Donny Fletcher undergoes a sweeping transformation, from loyal Union Army officer to wanted Southern guerrilla fighter and criminal. Ultimately, no longer willing to participate in such atrocities, he works with the Union once again to turn on Quantrill and the other guerrilla leaders, helping to bring an end to their reign of terror. This is largely a tragic tale, watching one man get caught up in circumstances beyond his control, but it does end on a positive note. Definitely worth reading, especially for readers interested in this period of history.

Benjamin Thomas

Featuring SPURS JACKSON AND HIS SPACE VIGILANTES

SPACE WESTERN COMICS

10¢ N045

"THE MOON BAT"

"TOMORROW THE UNIVERSE"

SPACE WESTERN COMICS 45
Charlton Comics
1953

"A disastrous combination of the western and SF genres."

Despite the numbering stating issue 45, this is the fifth and final issue of this title's incarnation as **Space Western Comics**, a disastrous combination of the western and SF genres. It contains four short colour strips in the standard American comic book format, all illustrated by Stan Campbell who turns in a competent job of clear line work and storytelling but is far from an unheralded talent and takes any opportunity to take shortcuts by simplifying his illustrations.

First strip 'The Valley That Time Forgot', has Native American Strong Bow venturing into Edgar Rice Burroughs territory as he deals with a voracious dinosaur who is besieging a jet pilot that has crashed on a secluded mesa. Next up is the absolutely bizarre 'Spurs Jackson and the Space Vigilantes' in which the crime-fighting posse pursue none other than Adolf Hitler, who is fleeing trial for war-crimes on a rocket into outer space. Landing on the nearest planet with human life forms, it's evident that Hitler hasn't learned his lesson, as he wastes no time in

installing himself as a dictator. Spurs and co could have saved themselves the interplanetary jetlag as, the by the time they catch up, Hitler's henchmen have turned upon him.

The Nazi-hunters return for 'Spurs Jackson and The Moon Bat' in which the cowboys lead a Moon expedition which uncovers precious rubies and the titular guardian. This was the best of a very bad bunch, with visuals reminiscent of classic SF-horror artists Al Feldstein and Basil Wolverton, to such an extent that I suspect they were swiped. Final strip 'Hank Roper and the Invisible Invader' has an escapee from a mental institution using his powers of invisibility to work with a team of cattle-rustlers, with a script that made little sense.

Although a fun enough oddity, the nonsensical scripts and workman like art mean that is all it is, and it is merely a reminder of a time before comics were made moribund by spandex and capes.

Justin Marriott

★ ☆ ☆ ☆ ☆

BITTER SAGE
Frank Gruber
1954

"Good guys, bad guys, plenty of action, a dash of romance, and no real profanity..."

Frank Gruber was a highly prolific writer of pulps and various novels, including many westerns. Twenty-five of his books were made into movies and he created three different western TV shows, in addition to writing sixty-five screenplays and a hundred television episodes. I note all of this because reading **Bitter Sage** is like watching a classic Hollywood western movie from the heyday of the 50s. Wes Tancred is one of the best gunslingers in the old west, but he's running from a violent past and a lie about who he is and what he's done that has taken on mythic proportions. Following a fateful intervention that sees him gun down three would-be thieves, Tancred ends up in Sage City, Kansas, a cattle town owned and lorded over by the crooked mayor, Jacob Fugger. Taking a job as a printer at the local newspaper, Tancred is inevitably pulled into a growing war between the upright citizens of Sage City and the forces of Fugger, who starts calling in hired guns to kill anyone who opposes him.

All of the classic tropes are here—good guys, bad guys, plenty of action (fistfights and gunplay), a dash of romance (but no sex), and no real profanity—just like those old-school Hollywood westerns. And that's actually meant as a compliment. There may not be anything surprising to be found here, but it is genuinely well written, moves at a great pace, and is never the least bit boring.

Steve Carroll

SADDLE THE STORM
Harry Whittington
1954

"A cohesive story of love, obligation, betrayal, hatred and violence ..."

An ambitious novel that follows three main narratives, a young couple in a rocky marriage, a bible-thumping rancher who feels that he has been spurned, and a mentally challenged boy whose actions are an enigma. All the action takes place during one hot Independence Day celebration in a small Texas town where Whittington effectively expands and merges the narratives into a cohesive story of love, obligation, betrayal, hatred and violence. This may have been Whittington's attempt to write

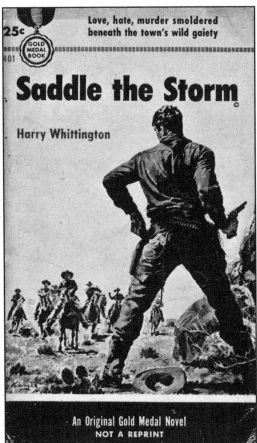

something more substantial than his excellent genre-focused crime and western books – his Great American Novel perhaps, and although it looks like a traditional western it is so very much more.

Ed McBride

SPUR TO THE SMOKE
Steve Frazee
1955

"The friction between father and son was kept hot until the finale..."

More action here than in a typical Frazee title, with young Lee Vale refusing to become an aggressive blowhard like his father, Roderick, boss of the Black Diamond ranch. The elder Vale is infamous around the Colorado Sapinero country for stringing up alleged horse thieves and being handy with a gun. As these things go, Roderick is a coward and cuckold, letting his right-hand man, Sam Harvey, take care of his honour—as well as his wife.

When folks around the town of Kebler hatch a plan to take over some of Vale's prime grazing land, they turn to the guidance of a whacked-out preacher, who assures them of their divine right. Only clear-headed Lee can save the day, but he's tired of covering his dad's ass.

Frazee takes his time setting up all the characters involved in the plot. In fact, I think the story would've been better with a few less hangers-on. Still, once I got into it, I liked the book a tad more than the previous Frazee I read, **Utah Hell Guns** (see page 28). In **Spur to The Smoke**, the friction between father and son was kept hot until the finale, and the romantic interludes for our young hero were more complex and pronounced—if not overly integral to the plot.

Richard Prosch

★ ★ ★ ★ ★

END OF THE GUN
H A DeRosso
1955

"A desperate fight for redemption and to start a new life on the right side of the law ..."

A dark novel telling the story of an ex-convict mustang wrangler, consumed by depression and anger bordering on psychotic, who battles everyone – his partners, ranchers, outlaws – in a desperate fight for redemption and to start a new life on the right side of the law. Things are complicated even more by two women who fall for him, as they somehow disregard his erratic temper and violent nature. Not a particularly good effort from a writer whose other works I have admired.

Ed McBride

★ ★ ☆ ☆ ☆

GO FOR YOUR GUN
Coe Williams
1957

"Fight through a roaring blizzard of ice and blistering hot lead to bring justice to the guilty ..."

Cattle rancher Morgan Letham and Ann Kershner were an item until Ann's father, Whit, was murdered, shot in the back and propped up in his saddle to drift lifelessly down the shoulder of Cache Mountain from the Mogul Plateau.

From Whit's initial disappearance, Morg suspects sheep rancher Ward Grafton of foul play. Grafton, along with young Ellen McCloud (who bought out part of his original outfit) has long hoped for a chance at the grassy valley owned by the Lethams and Kershers. Like their sheriff, Clyde Rybolt, the people of nearby Longbow are more interested in politics than the law and, hoping to avoid a range war, they give Grafton the benefit of the doubt and openly ridicule Morg's accusations.

After a humiliating public showdown with Grafton, Ward takes a second, more serious beating from the man and his thugs. Adding insult to injury, the cowman is rescued and nursed back to health by Ellen McCloud. But as events unfold, Ellen proves more trustworthy than Ann, and when his girl deliberately lies to help Grafton, it's to Ellen that Letham turns for help. If I'd had the chance to read **Go for Your Gun** by Coe Williams in manuscript form, I would have enjoyed a suspenseful build up, carried along by Letham's dawning realization that Grafton wasn't working alone.

As it was, I couldn't be surprised at the story's eventual revelation because some blabber mouth

WALT COBURN

His one chance of survival lay beyond a wall of savage bush fighters

VIOLENT MAVERICK

Original title: Wet Cattle

hack in charge of the book's back cover wrote '...grass-greedy Steve McKenna had already hired the toughest gun slicks in the valley to cut down his neighbours like butchered steers.' Still, by the time Letham and his confidants fight through a roaring blizzard of ice and blistering hot lead to bring justice to the guilty, I was engrossed enough to finish the slim novel in a second sitting.

This spare paperback was released by Popular Library Eagle Books in 1955 and is a longer version of a story called **Coroner's Range**, which originally appeared in **Ranch Romance Magazine**. I think it's a forgotten gem in the western genre.

About Coe Williams, I know next to nothing. The cover credits him with **Trouble Trail** and **Yellowstone Passage**, but there's nothing to indicate whether these are short stories or longer works. A web search offered little, with only one additional credit, **The Plundered Land**, from the Fall, 1957 edition of **Triple Western Magazine**.

Richard Prosch

★ ★ ★ ☆ ☆

WET CATTLE
Walt Coburn
1955

"A breakneck pace that had me finishing it in less than two hours ..."

Walt Coburn was first and foremost a cowboy. The Montana native was the son of Robert Coburn, the founder of Circle C Ranch. In the late 1800s, this was the largest ranch in the northwest (Montana didn't become a state until 1889). Coburn cut his teeth as a cowboy and served in WWI before becoming a full-time writer in the 1920s. From that period through the 1940s, the author contributed over a hundred stories to the pulps, predominantly **Dime Western Magazine**. From the 1930s through the early 1970s, he wrote over thirty western novels, including **Wet Cattle** in 1955. In 1970, the novel's title was changed to the much grittier sounding **Violent Maverick** via the Macfadden-Bartell line.

Penniless cowboy Pat Roper saved Mexican bandit Pablo Guerrero's life in a prior gun-battle. Pablo runs into Roper in a firefight over stolen cattle at the Arizona-Mexican border. Pablo gifts Roper the Two Block ranch, 25,000 acres of good feed, water and some start-up cattle. The problem is that Pablo is running guns through it to overthrow the Mexican government. Roper,

not digging into the devil in the details, accepts the gift and takes the ranch. He later finds out that Pablo's lifetime enemy, Wig Murphy, borders the ranch with his own cattle empire, and he's crushing the Two Block ranch out.

Coburn's validity as a real cowboy is a catch-22. While his books possess dirty, dusty realism, they are written in 'cowboy' terminology that's sometimes hard to decipher. It's this element that dampened what was otherwise a well-crafted story in **Wet Cattle**. It's a short read at 140-pages and has a breakneck pace that had me finishing it in less than two hours. Was I maniacally rushing so it was over quickly, or because I wanted to learn the fate of young sodbuster Pat Roper? Probably a little of both. The result is just another dog-eared, yellowed western that passes the time.

The Paperback Warrior

★ ★ ★ ☆ ☆

ESCAPE FROM FIVE SHADOWS
Elmore Leonard
1956

"The title of the book tells you what Bowen has in mind..."

Five Shadows is a prison camp run by megalomaniac Banda, who gets paid by another branch of the government for every hour of work he gets out of the prisoners. Subsequently, he works the men like dogs and uses the money he gets as sparingly as possible to barely keep them alive and pockets the rest. Bowen is in the camp for a crime he had no knowing part in committing. And the title of the book tells you what Bowen has in mind.

All the characters you could want are here: the bullied accountant, who gets trapped into help 'cook the books' for Banda's greedy enterprise; his gorgeous but selfish wife, who knows she hitched herself to the wrong wagon; Banda's sadistic hatchet man, Brazil; the tomboy who works at the post office/general store of the nearby small town and is, of course, a beauty in disguise; and her erstwhile father, holding council on her far-fetched theories on the doings in and around the prison camp.

Besides the obvious warden and guard threats, Bowen has other problems with his fellow inmates like the hot-headed young man bent on revenge and also the guy he went to prison with, who may be doing some canary work on the side. Bowen is an interesting character. When he sits back, he has the knack for seeing all the way through people and what motivates them; but

THEY STOPPED HIM ONCE
BUT BOWEN WAS PRIMED TO EXPLODE.

when he's in action, he gets downright bull-headed – sometimes to his own detriment. This was a good, solid read.

Scott Ranalli

★ ★ ★ ☆ ☆

THE KING AND FOUR QUEENS
Theodore Sturgeon
1956

"An unusual story, and Sturgeon gives us some very delightful characters to follow ..."

I've always known Theodore Sturgeon for his excellent SF, and this is the first time I was aware he'd written any westerns. Turns out he's just as brilliant in this genre, too, and with a very twisted plot. Four outlaws have stolen $100,000 and are blown to pieces by a posse. But one may have escaped. Their mother and their widows (but are they all widows?) are holed up in a burned-out town, but is the gold hidden there? The sheriff has the place watched carefully to see what happens. Enter Dan Kehoe, opportunist supreme and on the run from a bunch of idiots

who want to kill him. Can he play the women off against one another and discover the truth? For $100,000, it must be worth trying, right? But even if he succeeds, can he get the gold (if there is any) past the watching sheriff?

Certainly, an unusual story, and Sturgeon gives us some very delightful characters to follow – all with their own agendas. This is a novel based on a screenplay by Margaret Fitts, and which was filmed with Clark Gable (playing Kehoe, before you ask!). I must confess; I could see Gable as I read the story. And the book now makes me want to see the film. Recommended reading.

John Peel

★ ★ ★ ★ ☆

GUNSMOKE
Don Ward
1957

"Great short tales, and pure fun to read ..."

There was once a time when prime time TV in the US basically meant watching a western. And the biggest and best of these was **Gunsmoke**.

Upright Marshal Matt Dillon, comic sidekick Chester (Festus was later and dirtier), cranky Doc Adams and lady-of-questionable-virtue Kitty Russell were the stars, but it was always the stories that counted. Its height was the black and white half-hour shows, and they were almost all unremittingly grim and downbeat, with happy endings few and far between.

And we loved them.

This book collects ten of these earlier TV stories and turns them into riveting short stories, written with style and clarity. (It includes my wife's favourite story, **The Pest Hole**, which was a real feel-sorry-for-Chester story; a lot of those old shows were like that.) Matt Dillon must face all manner of criminals, from the hard cases to the 'I didn't mean to do it' kind, and he dispenses his own interpretation of justice.

Actually, these stories seem to be based on the original radio show scripts, not the TV ones – Matt smokes incessantly, which he rarely did on TV (except during the commercials, since the show was sponsored by a tobacco company), and Chester's surname is Proudfoot (it was Goode on the TV), and there's absolutely no mention of his famous limp. But they're great short tales, and pure fun to read. This is an absolute must for fans of TV – or simply of westerns.

John Peel

SUNDOWN AT CRAZY HORSE/THE LAST SUNSET
Vechel Howard (Howard Rigsby)
1957

"Involving you in every moment of their journey so that you savour them all..."

Retitled upon its reprint when Kirk Douglas purchased the book's film rights, **Sundown at Crazy Horse** has a fantastic mix of hardboiled and mythic elements. When a flawed but decent man with two great kids and a loving wife decides to pull up stakes and head out on a cattle drive, Cassidy, a charming gunslinger, decides to go with them, mostly because he wants to protect the woman and kids. He's joined by a man who's hunting him for the murder of his brother, but Cassidy convinces him to hold off, that they're both needed to get the Breckenridge family to safety on their ill-conceived venture. They agree that they'll settle things at the very end of the drive, when they reach the settlement of Crazy Horse.

Both Cassidy and his pursuer are principled men, at odds with one another, and drawn to Mrs Breckinridge. They must fend off challenges from rustlers and Indians and the environment, counter some of Breckenridge's choices, and work together even knowing that one of them is going to kill the other at the end.

It sounds like a simple mix, but Rigsby makes every moment work, developing every character, involving you in every moment of their journey so that you savour them all, hoping against hope that the two men you've come to like will somehow both survive. This is a wonderful book, a forgotten classic, and launched me into an exploration of Rigsby's other westerns, all of which I've found to be strong reads. Unfortunately, the movie adaptation is reputedly flawed.

Howard Andrew Jones

★★★★★

TEMPTATIONS OF VALERIE
Harry Whittington
1957

"A web of brutality, betrayal and deceit ..."

This short novel tells the story of an attempted murder from three different perspectives in an Old West courtroom setting. The beautiful newlywed Valerie, her menacing landowner husband, and the handsome new minister, who get entangled in a web of brutality, betrayal and deceit and who each give compelling and strikingly different testimonies. I liked the way that Whittington was able to tell the three stories without much overlap or redundancy. I watched the movie **Valerie** on YouTube and liked it a lot too.

Ed McBride

★ ★ ★ ☆ ☆

THE BIG COUNTRY
Donald Hamilton
1958

"A parade of great characters, some terrific dialogue and great action sequences ..."

I grew up in the Wild West. Okay, maybe not literally (I didn't get closer than Nottingham, England), but certainly in my imagination. Between TV shows and movies, comics and books, I felt like a cowboy, even though I am allergic to horses. Seriously. Anyway, despite my location and allergies, I loved the lone-cowboy-cleans-up-the-town stories.

That's not what **The Big Country** is about. Written by Donald Hamilton (creator of superspy Matt Helm) and later filmed (if you haven't seen the movie, your entertainment education is sadly lacking...), it's actually the reverse. An outsider – Jim McKay, a sea captain (retired) – turns up in Cowboy Country wearing... a bowler hat. He's there to marry the daughter of one of Texas's biggest cattle kings, but he's going to do it on his terms, and not theirs. He rejects the cowboy code, doesn't wear a .45, won't ride the bucking bronco and would rather get beaten up than indulge in brawling.

Is he crazy, or what?

And that is a large part of why this book is so much fun. Can an outsider who plays by his own rules even survive in Texas? There's a parade of great characters (most of whom don't make it into the movie), some terrific dialogue and great action sequences. If you've seen the film, there's lots of new stuff to discover. If you haven't seen the film, then this book will make you put it to the top of your 'to watch' list.

John Peel

★ ★ ★ ★ ★

FIVE RODE WEST
Lewis B Patten
1958

"The opening paragraph is a masterful example of how to quickly the draw the reader in and set the frame of the plot..."

Five Rode West is one of the first westerns I read, and still one of my favourites.

In the aftermath of the Civil War three friends ride towards the large Ute Reservation at White Valley. The local tribes are up north fighting with the cavalry following a bloody uprising. The three friends plan to grab the unattended cattle in the Valley, brand them and sell them. Along the way, they are joined by the lovely Lacy, who has her eyes on the leader Clyde, and the treacherous Hawken, who wants more than a fair share of the money.

It is a good, straightforward set-up and Patten handles it well. The tension between Clyde and Hawken is established very early on, as is the romantic tension between Clyde and Lacy, the younger sister of the woman who sent the three men on the dangerous mission. The story unfolds quickly and there are some well-staged fights between the five and bands of Utes and 'renegade whites' who are also after the cattle. There are also increasingly violent exchanges between Clyde and the 'yellow eyed' Hawken, which adds nicely to the tension.

Patten tells his story with an admirable economy and the opening paragraph is a masterful example of how to quickly the draw the reader in and set the frame of the plot, while still creating a visual image. The characters are an interesting mix and Clyde is a good hero: tough and brave, but not in an unbelievable way.

It is an enjoyable old-styled western that moves at a good pace and produces some good surprises as it heads to the final showdown.

Jeff Popple

★ ★ ★ ☆ ☆

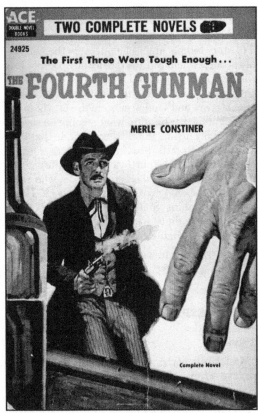

THE FOURTH GUNMAN
Merle Constiner
1958

"Full of great dialogue and intelligent characters with interesting little quirks..."

Constiner may be best known today for the mysteries he created for **Dime Detective**, and **Black Mask** tales featuring The Dean. But he also wrote more than a dozen westerns, all of which are enjoyable and about half of which are excellent. Each involve elements of mystery in addition to the western settings, with hidden motives and surprise plot turns. They're also full of great dialogue and intelligent characters with interesting little quirks – not to mention the requisite action and sudden, deadly violence.

The Fourth Gunman is one of Constiner's best, and by the end of its first chapter is already dealing its first surprises. We're introduced to George Netfield, the calm and deliberate proprietor of a saloon, apparently suspicious of a new hire and the influx of certain individuals into the town of Kirkville. Within a few pages the antagonists make their first move and we quickly learn that Netfield is far more than he seems; he's capable, decisive, and very, very smart. He's no slouch with a gun, either, although, unlike most western heroes, he swiftly learns he's not the fastest around.

The story follows him as he uncovers the schemes of the men who mean to transform Kirkville into the hub of their criminal enterprise. Netfield has to contend not just with his sceptical fellow shopkeepers and landowners, many of whom are too frightened or blind to what's going on, he has to somehow handle the three gunhands that have been sent to kill him, always alert for the appearance of the fourth and final one... This book is, simply, top shelf stuff. Those who enjoy this novel should look next to his book **Death Waits at Dakins Station**. If you like both of these, then you'll be in good hands for the rest of his westerns. Highly recommended.

Howard Andrew Jones

★ ★ ★ ★ ★

FORT DESPERATION
Frank Castle
1958

"Masterfully portrays the life in the fort, a career in the army, the tense feel of patrolling in Apache territory..."

A solitary review of a Frank Castle western I read some years ago was dismissive and put me off reading him. Now I regret that, because the first Castle book I read was pretty good and this, the second, was outstanding.

Fort Desperation opens in the middle of the action as Apaches assault a stagecoach. A young major, on his way to a remote western fort, thinks he's about to face his last moment.

He isn't, of course, but it's an attention grabber of an opening, introducing the greenhorn Wilding, the fat doctor that he and the reader might both underestimate, and the cool, lovely Selina, wife of a cavalry officer. Robert Wilding's been assigned to a distant fort as punishment after he duelled a French diplomat in DC. When he arrives, he's surrounded by veteran Apache fighters and hard cases, all commanded by a bitter superior, resentful he was never promoted and probably never will be. Worse, the young brave Wilding shot in the opening attack is the son of an Apache chief, now out for Wilding's blood. And as an added complication, Wilding finds himself tempted to be the third point of a love triangle with Selina and her husband, an officer he respects.

Castle masterfully portrays the life in the fort, a career in the army, the tense feel of patrolling in Apache territory, and Wilding's struggles with

his own self-worth. He's not entirely sure what he's capable of, and neither are we. Throughout, tension continues to mount, and Castle keeps doling out surprises, providing moments for even secondary characters to shine. Highly recommended.

Howard Andrew Jones

★ ★ ★ ★ ☆

SHOWDOWN AT WAR CLOUD
Lewis B Patten
1958

"The relentless sense of impending doom and escalating tension keep the story moving at a crisp pace..."

Like many Gold Medal Westerns this novel is essentially a crime story that takes place in the Old West. This setting helps to enhance the typical crime story concept in a couple of ways. First, bigotry against Native Americans and the mob mentality that goes along with it drives the plot, and second, the fear of a retaliatory Sioux

attack against the town, the relentless sense of impending doom and escalating tension keep the story moving at a crisp pace. The entire story takes place in a 24-hour period. An intelligent, thought-provoking and somewhat grim novel. I liked it a lot.
Ed McBride
★ ★ ★ ★ ☆

A TEXAN CAME RIDING
Frank O'Rourke
1958

"Did I mention there is a damn witch in this book?"

A hired gun named John Kearney arrives in the southwestern border town of Taos with a stack of letters. He presents these letters, some written by attorneys, judges and even a governor, to town sheriff Adolfo Montez. Kearney is searching for a criminal named Charles Malcolm, who's chosen Taos as a place to park all his wealth. As the owner of the mine and half of the area farms, Malcolm is a significant citizen. While never fully explained, apparently Malcolm raped a woman in the mid-west and cheated hundreds of God-fearing farmers out of land and stock.

We are introduced to Charles Malcolm and quickly realize he's a lunatic. Further, he keeps a witch by his side to cast spells and curses on his enemies. Malcolm has laid over half of the women in town, some carrying his offspring over to Mexico, others...well he doesn't even know about. His most prized possession is Rachel Perez, who's he most recently knocked up and placed at a nearby ranch. Kearney aligns with a sheepherder named Ed Shaffer, Rachel and sheriff Montez to uncover Malcolm's corruption in the town. Discovering an important upcoming transaction between Malcolm and businessman Don Roberto proves to be the key to uncovering Malcolm's corruption. The book's finale has Malcolm on the run as Kearney and his allies hone in.

Despite its mere 128-pages, **A Texan Came Riding** is an exhaustive effort to digest. The narrative is just implausible. Kearny has authoritative letters from various branches of jurisdiction citing Malcolm is a criminal. Why isn't he apprehended by the law? Why would Kearney, a rancher from Nebraska by trade, even be involved in this whole debacle? There's pages and pages of dialogue – displayed in lengthy paragraphs – between Malcolm, his witch and Don Roberto. Further, Kearney doesn't display any heroic traits whatsoever. Did I mention there is a damn witch in this book? **A Texan Came Riding** is terrible.

The Paperback Warrior

★ ☆ ☆ ☆ ☆

FORT SUICIDE
Gordon D Shirreffs
1959

"Torques up the tension with each chapter and delivers an unforeseen twist in the tail at the end..."

Travis Walker is an experienced cavalry officer with a keen instinct for survival. His only misstep is stopping by a remote outpost in the New Mexico desert on his way to his new posting on the Rio Grande. The fort and nearby town are threatened by Cuchillo Rojo and his growing band of Apache warriors. The fort's incompetent commander dragoons our hero into the forlorn defence of the doomed fort.

What Walker finds there is a company of soldiers and settlers turned against one another rather

Looking into the author more for this review uncovered a bunch of novels by him I never heard of. I'm going to remedy that now before this review is published!

Insider trading? Maybe.

Chuck Dixon
★ ★ ★ ★ ★

than focusing on the threat from without. Intrigue, betrayals, twists and turns confront his every effort to mount an effective strategy of defence and, this being a paperback original written in the '50s, there's more than enough horny frontier women to further distract him. Smouldering glances across the cantina floor abound.

A fine cavalry action story that torques up the tension with each chapter and delivers an unforeseen twist in the tail at the end as well as a satisfyingly violent conclusion. This author knows how to build suspense and keep the pages turning.

Gordon D Shirreffs is a favourite of mine who never failed to deliver a solid western action story. A very prolific novelist in both westerns and young adult novels, he wrote with a real authority, especially in stories set in Apacheria. His depth of knowledge about the Apaches and their tactics, as well as their capacity for cruelty, is always effective and, at times, frightening. The man knew how to stack up the stakes for his protagonist. He also writes action with clarity and just enough attention to detail to make it feel authentic.

LAST STAND AT SABER RIVER
Elmore Leonard
1959

"Rarely have I read a book which stood me in the shoes of so many of the characters ..."

One of the interesting challenges with reviewing a vintage paperback that is sixty years old is, do you review it based on the time it was first published, or based on the time in which you are reviewing it? Thankfully, Elmore Leonard's fourth book and western is so outstanding that it doesn't matter. I read a reprint edition from 1985, blissfully unaware that it had been first published decades prior to that. Its lack of spittin', cussing and wrasslin' may mark it out as originating from a gentler era, but its characterisation and dialogue are timeless in their grace and effectiveness. Leonard's portrayal of the Cable family and their troubles as they return home after being on the losing side of the Civil War is believable and nuanced. As they clash with the Yankees who have claimed their land, it plays out in a totally believable manner, with politics, greed and respect creating turmoil within all the antagonists.

Rarely have I read a book which stood me in the shoes of so many of the characters, with some sympathy for their motivations and sadness at how it might play out for them. When the violence escalates, it's even more powerful for the slow and inexorable build up. Perhaps the one aspect which might prevent this from the ultimate recommendation might be the simplicity of the plot. Either way, believe the hype with Leonard and his westerns.

Justin Marriott

LAST TRAIN FROM GUN HILL
Gordon D Shirreffs
1959

"Writes the claustrophobic scenario with tough, tight prose..."

In 1958, Gordon D Shirreffs (1914–1996) was asked to pen the adaptation of a screenplay by James Poe from a story by Les Crutchfield, **Last Train from Gun Hill**. The film was the bottom feature of a 1959 double-bill with **Gunfight at the OK Corral**. Both films were directed by John Sturges, starred Kirk Douglas, and were shot in the new wide screen format, VistaVision.

The story's a simple one, and Shirreffs delivers a compelling narrative in the book. United States Marshal Matt Morgan (played in the film by Kirk Douglas) is married to a Native American woman who, with their son, Petey, is waylaid on the road by Rick Belden, the drunken son of a rich cattle baron and his sidekick. Belden rapes and kills Mrs Morgan, setting up Morgan's hunt for justice, but with a twist—Belden's wealthy father is the marshal's old pal Craig Belden. Both book and film play out as you'd expect with Craig Belden trying to get his privileged louse of a son off the hook. Naturally, Morgan won't be bought and takes Rick into custody, promising him a fair trial back in Pawley. In a scene reminiscent of the film **3.10 to Yuma**, Morgan must wait in a besieged hotel room for the train to return and carry him home with his prisoner.

In the book, Shirreffs writes the claustrophobic scenario with tough, tight prose, superior to the

movie's portrayal (enjoyable though it is). The film uses the VistaVision process to show us a colourful wide-open saloon, some stunning location shots, and a rousing fire during the movie's climax that matched Shirreff's rock-solid descriptions. Or maybe it's the other way around—the adaptation playing it so close to the final shooting script of the movie, there's virtually nothing to differentiate the two.

Richard Prosch

MCCABE
Edmund Naughton
1959

"The tension increases, as does the sense of the inevitable outcome ..."

If three hired killers came to town for you, what would you do? If you are like the title character in **McCabe**, you hide in the church steeple, which seems like a good idea to me. But why are they there to kill him? In flashback, we meet McCabe, a gambler and alleged gunfighter who comes to the mining town of Presbyterian Church and opens a saloon and brothel. Soon Mrs Miller

An ex-gunman fights one last lonely battle for his life

McCABE

EDMUND NAUGHTON

McCabe, but instead bet with him on whether he will survive.

While the book can be somewhat difficult to find, I highly recommend that you search out a copy.

Tom Tesarek

★ ★ ★ ★ ★

SHADOW OF A STAR
Elmer Kelton
1959

"Lopes right along to a climax as nerve-wracking as it is ultimately satisfying ..."

Elmer Kelton (1926–2009) was a prolific writer, editor and eight-time Spur Award-Winner for western fiction. An impressive number, eclipsed by a bounty of additional accolades including an Owen Wister Award, honorary doctorates from at least two Universities, a lifetime achievement award from the National Cowboy Symposium, and many more.

Kelton is responsible for more than forty novels, and at least two genre classics—**The Time it Never Rained**, and **The Day the Cowboys Quit**. He wrote for television (**Maverick** and **Colt .45**) and his book **The Good Old Boys** was adapted for the small screen in 1995.

Kelton's fourth novel, **Shadow of a Star** (1959), grabs the reader from the git-go. Page one puts us in Coldridge County, Texas, where owlhoots Dencil Fox and his brother Buster watch fellow bank-robber Curly Jack die from a gunshot wound. The deadly slug inflicted during the gang's last attempted heist is almost certainly the result of Buster's own trigger-happy ways.

Leaving the boys to bury their dead, Kelton spirits us off to the town of Swallowfork and eager young deputy Jim-Bob McClain's eager point-of-view. He's equally ambitious as the villainous Buster, but in the opposite direction. Recklessly determined to become a lawman worthy to follow in his late father's footsteps, he takes more than a couple of cringe-worthy missteps.

For a few chapters, we follow Jim-Bob through his duties with sheriff Mont Naylor, watching the button goof-up at everything from his first encounter with a desperate cattle rustler to a couple of awkward encounters with the opposite sex. Despite it all, Jim-Bob's a likeable guy, which is a nod to Kelton's deft storytelling.

Before long, the Fox gang makes the scene, and the tension starts to mount. When Mont Naylor

comes to town and convinces him that she should run the brothel, as well as work there. However, the Snake River Mining Company wants to buy the whole town and convert it into a company mining town. When McCabe won't sell, the Company sends the gunmen to take care of McCabe.

As we switch between the present, as McCabe tries to deal with the gunfighters, and the past, which explains how he got to this point, the tension increases, as does the sense of the inevitable outcome. If you are familiar with the great Robert Altman movie **McCabe and Mrs Miller** with Warren Beatty and Julie Christie, you will find that the movie sticks quite close to this excellent book. Though it was written in 1959, this already had the feel of the '70s revisionist Westerns. Instead of a fantastic gunfighter, McCabe is a man with a reputation, even though he has only killed one man. McCabe and Mrs Miller have genuine care and concern for each other, but she doesn't stop prostituting herself. When it becomes clear that the killers are coming to town, the people don't rally around

is nailed in a fast gun back and forth with Buster, Jim-Bob takes centre stage—in town and in the story.

The plot is simple, the characterizations complex. There's even an undercurrent of legal philosophy as Jim-Bob struggles with some life or death decisions only he can make. The good news is Kelton never foregoes action for pedantic speechifyn' and **Shadow of a Star** lopes right along to a climax as nerve-wracking as it is ultimately satisfying. A highly recommended look at one of Kelton's early works.

Richard Prosch

THE THIRD RIDER
Barry Cord (Peter Germano)
1959

"Told at tremendous pace in a fast-flowing style that makes the book difficult to put down ..."

Peter Germano, writing as Barry Cord, creates some superb atmosphere throughout this book. Many scenes end in such a way that the reader shares the feelings of bitterness, loneliness, despair, and the sense of impending danger with lead character Mel Rawlins, Germano's choice of words vividly painting haunting images within my mind.

The story is filled with fascinating characters from the bad, the evil, and the innocent – the latter beautifully portrayed in the young girl Loan. Germano also hints that some, if not all, of these people may, or may not, be who they claim to be. The plot is filled with twists and turns, lies, treachery, mistrusts, and gripping action. Germano has Rawlins struggling to discover the hidden truths of what is going on in this small coastal town. The answers are kept from the reader too, and I never guessed what they were. Just what was the secret of the ship that unloaded only undercover of the fog? Who were behind the attempts on Rawlins life and why? Just what part did Loan have to play? And what had happened to the first and second riders?

All this is told at tremendous pace in a fast-flowing style that makes the book difficult to put down. Once again Peter Germano proves to be up there with the very best western writers. And of the few Barry Cord books I've read, this has to be one of my favourites.

Steve Myall

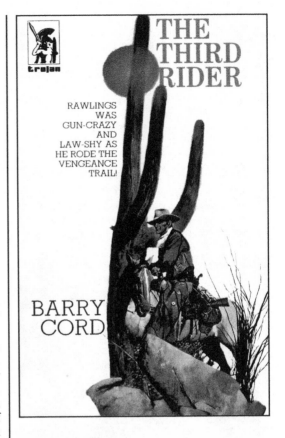

TOP MAN WITH A GUN
Lewis B Patten
1959

"Violence, vengeance and a good sense of western brutality ..."

While **Top Man with a Gun** isn't a standout western, it continues Patten's traditional western flair for violent and grim journeys by young protagonists.

The harrowing adventure begins with young Clay living in Lawrence, Kansas with his father and sister. Set in 1863, historians could probably guess what was about to unfold. Confederate militia, led by guerrilla fighter William Quantrill, descends on the city to root out the anti-slavery movement. The end result, known now as the Lawrence Massacre, left over 180 men dead and nearly 200 buildings burned. In the chaos, Clay is wounded and must watch his father's murder and his sister's subsequent suicide. He sees the face of the rider and vows to avenge their deaths.

As a classic Patten, the book is laced with violence, vengeance and a good sense of western brutality. As the author plunges readers into the narrative, we learn more about the man Clay is

name and others. Being innovative and original could be challenging under these genre tropes. Regardless, at 133-pages, **Top Man with a Gun** is an entertaining, action-packed western that didn't disappoint

The Paperback Warrior

★ ★ ★ ★ ☆

TRAIL OF THE RESTLESS GUN
Will Hickok (Chester William Harrison)
1959

"Enjoyable, even if the plot is rather unlikely ..."

TV tie-ins can be either very good or very bad, depending on whether the writer sees it simply as a quick way of making a few dollars or else a labour of love because they enjoy the show. This book, based on **The Restless Gun**, is – thankfully – one of the latter. There's more depth to the character than shown on TV, even if the resulting plot is a bit simplistic. It's credited to one "Will Hickok" (certainly a good name for a western author!), a penname for Chester William Harrison, an astonishingly prolific writer, and the plotline is rather unusual.

Hero Vint Bonner (John Payne on TV) has hunted down a dying outlaw, who comes up with a novel method of revenge – he leaves Bonner a half-interest in his ranch, and the other half to his remaining family. He figures that they will kill Bonner for him. (What if Bonner simply didn't bother claiming his half? Well, the villain didn't think of that!) Bonner decides to pretend to be an outlaw friend of the dead man and he decides that the killer's drunken father, slovenly mother, would-be gunman younger brother and trampish sister are not beyond saving. So, he goes to work on them, aiming to reform the remaining family. Naturally, though, they discover the truth, and all hell breaks loose.

It's a very different sort of a Western, and enjoyable, even if the plot is rather unlikely. But if you just want a good, easy read, then this is your book.

John Peel

★ ★ ★ ☆ ☆

becoming. Forced to ride with his sister's boyfriend Lance, the two are engaged in combat with Union officers, forcing deserter Lance to kill one of his own men. With both Clay and Lance on the run, the novel starts to find its own footing.

Soon, the duo rescues the beautiful Dolly from three armed criminals before heading across the frosty mid-west tundra to escape Indians, Union soldiers and law enforcement. While the first half ends with Clay and Dolly falling in love, the second half briskly moves the location to Texas and a robust cattle drive being handled by Clay and farmhands. Here the action heats up as Clay is forced to fight three men and a spoiled woman whom Clay rejected. This scorned lover's vengeance is about par for the course for a 1960s Gold Medal paperback – a fitting element that enhances this ordinary western tale.

This is my third Patten novel to date and I've really enjoyed all three. There are similarities in Patten's writing style – the weather elements, young heroes, revenge – but they are reminiscent of just about any good western story. Plus, Patten penned over a hundred novels under his

GOLD MEDAL WESTERNS

When I first started exploring noir and detective fiction I found a lot more places to turn for information than when I began hunting good westerns. A lot of the advice I received began and ended with the names Louis L'Amour, Max Brand and Zane Grey. Given that most of the time I'm after westerns that are less mythic and more hardboiled, these recommendations weren't terribly helpful.

Eventually I found my way to Fawcett Gold Medal westerns. Those of us in the know – and it seems that those numbers might be growing – have learned that there's a surprisingly high level of quality in the fiction produced between the launch of Gold Medal's paperback fiction line in the late '40s and sometime in the mid '60s (or possibly later, depending upon who you speak with). The GM editorial team seemed to know how to coax the best out of their writers, and

certainly seemed to know how to find talent. Unfortunately, while there's been a lot of discussion about which GM writers were crafting the best noir, or detective fiction, or juvenile delinquent novels, there's a dearth of information about their westerns. And all through the '50s, westerns were a major component of the Gold Medal line. Those numbers dropped off significantly by the mid '60s, but westerns never completely disappeared until the line itself ended. What, I wondered, were they like? I decided to find out.

In all GM published close to three hundred original westerns during a little over a quarter century. I've read a little over a third of them at this point, and while there are many authors I've yet to sample and many books I've yet to read, I can make some general observations. First, the standard level of quality is quite high. With a

GM western the plot's going to hang together, the characters are going to be well motivated, and the plot's rarely going to flag. Historical details, even down to how a riverboat operates or how a trail drive is run, are going to be well researched. These books were meant to be short and sweet, or, more precisely, short and mean, to get their hook in you and keep you going to the end. Characters don't spend a lot of time overthinking their problems or bemoaning their fates, they just get moving. Most of the books tend to be more on the hard-boiled, gritty end of the spectrum than the mythic side of things, which is admittedly my preference most of the time.

Quite a few authors wrote dependably for GM for years, so I was a little startled to learn how few of them used recurring characters even if they penned a dozen or more books for the publisher. The overwhelming majority of the books were standalones. The longest sustained GM series starred easy-going Texas drifter Buchanan, beginning with a few novels by William Ard and then continuing under a variety of other authors after Ard's untimely early death, all using the Jonas Ward by-line. All but one of the novels mention Buchanan's name in the title, so they're hard to miss. Only two other series come close in length, the Clifton Adams/Clay Randall **Amos Flagg** books, and the **Manhunter** books by Gordon Shirreffs. So far as I've been able to determine, there were only three other GM western series: the four **Clayburn** books by Marvin Albert (two of which are reviewed in this issue), three **Wyoming Jones** books by Richard Jessup writing as Richard Telfair, and, lastly, the two **Desperado** novels by Adams/Randall.

But which of the Gold Medal writers can you turn to for dependably good westerns? Well, as I mentioned, the line overall is fairly strong, but some writers are better than others. Keeping in mind my previously stated preferences, I whole-heartedly recommend any of the five Donald Hamilton westerns and anything by Marvin Albert, who sometimes wrote as Al Conroy. T V Olsen's always reliable, and in the same class as Hamilton and Albert. All three of these men can be depended upon to steadily deliver 4-star westerns. Two-time Spur Award winner Clifton Adams/Clay Randall wasn't always as gritty as these first three, but he was a true talent, and

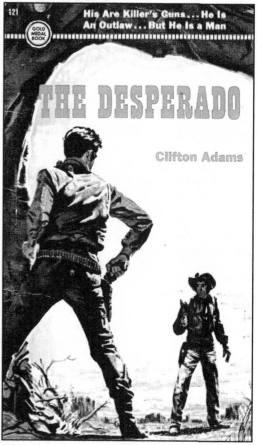

always came through, usually in the 3.5 or higher level.

Justly famed for his noir work, Harry Whittington wrote some fantastic westerns, including one of my favourites I'd classify as 5-star, **Desert Stake-Out**, reviewed elsewhere in the magazine. All of his GMs are good. Howard Rigsby, sometimes writing as Vechel Howard, didn't contribute as many westerns to the line, but all that I've read are reliably 3.5 to 4-star level, and one even rises to 5 stars. Lewis Patten is often strong as well, and I've read some Ray Hogan that impresses me.

I could suggest a dozen more specific titles that ranged from 3.5 on up but let me briefly mention a handful that are among the cream of the crop, all at least 4-star. **Desperado** and **A Noose for the Desperado**, by Clifton Adams as Clay Randall, are 5-star noir westerns, different from each other and both highly recommended. **Last Ride to Los Lobos**, by William Chamberlain, is the tale of a US cavalry unit sent south on a dangerous mission against a Mexican warlord. Two of L'Amour's very best were written for GM, the deservedly famous **Hondo** and the much less well-known **Last Stand at Papago Wells**, which is a great Apache-centric book.

A S Fleischman wrote some wonderful South Seas thrillers for Gold Medal, and one excellent western I'd rate at least as 4.5, printed as both **Yellowleg** and **The Deadly Companions** after it was turned into a movie. I cover one Richard Jessup/Richard Telfair novel in my own reviews, but I'll also mention the second and best (by a wide margin) of his three **Wyoming Jones** novels, **Day of the Gun**, which was a real page-turner. Robert MacLeod's **The Appaloosa** was another fine read and has me investigating his other works.

A number of the aforementioned titles are fairly simple to find. Starkhouse has been reprinting both Fleishman and Whittington, and even some Clifton Adams (thought not, alas, the **Amos Flagg** books, although they were reprinted so many times over their original run that it's fairly simple to find inexpensive copies). While I don't know the quality of the **Buchanan** series well enough to endorse them, I can point out that all the books are available in e-additions, and L'Amour is as easy to find as ever.

Most of T V Olsen's works were kept in print in the '80s and '90s through Leisure Books and can be had fairly inexpensively. Unfortunately, the work of some of the very best and most consistent of these writers can be more challenging to lay hands on. Donald Hamilton's westerns haven't

been reprinted, although many had large initial print runs. Rigsby/Howard seems to have only been recognized by the French and can be hard to lay hands on, much like the books of Marvin Albert, a true shame given his talent. It might be that Albert never quite delivered a classic, but there's something to be said for a writer with a large and varied body of work who consistently and dependably comes through at the 4-star level.

Howard Andrew Jones

1960- 1969

The western paperback forges its own identity.

Paperback editions from the genre's big names proliferate, but they are joined by new western authors who will make their mark on the genre, such as Gordon D Shirrefs, Lewis B Patten and Brian Garfield.

Recurring characters begin to emerge, such as The Man in Black, Amos Flagg and the much-loved Fargo.

British author J T Edson relocates the western to contemporary Texas.

When Buchanan saw the town, his first intention was to keep moving – but then he changed his mind . . .

BUCHANAN ON THE PROD

Jonas Ward

and a cool bath, but when he moseyed into the eye of a storm between two warring ranchers, he almost bit off more than he could chew. Tom did finally get that 'stake' though, four of them to be precise, but not exactly what he had figured. Staked out shirtless in the Arizona desert it was a toss-up if he'd be poisoned to death by rattlers or torn to shreds but vultures. But as old Tom would say, 'the devil looks out for Texans', and he wasn't lying as his luck changed and he sets off for a double dose of vengeance to the killers who left him to die.

Dave Karlen

LOUIS L'AMOUR

AMERICA'S FAVORITE STORYTELLER

FLINT

BUCHANAN ON THE PROD
Jonas Ward (William Ard and Robert Silverberg)
1960

"The devil looks out for Texans..."

Buchanan is a drifter who is as likeable as he is deadly, who seems to always be out of the frying pan and into the fire, but with a lightning fast draw and a little luck the big jasper endures from one tale to another. He was created in 1956 by hardboiled crime writer William Ard for Fawcett Gold Medal Books, writing the first five volumes under his Jonas Ward pseudonym until his untimely passing. **Buchanan on the Prod**, the sixth in the series was a work-in-progress which was completed by Robert Silverberg, with later volumes written by Brian Garfield and William R Cox.

Having practiced law for a spell in West Texas, I know exactly what Tom Buchanan would be like – tall and wiry with an easy smile and skin burnt to a crisp from a relentless sun, so I enjoyed reading **Buchanan on the Prod**, (western slang for looking for trouble or a fight). Passing through Arizona territory, all Buchanan wanted was to get off the trail and find him a $10 steak

FLINT
Louis L'Amour
1960

"It is fundamentally the perfect western..."

Deemed 'America's Favourite Storyteller', Louis L'Amour wrote eighty-nine western novels in his lifetime. Many fans and genre enthusiasts have compiled lists documenting the author's most outstanding literary works. These lists vary depending on the creator, but nearly all of them contain one fixture – **Flint**.

The book introduces us to James T Kettleman, a successful stockbroker from New York who has journeyed by train to New Mexico. Dying from an undisclosed illness (symptoms of cancer or tuberculosis), Kettleman plans to spend his dying days tucked away in a desert oasis reading his favourite books. We can imagine that Paperback Warrior readers are sympathetic to that impulse.

Through flashback sequences, we learn that Kettleman was snatched from a burning wagon train at the age of two by a man known as Flint. Passed around from family to family as an orphan, Kettleman became an exceptional student. Reuniting with Flint in his teen years, Kettleman learns how to fight and adapt in the hostile desert. These attributes eventually lead to Kettleman avenging the murder of Flint. Although that backstory alone would make for a great novel, again these are just flashback sequences that expand into a much broader narrative.

Kettleman's doomsday euphoria of peacefully dying in the desert surrounded by books is disrupted by Port Baldwin, the stereotypical land baron who desires the Kaybar ranch. Its owner is Nancy Kerrigan (not the figure skater), a strong-willed fighting woman who grew up on the ranch. Her property has no official deed, a common element found in real estate transactions with Indians. With land grabbers migrating from the east, her ownership is under heavy scrutiny.

As Kettleman finds himself an ally of the Kaybar ranch, he quickly finds he has feelings for Kerrigan. Using the moniker of 'Flint', Kettleman becomes the mysterious protector that engages in battle with Baldwin's faction. Utilizing numerous gunfights and the obligatory fistfight, L'Amour's portrait of the American west is a violent and gritty one. L'Amour thrives with the range war narrative and **Flint** doesn't disappoint.

It's easy to see why **Flint** ranks among L'Amour's best work. It is fundamentally the perfect western. Seasoned readers are very familiar with this type of story and the western fiction tropes, yet **Flint** proves to be a remarkable story worth retelling again and again. It's a valuable cornerstone for not only L'Amour's work, but the whole western genre.

The Paperback Warrior

SABADILLA
Richard Jessup
1960

"May feel as if it's going to launch into a standard gritty revenge novel, it almost constantly surprises..."

Though best known for his novel **The Cincinnati Kid**, and primarily known as a crime writer, Richard Jessup wrote close to a dozen westerns for Gold Medal in the 1950s and '60s, three of them featuring one of the line's few series characters, Wyoming Jones. **Sabadilla** is a standalone novel, however. Its protagonist is an exiled Mexican revolutionary famous both for his skill with a pistol and with a razor-tipped whip. He's not really looking for trouble when he's turned out of his native land, but then, in the desert, three men steal his horse and leave him to die.

After its gripping opening **Sabadilla** may feel as if it's going to launch into a standard gritty revenge novel, but it almost constantly surprises. Even when one of the toughs who took Sabadilla's horse turns out to be the son of a land baron, the tale still doesn't end up exactly where you expect. And then while western novels are full of tough loners, Sabadilla's remote, coolly formal manner and deadly efficiency is somehow different and compelling.

Jessup's writing is always excellent on a sentence-by-sentence level, and this is one of his best – well plotted, well paced, and full of action.

Howard Andrew Jones

SEVEN WAYS FROM SUNDOWN
Clair Huffaker
1960

"A great shoot-out between the mismatched pair of travellers and a gang of outlaws ..."

Clair Huffaker wrote the novel and the subsequent screenplay for **Seven Ways from Sundown** when it was made into an Audie Murphy movie. It is likely that both were done as a package deal, as there is a strong cinematic feel to the book in terms of the episodic telling of the story and the relationship between the green young Texas Ranger, Seven Ways From Sundown Smith, and the enigmatic, legendary gunfighter Jim Flood.

The book basically chronicles Seven's pursuit and capture of Flood and the long journey back to Texas with the outlaw in tow. Along the way, the pair develop a bond as they encounter various dangers, including Apaches, the weather and a gang of outlaws wanting to settle a score with Flood.

Huffaker tells his story with a nice economy and it proceeds at a brisk pace, while still conveying a good sense of the rigours of the journey. The relationship between Seven and Flood is at the core of the book and Huffaker develops it in a credible and affectionate way, often with good humour. The dialogue between the two is particularly enjoyable, especially when Flood is making fun at Seven's naivety:

"'You got t' stop askin' questions sometimes,' Flood laughed without much humour, 'because some of the questions you put mark you as unbelievably ignorant.'"

The action is frequent and well described, and there is a great shoot-out between the mismatched pair of travellers and a gang of outlaws. There is also a satisfying and poignant conclusion to the story.

It has been over thirty years since I first read **Seven Ways from Sundown**, but I enjoyed it as much this time as I did back then.

Jeff Popple

★ ★ ★ ★ ☆

TEXAS FEVER
Donald Hamilton
1960

"A surprisingly adult tale that isn't afraid to delve into some dark psychological terrain …"

While best known for his excellent **Matt Helm** espionage series, Donald Hamilton also wrote a fair share of westerns and it becomes obvious within the first few pages of **Texas Fever** that he was a genuine master of the genre. There is an immediate grasp of setting, characters, and purpose that sets the story into motion as we're introduced to young Chuck McAuliffe following his hardened Civil War hero father on a cattle drive from the McAuliffe Ranch in Texas through Indian Territory to Kansas. We enter the story in mid-drive and are alongside as their team runs into all manner of obstacles, from deadly bushwhackers in its opening pages to brutally enforced quarantines against potentially disease-carrying Texas longhorns in the border towns. Driving the narrative is a constant revenge-fuelled feud with the leader of the bushwhackers who murdered Chuck's brother and the sadistic and corrupt deputy enforcing the quarantine. Throughout the book, Hamilton

keeps subverting expectations and genre tropes to deliver a surprisingly adult tale that isn't afraid to delve into some dark psychological terrain. There's plenty of action—both with guns and fists—and a very frank sexual awareness that may have turned some heads in 1960 with anyone expecting a sanitized Hollywood-style cowboy oater. I quite literally couldn't put the book down and read it in a rush to see where the unexpected plot turns would take me next. This really is the very good stuff—highly recommended!

Steve Carroll

★ ★ ★ ★ ★

DESERT STAKE-OUT
Harry Whittington
1961

"A balance beam of thriller and suspense with the reader navigating the emotional states of these desperate characters …"

Whittington introduces readers to Blade Merrick, a former Confederate soldier who's contracting with the US Army to haul valuable

A Fawcett Gold Medal Book

KISSI 40¢

Bushwhackers and Indians had cut their number down—now a bunch of damyankees, still fighting the war, wanted to finish the job

TEXAS FEVER by DONALD HAMILTON

Author of the Bestselling MATT HELM SERIES

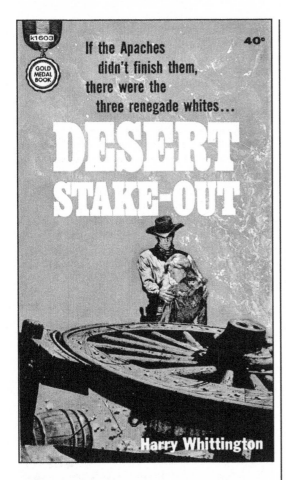

If the Apaches didn't finish them, there were the three renegade whites...

DESERT STAKE-OUT

Harry Whittington

40°

K1603

GOLD MEDAL BOOK

---

the outlaws will kill Blade, rape her and make off with all the supplies. Blade is stuck in a hard place knowing that San Carlos is experiencing a plague that desperately needs his supplies. But ultimately none of them will survive another Apache assault outnumbered and outgunned.

First, if you are looking for the rip-roaring 'Cowboys and Indians' western shootout I'm here to tell you **Desert Stake-Out** isn't it. Instead, this is a balance beam of thriller and suspense with the reader navigating the emotional states of these desperate characters. It increases tension and dread in all the right places, emphasizing how precarious the situation is for these six individuals. Just when you think you've figured it out, Whittington throws in a wild card; a grave that's been dug right there in Patchee Wells by Blade himself. Who's buried? Did Blade know these outlaws prior to meeting them at the watering hole? Little puzzle pieces are revealed as the reader sits in the rocks and dust waiting for everything to come full circle. The ending was extremely satisfying and painted a detailed portrait of this mysterious protagonist. I can't say enough good things about this one.

The Paperback Warrior

★ ★ ★ ★ ★

medical supplies to the town of San Carlos. Beginning at Fort Ambush, Blade must venture through the hot California desert amidst the dreaded Apache...solo. Why Blade has been chosen for this mission remains a mystery until the closing chapters. The mystery, intrigue and suspense are a solid wind-up through the middle portions of the narrative.

After a few days on the journey, Blade stops at a rocky watering hole called Patchee Wells. It's there that he stumbles on three outlaws – elderly Charley Clinton, his son Billy and the gunfighter Perch Fisher. They in turn have stumbled up on the gut-shot Jeff Butler and his wife Valerie. When Blade joins the group to assist, he learns they were attacked by the Apache with a second round of attacks coming. While Blade digs the bullet out of Butler, the table is densely set for alliances and betrayals.

The outlaws want to steal Blade's horses and supplies to head north away from the Army and Apache. Blade thinks they are the three guys that robbed a bank in Tucson. Butler's wife wants Blade's help to return to Fort Ambush where her husband can receive proper care. She fears that

FIGHTIN' BUCKAROO
Jeff Clinton (Jack Bickham)
1961

"All of which will bring him more trouble than a gunny sack full of weasels ..."

The fighting buckaroo of the title is Wildcat O'Shea – a fighting, whiskey loving, deceptively good-natured galoot created by western stalwart Jack Bickham under his Jeff Clinton pseudonym. To call Wildcat a disarming sight is an understatement. Wearing a battered blue hat planted over his shock of wild Irish red hair, he adds to his bold fashion statement by dressing in a red shirt, black vest, tan Levi's, green boots and fancy Mexican spurs, all while riding a painted orange saddle astride any nag willing to wear the rig. Despite his appearance, Wildcat is as tough, smart and determined as they come. In jail for public drunkenness and brawling, Wildcat is offered a get out of jail free card from the sheriff if he will go to Hog Creek and find out what happened to the deputy sent there to investigate a murder. Wildcat takes the job, figuring if can't be too hard, and is happy to be out from behind bars.

Constantly underestimated because of his appearance, Wildcat's goofy personality hides a

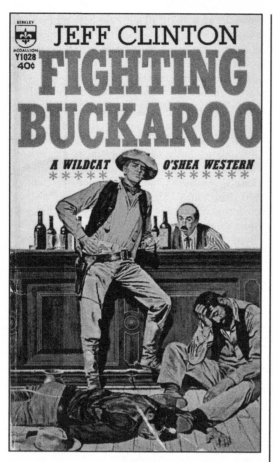

whodunit mystery with an everyman wrongfully accused of a murder who must work alone to clear his name. In this case, the everyman is Sam Dodge who has returned to the town of Bent River to attend the funeral of its fast-gun sheriff, Miles Ringo, who was gunned down late at night in the streets. Sam had a contentious relationship with Ringo, having been his deputy before a falling out over a woman sends Sam on to a hardscrabble life as a rancher barely making ends meet.

Upon his arrival back to town, everyone questions his motives. But Sam Dodge has come to flush out the murderer of his former friend and decides to set a trap. However, the device of the book's title ensnares Sam himself as he fakes a drunken scree at the local saloon where he brags about killing Ringo himself to draw out the true killer. This plan fails spectacularly as Sam is framed for yet another murder and ends up in a gunfight where he is forced to gun down three members of the town's criminal population. It all ends in a courtroom where a recovering drunk lawyer represents Sam as he fights for his life and to uncover the conspiracy that has befallen him.

This is a short, fast read and although not action-packed, it is never boring and is written in

rock-hard core of granite punching, fast shooting, stubborn fighting man. Within twenty-four hours of arriving in Hog Creek, he breaks up a domestic dispute, tosses the town bully out a window, gets shot at, gets his head clobbered, drinks more whiskey than he should, picks up the undying friendship of Simple Simon (who in less politically correct days would be called the town idiot), and slicks his hair back for a date with the town's prettiest saloon belle—all of which will bring him more trouble than a gunny sack full of weasels. Much mayhem ensues before Wildcat gets to the bottom of murder and fraud.

Paul Bishop

A TRAP FOR SAM DODGE
Harry Whittington
1961

"Written in a terse, clipped manner that immediately engages the reader ..."

Even though **A Trap for Sam Dodge** is a western, it still clearly adheres to the format of a classic

a terse, clipped manner that immediately engages the reader.

Steve Carroll

★ ★ ★ ☆ ☆

WAR IN SANDHOVEL COUNTY
Wayne D Overholser
1961

"Even the good guys tend toward the grey side of the scale ..."

I've been wanting to read a Wayne D Overholser western ever since I saw him referenced in Stephen King's novel **Wolves of the Calla**, part of King's **Dark Tower** saga. Overholser was among the earlier group of American western writers and, in fact, won the very first Spur Award in 1953 for his novel, **Lawman**. Like many others of his time, Wayne cut his teeth in the pulps, his first story published in 1936.

In this book, Jeff Ardell is a man caught in the middle of a range war. He begins the book as part of the 'Big 4' ranchers in the high prairie region of the fictional Sandoval County, Colorado. An ugly cattle-rustling problem causes the leader of the Big 4, Ben Shortt, to call in a 'livestock detective' to find proof of the re-branding activity. However, the man he secretly calls in, Sam Marks, is a notorious killer, known for his cowardly way of shooting unsuspecting men in the back. Jeff sees Shortt's power-grab for what it is and decides to pull out of the Big 4. But trying to determine who his friends are and who might be selling him out to the killer is only part of his problem now. While that plot sounds straightforward, it doesn't play out in the expected ways. And considering that Shortt's granddaughter is Jeff's fiancé, you can imagine that this place is ripe for combustion.

This book has plenty of gun-slinging action and backstabbing twists as Jeff stubbornly takes on the existing power structure. It's not just about how Jeff tries to outmanoeuvre his foes but figuring out how to lead his side against all the people arrayed against him. Even the good guys tend toward the grey side of the scale, so Jeff has some moral dilemmas to wade through.

An enjoyable read with a satisfying ending that makes me want to hunt down more of Overholser's work.

Benjamin Thomas

★ ★ ★ ★ ☆

GOPHER GOLD
Todhunter Ballard
1962

"Takes us into a claustrophobic town affected by the plague and the people who are being killed by it..."

When the plague came to the mining town of Gopher, men began dropping like flies. But why won't the remaining men leave? Well, in town, there sits an over one-ton ball of gold. And all the remaining men who are not infected with the plague have gold fever. The gold was formed into a ball by two men, the notorious Sam Dohne and Clint Collins, who believed that by creating it into the seemingly immovable one-ton ball, that they were free from being robbed of it. A young doctor named Adam Patch heads to the godforsaken town of Gopher along with Mary Collins, who is searching for her husband and Lindsey Stewart, who's motives we are unsure of. Adam, a man of many skills, is going because, as a doctor, he feels he must try and assist the people of the town, even though he could become infected. He lands in the middle of not only an epidemic but of a town of some of the most despicable and desperate characters ever assembled. And all the men in town are all angling to get out of town with the gold ball. The loathsome Kid Beale and his gang decide to get the ball and head out of town, heading towards Mexico. The gang takes the beautiful Mary Collins along for insurance, but Kid Beale has rapist designs on her. Adam and Lindsey head out after the band of vicious outlaws to save Mary from the sadistic Kid Beale. Adam Patch, though, is not your average doctor, a man of the impeccable skills of a surgeon, but also an excellent gambler and gunman. Adam Patch presented as a man of high character, is a doctor who aims to help people, but a man who can handle himself in the direst situations. Adam Patch always seemed to be in control, except when it came to Mary Collins. And for her, he would do anything.

Todhunter Ballard creates a stunning piece of fiction in **Gopher Gold**. Having a highly moralistic character such as the doctor Adam Patch enter a den of thieves and outlaws, all trying to stay alive and get their hands on that luring gold ball, is a fascinating angle. Ballard takes us into a claustrophobic town affected by the plague and the people who are being killed by it. Placing us squarely in the middle of the mining town of Gopher, a lawless town, brimming with veterans of the gold rushes, men who will risk it all for the gold they crave. The men in the town of Gopher are afflicted by either the plague, gold fever or (in the case of Adam Patch) love. Out of a world of greed, death and disease, Ballard's message to the reader is that all the gold in the world can never take the place of love. The copy reviewed was the 1969 release under the title **Blood and Gold** and published by the great Belmont Books!

Mike Hauss

★ ★ ★ ★ ☆

LANDO
Louis L'Amour
1962

"You'll be hungry for more of the same as soon as you finish this one..."

I'll admit that when I decided to dip my toe into trying a new western author, I found the sheer amount of output from Louis L'Amour somewhat intimidating. Where on Earth does one start? Thankfully, more than one friend suggested I give **Lando** a try. Although this is book seven in the Sackett family saga, it can be read as a standalone novel.

Orlando (Lando) Sackett has been left with friends of his father's to be schooled and raised with them. Along with Lando came a huge sack of gold to pay for his education. As you might expect, the gold is spent on the friend's son and the purchase of a cattle ranch. Lando is left to fend for himself and hastily leaves the family to live in a mill. There he matures and grows until a travelling tinker offers him passage to distant lands. Lando grabs the opportunity and heads off, little knowing that word of his existence and the rumour of missing gold has spread far and wide.

It's not long until he gets in trouble and right on the border of Mexico, he lands himself in prison. He spends some years here, but the time is not wasted as he becomes an accomplished bare-knuckle fist fighter. Fortuitously, he is eventually released and the book flows into a somewhat open-ended conclusion which will naturally lead to the next instalment in the series.

L'Amour's writing style is effortless and I'm certain you'll be hungry for more of the same as soon as you finish this one. Perhaps consider

starting with the first book in the Sackett saga though, **Sackett's Land**.

Jules Burt

★ ★ ★ ★ ☆

RIO DESPERADO
Gordon D Shirreffs
1962

"A depth of character and a literary flair to this book that belies its pulp roots ..."

As **Rio Desperado** opens, gunslinger Burke Dane cuts down the lynched body of his half-brother on the outskirts of a town where the young family man had gone to buy cattle. Dane's only clue is the unique style of braided rawhide reata that was used to hang his brother. Armed with basic knowledge of the town and the power-hungry cattle baron who runs it, Dane sets out to find those responsible and exact justice. He also intends to retrieve the $5,000 in poker winnings that was stolen from his brother's corpse so he can give it to his brother's widow and children. This basic set-up is all that is necessary in the hands of a pro like Shirreffs, who wrote over seventy novels in his day. There is a depth of character and a literary flair to this book that belies its pulp roots. Dane saves the life of Jesse, hotheaded young hired gun working for the town's dictator-like boss. A friendship slowly develops between these two although evidence would appear to point a potential finger of guilt at Jesse, who is trying to find his special reata that is missing. The central mystery is sufficiently intriguing, and it's all punctuated by some excellent action sequences. Everything climaxes with a protracted chase and gunfight through the canyons during heavy thunderstorms as floods threaten to wash out the only bridge to freedom while a small army of cutthroats closes in. The best endorsement I can give **Rio Desperado** is that it makes me want to read more by Gordon Shirreffs!
Steve Carroll

★ ★ ★ ★ ☆

VENGEANCE RIDER
Lewis B Patten
1962

"I can never provide enough praise for Lewis B Patten ..."

Despite the lack of witnesses or evidence, rancher Ross Logan was convicted of killing his wife Ruth. Logan was sentenced to fifteen hard years in prison. In Patten's opening pages, Logan is released from confinement after serving his full sentence. From high atop Cheyenne Ridge, Logan looks down at his condemner, the small town of Vail and what was originally his sprawling Horseshoe Ranch. He is determined to locate Ruth's killer and seek redemption from his former friends and peers. But as we quickly learn, the town has no interest in Logan's proclamation of innocence. They have simply moved on.

Out of money, food and supplies, Logan goes to work for the new operator of Horseshoe Ranch, a brutal man named Caine. Smitten with Caine's much younger wife, Lily, Logan begins earning just enough money and food to bide some free time to investigate Ruth's murder. Patten's panel of suspects seems promising: town founder Tobias Vail, judge Millburn and Logan's long-time friend Phil – all who have vested interests in Horseshoe Ranch.

The most likely suspect is Millburn, who was Logan's attorney fifteen years ago. After Logan's conviction, Millburn sold the neglected Horseshoe Ranch cheaply to Caine to raise enough money for Logan's legal fees. But, after

SIGNET BRAND WESTERN • 451-AE2621 • (CANADA $2.75) • U.S. $2.25

Framed and sent to prison, Logan was back to catch his wife's killer—even if it cost him his life...

SPUR AWARD-WINNING AUTHOR

LEWIS B. PATTEN

VENGEANCE RIDER

investigating the books, Logan learns that Millburn had Caine quickly sell the ranch back to him. Could Millburn have set the whole thing up to acquire the ranch for pennies on the dollar?

Determined to prove Millburn is the culprit, Logan begins to connect the dots while secretly meeting with Lily. Soon, Logan finds that's he's under arrest for yet another murder – Caine's! On the run from a posse and the law, Logan now must find who has killed Ruth and Caine or face the gallows.

I can never provide enough praise for Lewis B Patten. I've now read a handful of his western novels and all of them have been top notch. While never overly violent, Patten is a bit more subdued with **Vengeance Rider**. Here, the author uses a popular crime fiction element – the convicted defending their innocence – and places it in the harsh American West. Brimming with fights, romance and the thrill of the chase, Patten's **Vengeance Rider** works exceptionally well as both a western and a crime novel. Read it, you'll love it!

The Paperback Warrior

WILD SKY
Harry Whittington
1962

"An interesting story that uses the 'past catching up' theme …"

The beginning of the novel introduces readers to Josh, his pregnant wife Fran and four-year old daughter Joanie. It's the young family's thirty-third day of travel from the East Coast, a long and perilous journey to Wyoming. Whittington paints this rather basic introduction with heightened tension, an impending doom that is evident with Josh's frequent glances over his shoulder. Soon, a young Native-American rides towards the wagon, non-pleasantries are exchanged and soon Josh and the family are riding away as the brave lies defeated with a broken arm. This brief exchange proves the validity of our protagonist – Josh is a fighter.

The family settles on a beautiful stretch of valley with Josh building a cabin and planting crops. I really enjoyed the author's descriptive narrative on hunting deer and tracking through the mountains. It's these scenes that are often ignored by western writers, something that L'Amour excelled at with his early Sackett frontier stories. Once settled, Josh reflects on why his family has retreated to the wilderness.

Back east, Josh ran a mercantile store with Fran and the two had a picturesque life together. One night while leaving work both Josh and Fran are attacked by a belligerent man named Can Kirby. It's a brief encounter, but Kirby strongly advises Josh that he will kill him soon and encourages him to start wearing a gun. Josh, at this point a pacifist, doesn't accept violence as the answer. But this is the 1800s wild west and Josh has a family to protect. Why has he sworn off violence? Why does he keep his pistol in a bag under the bed?

Ultimately, Whittington creates an interesting story that uses the 'past catching up' theme to place Josh and his family in dire straits. We know that he can't run from his past, but it is interesting to see how it creeps up from behind. While only 103-pages, the author writes a propulsive narrative that incorporates another wilderness family to pad out the dialogue (and create alliances for the impending doom). Overall, a solid western tale worth pursuing.

The Paperback Warrior

CATLOW
Louis L'Amour
1963

"Has a stripped-down charm I found satisfying …"

Ben Cowan and Abijah Bijah Catlow had been bound as friends since childhood. By the time they reached manhood, however, they had drifted apart. Ben had taken the path to wearing a tin star, while Catlow followed a more serpentine trail to becoming a top cowhand with a wild streak who followed the spirit of the law if not the letter. By mutual consent, they avoid each other so as not to force a confrontation. But after a disastrous confrontation with a band of greedy ranchers, Catlow is branded an outlaw and it is US Marshal Ben Cowan's job to bring him in alive—if Catlow will let him.

When Catlow escapes to Mexico, determined to pull off a Confederate gold heist and retire, Ben is hot on his trail. But circumstances will force the two men on opposite sides of the law to become allies again, fighting for survival as they are pursued across the harsh Mexican desert by forces who want them both dead.

While **Catlow** is clearly from the early stages of L'Amour's writing career, it has a stripped-down charm I found satisfying. I enjoyed the interplay between Catlow and Cowan—friends turned reluctant adversaries—and found myself rooting for both characters to win. L'Amour was a master at creating this type of reader engagement and, because **Catlow** is so stripped down, an attentive reader can get a glimpse of the behind the scenes writing mechanics. I found this fascinating. There is some justification to believe **Catlow** was an unsold pulp story L'Amour whipped into shape quickly to keep up with the demands of his publisher's schedule after he (justifiably) took too long expanding the novelization of the movie **How the West Was Won**.

Paul Bishop

HARDCASE FOR HIRE
Clay Randall
1963

"A glimpse into the fragility of the human psyche without skimping on the action..."

Dogtown, a sad dead-end left to die along the tracks gets a jolt with the arrival of Bella Steffino, a socialite and chanteuse from back East. She's a woman on a mission to find her errant husband who's fled into the Choctaw Nations to serve as a doctor to the outlaws who hide out there. To bring back the doc, Bella hires Jess Henry, the hardcase of the title and a man who knows the sawtooth ridges and dark hollers where the Butler brothers are bandit kings. What follows is a manhunt tale complicated by a femme fatale with questionable motives. Randall's taken what would have been a sturdy plot of a hardboiled crime story (and probably was) and restaged it in Arkansas in the 1880s. The prose is lean and written with the authority of someone who knows the country. That's the biggest challenge, for me anyway, in writing westerns; making the terrain come alive. Randall excels at that that as well as ratcheting up tension and delivering on the action when called for. His dialogue touches are unique and have the feel of authenticity. He stays away from anachronisms when characters are speaking. Not so much in the descriptions which often use out-of-period words and phrases. But that's a pardonable sin when you're writing on tight deadlines for pennies a word, right? Despite the lack of pretence to art, this is a well-written, intelligent story that provides a glimpse into the fragility of the human psyche without skimping on the action. Randall writes with the invisible hand, allowing the characters' personalities to grow out of their actions rather than exposition. This brand of writing, which I prefer, allows the reader to discover the players in the story rather than be schooled on them. A tidy shoot-'em-up that gets high marks in lowbrow entertainment.

Chuck Dixon

MONTE WALSH
Jack Schaefer
1963

"A special book that made me laugh and made me cry ..."

This is a wonderful novel telling the story of likable cowboy Monte Walsh and his faithful friend Chet Rollins in a series of vignettes that can be humorous, exciting, or touching. Shaefer provides a truly vivid and likely accurate portrayal of cowboy life in the latter half of the 19th century from the simpler times when ranch and cowboy activity was at its prime to when the influx of technology such as automobiles began to signal their coming decline and the end of a way of life. The story begins with Monte as a young man, fun loving and a bit wild, and follows him as he matures into middle age with the

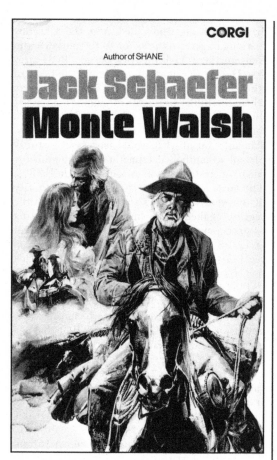

CORGI

Author of SHANE

Jack Schaefer
Monte Walsh

is forced to be a witness to the hanging of the three accused to ensure his silence. Everyone, including the town sheriff, is convinced of the trio's guilt. There has even been a failed attempt to achieve a change of venue for the pending court trial to avoid just this very outcome due to the toxic atmosphere within the town toward the accused men. The bulk of the book consists of Murdock on a self-imposed journey throughout the Southwest and into Mexico to notify the families of the lynched men of their fates. However, it quickly becomes apparent that he's been followed by killers from Ute Crossing intent on keeping him from accomplishing his mission. The book slowly morphs into a mystery as the clues Murdock gathers on his journey begin to unravel the case against the three hanged men. It is quickly apparent that murder has been committed and there's a conspiracy afoot. Mix in a little romance and several gunfights and you've got a solid straightforward western that may meander a bit and wraps up a little too quickly in the climax but entertains throughout.

Steve Carroll

★★★☆☆

changes that accompany that process, something that many of us can relate to. This is a special book that made me laugh and made me cry. It transcends the western genre, much like **Lonesome Dove**, or **The Time it Never Rained**. One thing's for sure. Anyone that reads this book will wish that they had a friend like Chet.
Ed McBride

★★★★★

BLOOD JUSTICE
Gordon Shirreffs
1964

"A solid straightforward western that entertains throughout..."

Gordon D Shirreffs was a prolific writer, publishing five novels and two children's books in 1964 alone. **Blood Justice** represents a more adult, less pulpy approach from other Shirreffs books I've read. Jim Murdock was almost lynched in the town of Ute Crossing for a crime he didn't commit and is returning to the town for the first time in years. As fate would have it, he arrives just as another lynching is underway and

SIGNET WESTERN · P3991 · 60c

He'd escaped lynching himself. Now he swore justice on the graves of three men who were railroaded to the rope...in a hanging at dawn

BLOOD JUSTICE
GORDON D. SHIRREFFS

HANGING WOMAN CREEK
Louis L'Amour
1964

"Loaded with atmosphere and mystery…"

Set in frosty Montana, L'Amour introduces us to the rough and tough Pronto Pike. He's a down on his luck journeyman who drifts from job to job all over the country. Like many paperback cowboys, Pronto is decent with his fists and Hell with a rifle. He's a great cattle guy, a hard worker…but his temper has been the bane of his existence. So, it's fitting that the book opens with Pronto being released from an overnight stay in jail along with a couple of other drifter types – Van Bokkelen (who may be wanted for murder) and an older African American boxer named Eddie Holt.

After separating themselves from Bokkelen, both Eddie and Pronto team up to find work before the bulk of winter hits the Montana timbers. After asking around, the duo find a great stint punching cattle for a rancher named Bill Justin. It's a good gig – warm cabin, plenty of wood, a few books and the calm day-to-day activities of babysitting cattle through the winter. Eddie, while not a skilled rancher, earns his keep by preparing good meals and teaching Pronto some boxing lessons. In turn, Pronto shows Eddie how to punch cattle. However, the good vibe at Hanging Woman Creek doesn't last long.

L'Amour slowly envelopes the story with an impending sense of gloom, enhanced by the cold, rural landscape. After learning that cattle rustlers are among them, Pronto finds a murdered man in the snow (with a few mysterious horse prints). With tensions high and both men feeling watched and unsettled, Pronto rides into town to present the dead man and to make a sworn statement. There, he finds an Irish beauty named Ann Farley, the sister of a nester named Philo Farley, an old friend of Pronto's. Ann explains that her brother could be in trouble and needs a ride out to his cabin just shy of Hanging Woman Creek.

The heart of the book is ultimately a classic western…but it's loaded with atmosphere and mystery. Where's the rustlers, who's leading them and what's behind the murders? How are Philo and Ann Farley tied to it? While the first third of the book develops great characters, the middle really expands on that and introduces mystery and intrigue. The last third is Hell bent for leather, matching the book's cover perfectly.

L'Amour is a master storyteller and this one has all his best ingredients. Action, mystery, interesting (and lovable) characters and a frantic sense of pacing. It's a short read packed with atmosphere and firepower. **Hanging Woman Creek** is highly recommended…and won't let you down until that noose snaps tight.

The Paperback Warrior

THE PROFESSIONALS
Frank O' Rourke
1964

"Action flows fast under a sun as relentless as the kidnapper's deadline. …"

Frank O'Rourke's novel **A Mule for the Marquesa** underwent a name change to **The Professionals** when it moved from page to screen. Movie tie-in versions and subsequent reprints all retained the punchier title. **The Professionals** begins as a straightforward western actioner but packs a kick by the time the last page is turned. Set in the sixth year of the Mexican Revolution, a group of Mexican rebels kidnap Angelina Grant, the fiery Mexican wife of American cattle baron Augustus Grant. The purpose of their actions is three-fold – obtain pardons from Pancho Villa, reward, and ultimate revenge against Grant.

The arrogant, very rich, Grant recruits a band of five larger-than-life soldiers of fortune – led by ex-cavalryman turned arms dealer Henry Fardan, who combines a taste for adventure with a penchant for retrospection. Each man is a hardened expert in logistics, combat, explosives or improvisation. Their job is to cross the desert and rescue Grant's kidnapped senorita. The action flows fast under a sun as relentless as the kidnapper's deadline. Straight shooting leads to the inevitable rescue, but there is a surprise twist. The caper – five men against a hundred – is ingenious, exciting and vividly told.

Paul Bishop

★ ★ ★ ★ ☆

THREE RODE NORTH
Marvin Albert
1964

"Clean, sharp prose, driving action scenes, and compelling characters ..."

One of the four novels featuring Albert's Clayburn character, this novel can be found published both under his own name, and his Al Conroy pseudonym, in printings from multiple publishers. Skilled and versatile right from the start of his career, many of Albert's works were converted into movies, beginning with his very first western, **The Law and Jake Wade**. A Shamus award-winning mystery novelist, Albert wrote thrillers, men's adventure novels, detective stories, historical fiction, noir and –naturally – westerns. I've enjoyed his clean, sharp prose, driving action scenes, and compelling characters so well I've read through most of his work and I'm almost never disappointed.

Three Rode North is the third of the books featuring Clayburn, a gambler and skilled gunman, a hero who tends to wander into problems and then solve them with tenacity, wit, fists and, when necessary, lots of bullets. Albert is a skilled action writer, and you can see his chops on display throughout **Three Rode North** as Clayburn tracks down the assassin who killed his oldest friend and mentor. Though this novel begins like a simple tale of revenge, it turns out that the assassin is the right-hand man to a corrupt Mexican revolutionary, a general holed up with a small army in a hidden desert fortress. He's a powerful enemy, and one Clayburn

eventually realizes he'll have to contend with if he wants to keep breathing.

You want cinematic action, surprises, and great characters? You're in good hands with any of Albert's works, but this may be the best of the four Clayburn novels in particular – even though it was another from the series, **The Man in Black**, that was made into a movie retitled **Rough Night in Jericho** (and, oddly enough, novelized by Ben Haas under his Ben Elliot pseudonym).

Howard Andrew Jones

★ ★ ★ ★ ☆

THE MAN IN BLACK
Al Conroy (Marvin H Albert)
1965

"Fast and free with his fists and never hesitates to fight dirty ..."

The Man in Black is the second in a four-book series featuring the gambler and gunman known as Clayburn. Like many tough guys, Clayburn has no first name. A former army scout, Clayburn's past includes a stint as a town tamer for the Remsberg Detective Agency. He chooses to dress in black when he's in town gambling, but being a realist, he wears buckskins and Levi's when out on the trail. Clayburn is a smart tactician, favouring brains over violence. But when violence is called for, he doesn't worry about being fast with his guns – believing accuracy is more important. He is, however, fast and free with his fists and never hesitates to fight dirty.

In **The Man in Black**, Clayburn has invested his gambling spoils into a new stage line run by Greco, his old partner from his detective days. Looking to protect his investment, Clayburn is riding shotgun when the stagecoach is shot up by a sniper, shredding the stage and leaving Greco wounded. Attractive widow Velma Lang, Greco's business partner, has refused to pay protection money to the Cole Wheelock gang, who control the town. Wheelock's orders to shoot up the coach were carried out by Alex Flood, Wheelock's top enforcer—a killer marksman who specializes in long-range ambush. To salvage his financial investment, Clayburn must take on Wheelock, his gang of hard-case killers, and Flood – the deadliest killer of them all. But Clayborn has a plan. As he puts it, 'The difference between an amateur and a professional is, a professional figures out a way to cut down the odds before he makes his move.'

Paul Bishop

THE NIGHT IT RAINED BULLETS
Brian Wynne (Brian Garfield)
1965

"Different characters and threads intertwine and connect in explosive ways..."

One of Garfield's novels starring Marshall Jeremy Six and written in the decade before he became famous for the **Death Wish** novel and the movie that followed, **The Night it Rained Bullets** is a great western read and the book that put me on the alert for anything with Garfield's by-line – pseudonym or not. Six is the Marshall of Spanish Flat, a community that comes with some of the trappings you'd expect from a western lawman series, including the beautiful saloon owner, Clarissa, who has a sort-of unspoken relationship with the lead.

In the dead of winter, the Madden gang returns to Spanish Flat to seek revenge against Six. Under cover of a blizzard that pretty much reduces every building in the little settlement to

an island, they kidnap Clarissa and wait for Six to come and get her. But there's much more under way at the same time, including some wildcards that the gang hadn't anticipated, like a visiting gunfighter, a gambler, and the hot-headed owner of a nearby mine, as well as his determined young sister. The different characters and threads intertwine and connect in explosive ways. It only takes a few pages for the book to launch propulsively forward and then you're hooked until the very end.

I've read a number of the other Six novels (there are eight of them, and then another ghosted by Dudley Dean) and they're all enjoyable. Hopefully one of the later ones will prove as excellent as this second entry; some of his standalones have been.

Howard Andrew Jones

THE BRAVOS
Brian Wynne (Brian Garfield)
1966

"A journey that ultimately is one of self-discovery and redemption ..."

As mentioned above, under the pen name of Brian Wynne veteran author Brian Garfield (best known for **Death Wish**) wrote a total of eight westerns featuring Jeremy Six, marshal of the town of Spanish Flat. Lean and mean, **The Bravos** sketches in the basics of Jeremy Six in its opening pages as he tracks down and captures a killer wanted for murdering a woman back in Spanish Flat. We quickly learn that Marshal Six is methodical, calculating, and deadly with any form of gun. He succeeds in subduing his man, but upon arrival back in town, Six is overpowered by a mob who lynch his prisoner. Six is so disgusted by this complete lack of respect for the law that he abandons his badge and Spanish Flat, embarking on a journey that ultimately is one of self-discovery and redemption as he tries to sort out his place in a world where the law has no value or respect. He soon finds himself travelling toward the town of Rifle Gap with two unwanted companions, Rafferty, a newspaperman, and Story, a recently released ex-convict with a secret backstory. Rifle Gap is in the grips of a land war between two powerful ranchers and the town is caught in the crosshairs as each land baron is calling in gunslingers to bolster the ranks of their personal armies. As tensions escalate and a personal deadly toll is exacted upon a friend of Six's, it becomes clear that the marshal will need to rise above his disillusionment and do whatever is necessary to take control of the town away from those who would harm the innocent with no regard. This is a solid fast read at only 126 pages and is recommended, even if it offers nothing especially new to a classic formula.

Steve Carroll

KILLER LION (BONANZA)
Steve Frazee
1966

"Kept me entertained and feeling nostalgic…"

I would have really loved this book if I had read it when I was 12 years old. Author Steve Frazee was a prolific writer of westerns, several of which have been made into films, and many TV tie-in novels. He was an excellent choice to write the **Bonanza** books, giving them the authenticity of the Old West while capturing the essence of the beloved Cartwright family members. The novel tells the story of kind-hearted Hoss who takes in an orphaned mountain lion cub only to find it hopelessly dependent upon him. Unable to rid himself of the friendly cub, Hoss finds himself in

a predicament when local ranchers organize a mountain lion hunt to avenge a mysterious killing. All in all, an enjoyable, albeit somewhat juvenile, book that kept me entertained and feeling nostalgic.

Edwin McBride

A BADGE FOR A BADMAN
Brian Wynne (Brian Garfield)
1967

"It may not stand up to a lot of scrutiny after the fact, but Garfield is a pro…"

This is the sixth of the eight westerns featuring Jeremy Six, marshal of Spanish Flat, written by Brian Garfield under the penname of Brian Wynne. **A Badge for a Badman** kicks off in fine form with an excellent and suspenseful sequence detailing Marshal Six, his deputy, Dominguez, and a small group of devoted friends as they go into covert action upon realizing that Buel Marriner and his gang have arrived in town to steal the Reservation consignment from the town bank. Burl is a hardcase whose son, Cleve, and a nephew, Wes, both share a history with Jeremy Six. It all ends with Six outgunning the elder

Marriner and capturing an injured Cleve. The real villain of the book though is the now widowed Ma Marriner, who immediately pulls together a large group of outlaws and sets off to free her son and kill Marshal Six. Realizing that this will endanger the entire town, Six decides to hit the trail with Cleve in an attempt to beat the gang to a larger town where Cleve can be more safely held until trial. Despite some convenient coincidences and occasionally confusing character motivation, this is a fast and enjoyable read. It may not stand up to a lot of scrutiny after the fact, but Garfield is a pro and knows how to spin a fast and compelling read that features good, concise action and stronger than expected dialog.

Steve Carroll

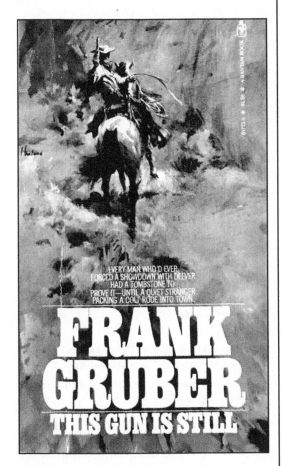

THIS GUN IS STILL
Frank Gruber
1967

"Drama, romance and courtroom intrigue..."

The book begins with what could be the best opening pages of any western I've personally read. It's a bold statement – but true. A Wells Fargo stagecoach is racing across the hot White Sands as Apache warriors descend from the hills. In a rapid-fire delivery, we read that the stagecoach driver is killed, and the carriage is tipped onto its side. With at least a dozen warriors outside, the two passengers, Jim Forester and Lily Bender, prepare for death. Forester, with only six bullets and a Navy Colt, begins firing from the window, hitting warriors within ten feet of the coach. He makes five shots deadly but debates the final shot – kill the girl so he alone can be tortured and ravaged by the Apaches or fire one more deadly shot at the braves and await the grizzly inevitable. Thankfully, a lone cowboy rides in with a Winchester rifle and kills enough warriors to make the war party scatter. Jim Forester meets Wes Morgan.

We learn that Forester works for a bank in Chicago called Davenport. He's come to the town of Stanton to collect on a default loan from one of two store owners. After the owner dismisses the delinquent $8K, Forester obtains a warrant to shut the store and owner down. The Justice of the Peace provides an interesting backstory on Stanton's rather odd situation. The town's wealth lies in two factions, Bender and Deever. Bender has a large and very profitable cattle ranch and is a passive man. Deever is a former Major who makes his living stealing from Bender and running his own cattle ranch off the theft. Bender has enough wealth and cattle and simply doesn't care. However, Deever, in a rather bold authority, hates Bender and only wants the town to support him. Deever asks that Forester and his company only conduct county business with him, starving and depleting the other businesses and ultimately 'gifting' the town to Deever. Forester refuses and that's where the story thickens.

In a wild chain of events, Forester quits his job and takes over the store as its new owner – partly for a change of scenery but also because he refuses to see Deever win. Complicating things is Wes Morgan, a wanted outlaw who saved Forester but who may be working with Deever. Discombobulating it further is the lovely Lily, Bender's daughter and former Morgan lover. She may or may not be falling for Forester, who has a number of decisions to make once Deever and his hired guns start threatening violence. Tuck tail and run, align with the law or fight Morgan and Deever. It's a western, so you know which way it will eventually go...but it is a thrilling journey to get there. Overall, Frank Gruber is fantastic here and expels just enough drama, romance and courtroom intrigue (yes, I said courtroom) to make this a well-told western. If you are looking for something that isn't the traditional western fare, this one is a must-read. Recommended.

The Paperback Warrior

MAD RIVER
Donald Hamilton
1967

"Times when the histrionics border on soap opera ..."

Before he solidified his reputation as the author of the **Matt Helm** espionage series, Donald Hamilton wrote several westerns, some of which started life as serialized stories for **Collier's Magazine**. Such is the case with **Mad River**, originally printed by Collier's in 1956 and then lengthened into a novel and republished by Gold Medal in 1967.

While **Mad River** is well written (I've yet to read anything by Hamilton that wasn't) and features a few standout action sequences, it bears the tell-tale signs of a shorter work that was padded to hit a required word count rather than a justifiable plot expansion. Boyd Cohoon is released from Yuma prison following a five-year stint for a crime he didn't commit; he agreed to serve his sentence in order to protect the brother of the woman he loves, who has pledged to wait for him. However, nothing goes as planned once Cohoon returns to his hometown and a rather convoluted and sometimes confusing series of events transpire with varying degrees of believability. There are times when the histrionics border on soap opera as everyone is hiding secrets from each other which hold the power to tear families and the entire town of Sombrero apart. The cast of characters is larger than is needed and loses focus early, never quite recovering.

To top everything off, the ending feels rushed, and it all comes together a little too tidily. All in all, a disappointing slog that took far more time to read than I would have expected given the author's pedigree.

Steve Carroll

NOBODY LOVES A DRUNKEN INDIAN
Clair Huffaker
1967

"A few dozen plot twists and turns that make it seem like you've been on a bucking bronco..."

Flapping Eagle is a Paiute Indian who decides that it's time for some payback on the White Man. But it's 1967, and there isn't exactly a warpath to go on anymore. So he evolves a plan to use public relations to highlight the plight of the remnants of his tribe – abandoned by the Government, living in poverty and powered by moonshine. He and his friends on the washed-out reservation cook up a plan that starts with them desecrating an ancestor's grave to fake an ancient Indian burial site – and it gets wilder and more wonderful after that. He has some odd allies, but a lot of unpleasant foes that eventually include the entire city of Phoenix.

I wouldn't go quite as far as the **Saturday Review** reviewer who calls the book 'uproarious', but it's certainly funny. It's also truthful and moving. And there is a lot of booze (hence the title). Vivid characters, insane plot developments (wait until the helicopter gets lassoed...) and a few dozen plot twists and turns that make it seem like you've been on a bucking bronco. It's a hell of a ride.

The novel was filmed in 1970 as **Flap**. Ironically, the movie indirectly makes the book's point about the Indians being exploited, since all of the major characters are actually played by white actors...

John Peel

THE GODLESS BREED
Gordon Shirreffs
1968

"Making the reader feel the wind and the sun and the harshness of the surroundings ..."

The Godless Breed opens with gunrunner Lee Hunter pinned down by Yaquis warriors in a dead-end canyon. Joined by his hated nemesis Jack Priest, the pair try to make a break for it, only to be captured by Mexican soldiers. They are given a choice –death by firing squad, or ride further south into Mexico and recover the Treasure of the Lost Virgin, which is reportedly in Apache territory and guarded by a fanatical cult. It seems an impossible task, but marginally preferable to being shot on a cold morning by a Mexican firing squad.

Shirreffs' novel falls somewhere between the traditional westerns of Louis L'Amour and co, and the much tougher fare by the Piccadilly Cowboys, which were then on the horizon. The violence in **The Godless Breed** is strong and frequent, but not overly graphic, and there is much mention of the cruel killing practices by the Apaches and the Yaqui. None of the characters are respectable or engaging, although Lee Hunter does have a shabby heart of gold.

Shirreffs takes a little while to set his unlikely story up but, once underway, it is a quickly moving tale with some well-orchestrated shoot-outs. The descriptions of the tough Mexican terrain are simple, but very effective and evocative, and Sherriffs is adept at painting a scene and making the reader feel the wind and the sun and the harshness of the surroundings.

This is an enjoyable, entertaining tale that is only slightly marred by the fanciful ending.

Jeff Popple

THE PROFESSIONAL KILLERS
J T Edson
1968

"Larger-than-life heroes that are chisel-jawed and characterised with no moral ambiguity ..."

J T Edson was the UK's premier writer of westerns during the 60s, producing more than a hundred books and selling huge numbers of copies of each. Now Edson is something of a joke due to his politics and peccadilloes, especially his habit of featuring cat-fighting blondes, but he is a solid and competent author. **The Professional Killers** is the fourth in Edson's **Rockabye County** series of modern westerns set in contemporary Texas, recycling material he originated for his earlier scripting work in British comics.

It opens with the titular crew carrying out a hit on a Texas lawman, with his enraged colleagues Bradford Counter and Alice Fayde (the recurring characters in the series) called in to unravel the motivation for a seemingly random shooting and track down the assassins.

It's archetypal Edson: crystal clear storytelling, an involving plot that marches forward with an undeniable logic, larger-than-life heroes that are chisel-jawed and characterised with no moral ambiguity, plentiful action without excessive bloodletting or sadism. I can totally understand why this material was popular at the time, but also why it ushered in the Piccadilly Cowboy era

of brutal and cynical stories. You could do worse than pick up an Edson.

Justin Marriott

THE RED SABBATH
Lewis Patten
1968

"Many exciting, and tense, scenes throughout ..."

This whole book pretty much takes place over that one bloody Sunday known as The Battle of Little Big Horn, moving into the next day for the conclusion. The story is told in the first person through Miles Lorette and his back-story is explained through a series of flashbacks during lulls in the battle.

There are many exciting, and tense, scenes throughout, one of the best for me being the desperate attempt to get water. Patten superbly portrays the fear of discovery and the frantic race back to the soldiers' lines when discovered.

Lorette finds himself with Reno and Benteen's commands, pinned down and helpless to go to

Custer's aid, hoping for Custer's death but saddened by the thought of the loss of the men with the General. Lorette isn't the only man who has these wishes, for most of the characters Patten features in his novel also want to witness Custer's death for past wrongs.

Lewis Patten captures the atmosphere of the battle and its immediate aftermath in moving and visual prose. Even though the outcome of this savage clash between white men and Indian is well known, I still found myself swept up in the story, eagerly turning the pages to see what happened next, the final scenes of Lorette riding through the masses of dead making for a powerful ending to the book.

The Red Sabbath is a must-read for anyone with an interest in Custer and/or the Indian Wars, and, of course, for fans of Lewis Patten's work. This book was the winner of the Spur Award for best western historical novel in 1968.

Steve Myall

★ ★ ★ ★ ★

CHARRO!
Harry Whittington
1969

"Written with the lean muscular prose for which he was renowned ..."

Charro! is an excellent novel based on a bad film. Harry Whittington developed his novelization of **Charro!** from a story treatment by Frederick Louis Fox. The original treatment contained many violent and sexually related scenes, which the director of the movie deemed too objectionable. Whittington didn't have any such proclivities, putting all the sex and violence back when he wrote the novelization, making Whittington's book much better than the film on which it is based.

To take timely advantage of a movie's initial release, many novelizations are written based only on a brief outline known as a treatment. As a novelization's author is rarely privy to the full elements of characterization, mood and tone of a finished film, a novelization can be substantially different. The best novelization writers rely on their own imagination to flesh out motivations, plot points and even new characters in order to produce a coherent story. In the hands of a top pro like Harry Whittington, the novelization can become a special entity all its own—as with Charro!

A gold-plated Mexican cannon belonging to Emperor Maximilian has been stolen by an outlaw band. The Mexican army, various Mexican thugs and bounty hunter Jess Wade are after the two-thousand-dollar reward for the return of the cannon. As the story progresses, the outlaws want to ransom the cannon back to the town from where it was stolen. By this time, they have trapped Wade into working with them as they use the cannon to terrorize the town into capitulation. Tension and violence soak Whittington's take on the story, written with the lean muscular prose for which he was renowned.

Paul Bishop

★ ★ ★ ★ ☆

ESCAPE FROM YUMA
Frank Castle
1969

"It's hard to put this one down ..."

Our introduction to Boone Wade is a rather cramped one – tucked inside the cold steel of Yuma prison. Wade, just the average Joe, was a rancher who joined criminal McGare for a one-time train robbery. The hit and run went off as

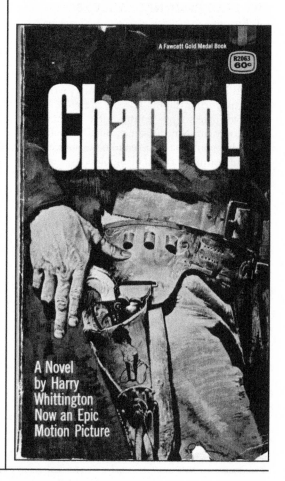

expected for everyone but Wade. McGare's gang made a successful break and Wade was left behind to face the worst prison in the west.

The 24-year old has become hardened after two years of breaking rocks and succumbing to nightly beatings. So, it's with great surprise that Wade finds that someone has tossed him the keys to his cell in the dead of night. After running towards the river, Wade finds a woman and her grandfather waiting with a boat to usher him to freedom. What's the price of his freedom?

Frank Castle uses a familiar crime fiction ploy to lure readers into this engaging western tale. A lawman named Rambo rigged the escape from Yuma as bait to lure McGare. Rambo wants Wade to rob three trains, all fabricated to the highest degrees of safety by Rambo and his men. Once the news of the robbery, combined with the prison escape, reaches McGare's gang they will want in on the action. That's when Rambo will swoop in for the snatch and convince judges to pardon Wade. But can Rambo be trusted? Perhaps he's really a criminal himself and the train robberies are legit. That's the ultimate question as Wade is forced to choose between cooperating with what he hopes is the law or furthering his escape by fleeing into Mexico.

At 155 pages of intense action, it's hard to put this one down. I nearly read it in one sitting and found Castle's writing to be intriguing. He doesn't spill the beans until the end, using patience to make for a more entertaining finish for his readers. It's this reservation that glues the book together. Will Wade flee, fight or submit in hopes of the greater good? That's the focus of the narrative and it's enough to create a winning formula. Western and crime fiction fans should equally enjoy **Escape from Yuma**.

The Paperback Warrior

FARGO
John Benteen
1969

"Beyond the scope of traditional Westerns ..."

Neal Fargo – adventurer, lover and fighter. He lives with a gun in one fist and a stick of lighted dynamite in the other. Want to start a revolution? Want to stop one? Send for Fargo. Want to blow a bridge, stage a prison break, rob a bank? Get Fargo. Tall and weather beaten, he still wears much the same outfit he wore in the service: cavalry boots, campaign hat, jodhpurs or khaki pants, comfortable shirt. His weapons of war include a .38 in either a hip or shoulder holster and loaded with hollow points for greater stopping power. He also carries a razor sharp Batangas knife made by Philippine artisans, its ten-inch blade flashing open with the flick of a wrist.

In this debut outing, Fargo heads down to Mexico to help a mine owner under siege by a gang of bandits. Fargo's job is to get a fortune in raw silver and the mineworkers across the border to safety. Things do not go smoothly. If they did you wouldn't need a man like Fargo, who it at his best taking on all comers and against all odds. One of the aspects I find most enjoyable about **Fargo** and the other books in the series is that the books go beyond the scope of traditional westerns. Each one retains the structure of a traditional western, but take place in not only the west but also diverse locations such as the Philippines, Argentina, Nicaragua, Alaska and Peru. This distinction is part of the fun and makes **Fargo** stand out among its contemporaries.

Paul Bishop

Fargo is a specialist in sudden death. Want to blow a bridge, stage a prison-break, rob a bank? Send for Fargo.

John Benteen

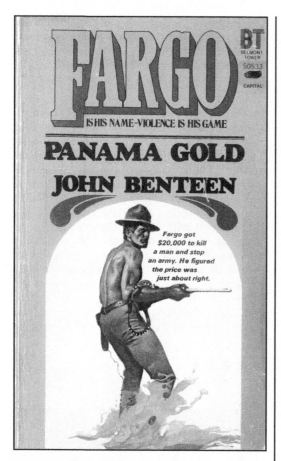

Fargo got $20,000 to kill a man and stop an army. He figured the price was just about right.

PANAMA GOLD (FARGO 2)
John Benteen (Ben Haas)
1969

"Never lets a reader down on this thrill ride of a series..."

What do most balding, mild-mannered tax accountants like me read on their lunch break? If we're lucky, one of the twenty-three volumes of Belmont/Towers **Fargo** western series to kickstart our humdrum lives. Even though the early cover art on these undiscovered gems looks like straight western fare, the books are anything but that. The blood and thunder world of Neal Fargo is set in the 1910s, after the Wild West has been tamed. Fortunately for us, somebody forgot to tell Fargo. The blistering prose of writer Ben Haas, under his John Benteen nom de plume, never lets a reader down on this thrill ride of a series. Later printed covers finally got the true image of this mountain of a man correctly. Now clad in his Rough Rider uniform, with shotgun blazing, this two-fisted hero practically jumps off the page in every adventure. My favourite entry is the second book, **Panama Gold**, published in November of 1969. Here we find Teddy Roosevelt summoning his old friend Fargo to help him stop an act of sabotage on the Panama Canal before it is completed. An old enemy soldier with a chip on his shoulder for Fargo, Cleve Buckner, has rounded up the most coldblooded killers from all over Central America to stop the canal dead in its tracks. Neal is offered $20,000 by the Colonel to kill this man and stop an army, and that's exactly the kind of tough job he likes.

Dave Karlen

★ ★ ★ ★ ★

THE GUNS OF GREED (NEVADA JIM 13)
Marshall McCoy (Leonard Meares)
1969

"Characters don't always turn out the way you expect..."

Sheriff Ben Courtney has an appointment with a traveling dentist, so when the Luscombe gang robs the Cornerstone, Nevada bank, the lawman is asleep in the ether. Inside the bank, wealthy landowner Avrill is defiant, so Luscombe kills him.

As the gang makes their getaway, the mayor of Cornerstone rushes forward with a gun. He's shot, but not mortally wounded, and luckless drifter James Malloy picks up his gun. Malloy is no hero, but stumbles, fires the weapon and takes out one of the gang, an action half-seen by loudmouth store proprietor Dave McHenrey. Believing Malloy to be a sharp shooting gunfighter, and in absence of the law, (or Nevada Jim Gage), McHenrey recruits him along with several town folk to join his posse.

Almost immediately the group is joined by Verna Avrell, cool and ruthless daughter of the murdered landowner. Encouraged by lusty cheers from the citizenry, they set out after the bad guys.

Naturally, when the Sheriff wakes up, he and Nevada Jim follow fast on McHenrey's heels, hoping to avert more bloodshed.

James Reasoner makes the comment on his blog that in Nevada Jim novels, characters don't always turn out the way you expect, and this is true of reluctant vigilante Malloy and a few additional players.

Author Leonard Meares understands heroism, and by the end of the story, his characters do too. For such a short novel, there's a surprising amount of character development. Packed with lots of humour and action, this entry in the long running series is a winner.

Richard Prosch

★★★★☆

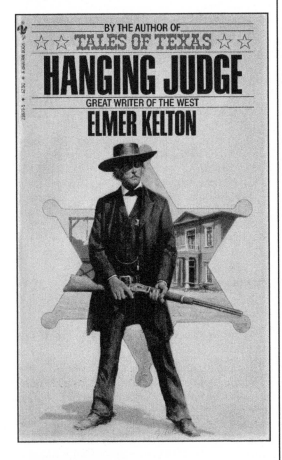

HANGING JUDGE
Elmer Kelton
1969

"Engaging characters and an authentic frontier justice system ..."

Judge Isaac Parker (who also featured in the 1968 novel **True Grit** by Charles Portis, published just one year earlier) was known as the **Hanging Judge** for a perception of sentencing a large number of convicts to death during his time as a US District judge in Fort Smith, Arkansas. Considering Judge Parker, over the course of his twenty-one-year career on the bench, tried 13,490 cases, but only sentenced 160 people to death and only 79 were ever actually executed leads me to believe that perhaps his reputation was over-hyped. However, this novel is not about him, although he does cast a long shadow over the events depicted.

Instead, the main character in the novel is 22-year-old Justin Mofitt, a newly sworn-in deputy marshal to Judge Parker. He's assigned to veteran Marshal Sam Dark for training, a hard man with an intriguing past who quickly becomes Justin's mentor. Life as a deputy marshal is not one for the faint of heart; history tells us that Judge Parker lost one law officer for almost every criminal he hanged. When Sam Dark brings in wanted fugitive Barney Tankard, killer of a friend in a drunken brawl, Justin finds himself questioning the law and his newfound role in it. The Tankard family believes the real culprit is none other than Harvey Oates, who runs a large illegal bootlegging operation. When the rest of the Tankards get in Oates' way, the resulting bloody violence prompts Justin's friend, Mathew to go after Oates for revenge. Justin must decide if he will fulfil his marshal duties or help his friend in a righteous cause.

Elmer Kelton is one of the most-loved Western authors of all time. And with this novel it's easy to see why. Not only does he bring lots of realistic gun action to this story, he combines it with engaging characters and an authentic frontier justice system, warts and all. His characters, even the good guys, are often flawed. The ending, while satisfying, does not tie up all loose ends, leaving the reader to come to his or her own conclusions about Justin's future.

Well-written prose combined with an authentic, engaging plot demands I start looking for my next Elmer Kelton novel.

Benjamin Thomas

★★★★★

TEXAS GUNS
Ray Hogan
1969

"The reader is kept constantly on edge..."

Author Ray Hogan wrote a hell of a lot of books during his career. **Texas Guns** is one of them. And it's a good one. Adam Rait is the protagonist here, a man who was damaged in both body and mind by the Civil War and now wants nothing more than to live a peaceful life where life and death decisions no longer rest upon his shoulders. When a job with the promise of minimum responsibility comes up to escort a wagon train with a mystery cargo to its destination, Rait eagerly accepts, viewing it as easy money. In this supposition, he is soon proven wrong.

Before long, the mystery cargo is revealed to be a

shipment of weapons, the Texas guns of the book's title, meant for the Confederacy. Before they can be delivered, the Civil War comes to an end. Rait soon finds himself contending with rival groups vying for the firearms, his own gang of surly teamsters, and the beautiful Angela de Acera, a woman who may not be as pure and innocent as she seems.

Texas Guns is an exciting read. The reader is kept constantly on edge as, like Adam Rait, we never know where danger will spill from next. Attacks by outside factions are often just as dangerous as the bad-tempered teamsters under his employ, a situation that only worsens when a lone beautiful woman is introduced to the mix. It's a recipe for disaster. Pick up a copy to see how it all plays out.

Dan Shanahan

★★★☆☆

VALLEY OF THE GWANGI
Dell Comics
1969

"Its visual impact is undermined by the workmanlike art..."

Dell Comics were one of the smaller comic book publishers and had a successful strategy of producing tie-ins to movies and TV series. This included western characters and shows such **The Lone Ranger**, **Roy Rogers**, **Laramie**, **Wyatt Earp**, **Cisco Kid** and many more. **Valley of the Gwangi** combined both, being a 32-page, full-colour comic book adaptation of the 1969 cowboys-meet-dinosaurs movie. The film was originally conceived by Willis O'Brien, which is perhaps why it shares some themes with his **King Kong**, and had stop-animation effects by Ray Harryhausen. As an adaptation it faithfully follows the film, albeit in a scaled down manner, but does concentrate on the elements with the titular Allosaurus. Unfortunately, its visual impact is undermined by the workmanlike art of Jack Sparling, whose rough-hewn style and sound human figure-work suits the cowboys but is unconvincing on dinosaurs. Especially the Gwangi, whose anatomy and in particular, tail, looks ridiculous.

Justin Marriott

★☆☆☆☆

THE AMOS FLAGG SERIES
Clifton Adams writing as Clay Randall
1964 - 69

"The books are solid and entertaining, if not standouts..."

Clay Randall is one of several pseudonyms for the two-time Spur award-winning Clifton Adams, the versatile author of well-regarded hard–boiled noir novels as well as westerns. He's also one of the few Gold Medal authors to create series characters, and has the distinction of being the only one of them to create two – Tall Cameron, featured in **The Desperado** and **A Noose for the Desperado**, and Amos Flagg, the central character of six novels, starting with **Amos Flagg, Lawman**, in 1964. The Amos Flagg books were later reprinted and misnumbered; the actual chronology is on the opposite page.

In the first few Flagg novels Adams seems to be getting himself set. The books are solid and entertaining, if not standouts, although there are distinctive touches that make them memorable, particularly the presence of El Cazador, the tomcat, who hangs out in Flagg's office and who is occasionally a point-of-view character – an idea that may sound farcical, but one Adams pulls off so well that a lot of readers find themselves looking forward to the cat's occasional appearances.

Flagg is a Texas lawman, sturdy, laconic and unimaginative, but wilier than his opponents expect. Anyone who's watched **Gunsmoke** will be familiar with the kind of recurring characters that pop up in each book. Naturally there's a lovely saloon owner, and a crusty doctor. More originally, there's Flagg's old man, a former convict who's always wheeling and dealing and causing trouble, even though he's allegedly reformed. Flagg's character develops so that while he's always taciturn he's actually much sharper after the first few books, as well as a seasoned lawman who understands human behaviour.

By the time he wrote **Amos Flagg Rides Out**, Adams was so comfortable with the formula he'd begun to stretch his muscles and deliver more surprises. In **Rides Out**, Flagg must address multiple problems, not the least of which is the sudden challenge he faces when he's up for elections and his own deputy and close friend decides to run against him. There's also the minor matter of a criminal conspiracy and a deadly, capable agent of a Chinese tong who's undercover on a secret mission. Come **Bushwhacked**, the focus shifts to his father, Gunner Flagg, who's loyalty to an old friend and his own son is tested to the breaking point;

Adams had become so familiar with his characters that he could shift focus away from the star and still deliver a satisfying tale.

The last two books are probably the best and show what Adams might have envisioned all along – Flagg has to deal with the scheming and idiocy and selfishness of various folk to keep the peace in his little community and it's truly entertaining stuff. **Showdown** is so fluid and polished, from start to finish, even from the way El Cazador is used to open and close the novel, that it's a pleasing little gem, and a wonderful finale. It seems clear that Adams was having fun and I can only imagine he would have written more Flagg novels if not for his untimely death.

Howard Andrew Jones

The series
1. Amos Flagg: Lawman ★★★☆☆
2. Amos Flagg: High Gun ★★★☆☆
3. Amos Flagg Rides Out ★★★★☆
4. Amos Flagg: Bushwhacked ★★★☆☆
5. Amos Flagg Has His Day ★★★★☆
6. Amos Flagg: Showdown ★★★★☆

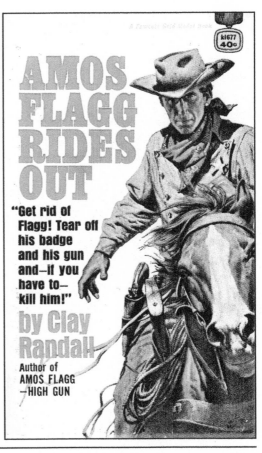

1970- 1979

The western paperback gets violent.

A group of British authors who had never travelled West of Piccadilly (tube station) bring unheralded levels of violence and sadism to the genre.

The Americans respond with the adult western, introducing unheralded amounts of sex to the genre.

The Europeans have been combining these in their comic books already.

THE BANK ROBBER
Giles Tippette
1970

"The darker side of the story is often balanced with moments of humour ..."

The story is told in the first person, through Wilson Young, who makes for a very strong central character. He's tough yet can make simple mistakes that put him and his two companions (childhood friends) into deadly danger. Fallen on hard times, the three main characters struggle to make money – their careers as outlaws don't always go according to plan. This leads to squabbles between them that could become their downfall. During all this Wilson Young becomes infatuated with a Mexican girl, a beautiful woman who could become part of his future...

This is the first book by Giles Tippette I've read, and it certainly won't be the last. Tippette's storytelling is captivating, gritty and well plotted. His dialogue is believable and the action scenes, and their aftermath, are hard-hitting. The darker side of the story is often balanced with moments of humour.

This became the first of a nine-book series. It was also filmed as **The Spikes Gang**, directed by Richard Fleischer and starring Lee Marvin as Harry Spikes, Gary Grimes as Wilson Young, Ron Howard as Les and Charles Martin Smith as Tod. It's been a long time since I've seen this film (it can be viewed in its entirety on YouTube). Parts of it are taken from the book, including the character Kid White (played by Arthur Hunnicutt), but the main difference is that Lee Marvin's character doesn't exist in the book! As is nearly always the case for me regarding books made into films, I found the book to be the most enjoyable of the two, but both are very entertaining.

Steve Myall

FOUR UGLY GUNS (THE BUFFALO HUNTER 2)
Ralph Hayes
1970

"Short on mercy but long on revenge ..."

Remember Henry Bemis in the **Twilight Zone** after the bomb dropped and he was stacking up books to read before he accidentally broke his glasses? If you look very closely, I think I saw on top a copy of Ralph Hayes **Buffalo Hunter #2**,

Four Ugly Guns. It's a crying shame the meek bank teller missed out on this explosive volume of the eleven-book western series by Leisure Books which debuted in 1970. Hayes has done it all over his near hundred book writing career, but his real talent is writing westerns. The author describes his cowboy hero, O'Brien, as a rugged, intimidating, wild-country survivalist who can't read or write but speaks several Indian tongues. In this simple but bloody yarn, four savage outlaws murder O'Brien's friends for kicks, so he takes a vacation from hunting buffalo and starts hunting men. Like a slow burning fuse, the hunter follows the signs across the first 73 pages before the powder keg blows and the action really starts. The sidewinders flee into Indian territory and with the heat turned up, the reader sweats as they experience each kill with O'Brien. On Indian land, the law had no jurisdiction but that doesn't rile up our hero as his ideology was to speak softly and carry a big Sharps Rifle. Short on mercy but long on revenge, by the end of the trail the title should have been changed to Four Ugly Deaths!

Dave Karlen

and Welsh factions while currying the favour of the local Chinese Tong leader and ends up in bed with a couple of different women over the course of the slim, large print book. The truth is, while competently written, the whole book has a laconic, laid-back pace with no sense of urgency whatsoever; it takes over half of the book before any real plot starts to coalesce. There are a few action scenes, but overall the whole thing feels half-baked and padded with a rushed and unsatisfying climax hurriedly tacked on in the last few pages.

Steve Carroll

★ ★ ☆ ☆ ☆

FUNERAL BEND (LASSITER 12)
Jack Slade (Peter McCurtin)
1970

"Has a laconic, laid-back pace with no sense of urgency whatsoever..."

The **Lassiter** series, credited to house name Jack Slade, was written by a variety of authors over the course of numerous books with multiple publishers in the US and across Europe, although deciphering information on actual authors and correctly numbered editions is a bit daunting. The consensus seems to land on **Funeral Bend** being the work of action/adventure stalwart, Peter McCurtin. We are introduced to our anti-hero, Lassiter, as he arrives in the town of El Dorado, formerly known as Funeral Bend. It's a violent mining town with no law to speak of and plenty of intermingling immigrants (Welsh, Irish and Chinese). Lassiter takes out three troublemakers in one of the town's saloons early in the book and is offered a job as marshal, which he takes. However, we soon learn that Lassiter has a plan to steal the town's gold reserves through information he gains as the local peacekeeper. He ends up angering the Irish

MATT MARRIOTT – ZINCVILLE, COLORADO
Jim Edgar and Tony Weare
1970

"Edgar's script is sharp and complex...Weare's art is outstanding..."

Newspaper strip **Matt Marriott** began its over thirty-year run in the **London Evening News** in September 1955, during a boom in western comics in the UK. The son of poor Kansas farmers killed when ruthless cattle barons ride their steers roughshod over the family's land, Matt and older sidekick Jason 'Powder' Horn subsequently wander the US, righting wrongs and defending the poor and needy. All the Matt Marriott stories were written by talented comics scribe Jim Edgar, with Tony Weare drawing every three-panel episode, six days a week, until he left the strip in 1977.

Matt and Powder visited the town of Zincville (stories were never actually titled in the paper itself) in the **Evening News** from June to October 1970. The place is beat up and run down, the nearby silver mines worked out many years past. Yet ever hopeful Swedish miner Nils Ericcson is convinced there's still a fortune under the plot he owns. He's right enough, but – needing money to actually dig the silver out – kills a man in a rashly-conceived stick up job before losing his own life trying to outrun the sheriff and his posse. The greedy burghers of Zincville then set about trying to bilk Ericcson's widow out of her inheritance. That is, until Matt steps in...

Edgar's script is sharp and complex, with the scheming townsfolk of Zincville deftly characterized and the plot (despite the strictures of the short, sharp, episodic format) satisfyingly twisty. Weare's art is outstanding – gritty and distinctive, with plenty of variety across the panels and some excellent portraits. Tragically never properly collected in the UK, Matt Marriott is like Ericcson's silver – a rewarding find for anyone who can track him down.

Jim O'Brien

★ ★ ★ ☆ ☆

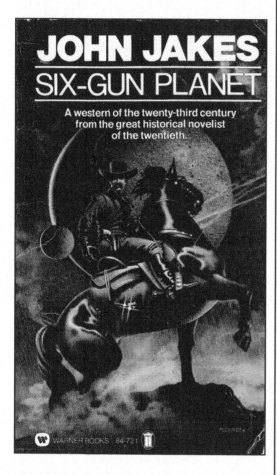

SIX-GUN PLANET
John Jakes
1970

"Just too earnest and desperate to be important to be truly enjoyable."

Pre-dating the more famous **Westworld** by three years, **Six-Gun Planet** is an SF-western with a core of social satire. In the 23rd century on a planet named Missouri, where the inhabitants have chosen to live in the style of the 19th century Wild West, with robot horses and pearl-handled laser pistols, pacifist Zak Randolph is facing into the threat of a planet-hopping master gunman. This is one of Jakes' books in the period where he was working full-time and writing in the spare time, to indifferent sales figures and was on the verge of throwing the towel in. It's no surprise based on this slim but surprisingly difficult to get through novel, which is solid enough – well-written and with clever ideas – but just too earnest and desperate to be important to be truly enjoyable. SF-western was a derisory term employed by the more snobbish members of the SF community, but in this case is entirely fitting.

Justin Marriott

★ ☆ ☆ ☆ ☆

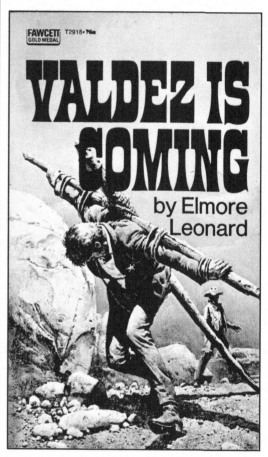

VALDEZ IS COMING
Elmore Leonard
1970

"Taut, gritty and utterly compelling…"

I'm probably not alone amongst contributors here in picking a title to review that I knew next to nothing about prior to reading but which sounded like it could have potential. In the case of **Valdez is Coming** 'sounded like' because I had read and loved plenty of Elmore Leonard's crime and thriller titles over the years but had never touched one of the man's westerns. Somewhere early on in my Leonard reading, I seem to have decided (based on little more than a total lack of knowledge of the subject) that the westerns were 'early works' and were 'not as good as' the modern, urban noir titles by the great writer that I was getting into it. Oh, how wrong was I: **Valdez is Coming** is a superb book – taut, gritty and utterly compelling. The story is simple enough: tricked into killing an innocent man by heartless horse and cattle trader Frank Tanner, Bob Valdez (lowly parish constable and hired gun for the local stagecoach company) determines to extract compensation from Tanner for the dead man's widow. The brutal Tanner of course declines Valdez's courteous suggestion and the bulk of the book then sees through to its inevitable conclusion the clash between the complex but essentially moral Valdez and the utterly amoral Tanner. The period (early 1890s) and the place (Texas, close to the Mexican border) are perfectly captured and the frontier as pictured by Leonard is a wholly credible place full of boiling class, ethnic and gender tensions. The book has one great iconic sequence, which I won't spoil entirely but which features a kind of western crucifixion that is hard to beat as a set piece. As always with Leonard the dialogue is crisp, natural and extremely cool. Highly recommended.

Jim O'Brien

★ ★ ★ ★ ★

WILDCAT'S CLAIM TO FAME
Jeff Clinton
1970

"A wonderful tall tale told to you in a rough bar by a big galoot ..."

Wildcat O'Shea had me hook-in-and-sinker. From page one I knew I had found a new friend. Wildcat lives up to his name, he's a literal colourful character that stands out among the crowd of cowboy heroes. He fights, drinks, chases the ladies around and lands headfirst into trouble. In other words, my kind of guy. Wildcat's favourite author Ned Shipwright is rolling into town. Problem is that Ned's a bit of an ass and then he steps into the wrong kidnapping; a real one not the one he planned as a publicity stunt. It falls onto Wildcat to save his bacon and maybe get the chance to become a dime novel hero.

Jeff Clinton was really Jack Bickham and under any name the guy could write. Wildcat keeps himself in trouble but instead of facing danger with a steely glint, he faces it with a broad grin.

The humour of the character is a breath of fresh air in a crowded room of dusty and musty cowpokes. He reminds me of my favourite western series Hashknife Hartley and Sleepey Stevens by W C Tuttle, who also shook things up by injecting humour into the classic action/adventure western mould. The humour is well used: it never bogs down the narrative or the fast, well written action that Clinton puts on the page. The book is a wonderful tall tale told to you in a rough bar by a big galoot, it can't all seem to true. But you sure wish it is.

Roy Nugen

★ ★ ★ ★ ★

A MAN NAMED YUMA
T V Olsen
1971

"Top-shelf, gritty stuff, crammed with action and well-sketched characters..."

Olsen published a fair number of westerns from Fawcett Gold Medal starting in the 1960s and kept at it well into the 1970s. Olsen himself was the prolific writer of standalone westerns, and

was dependably good, with a knack for quickly drawing his readers in and playing with familiar tropes in surprising and satisfying ways. He's one of my favourite recent discoveries and –apart from some formulaic early magazine work – has seldom let me down. If you find L'Amour a little too mythic and predictable and wish he was more hard-boiled, you might want to give Olsen a read.

The central character of **A Man Named Yuma** is a half-breed Apache and occasional Army scout who happens upon the aftermath of a massacre and saves the life of a traumatized woman who wants nothing to do with him. Before too much longer he has to throw in with a band of travellers riven by their own petty dramas, pursued the while by a band of Apaches on the warpath led by none other than Yuma's traitorous half-brother.

This is top-shelf, gritty stuff, crammed with action and well-sketched characters. Olsen is a steady hand, telling a strong tale but never one on rails because, like other work written in his prime, it never quite ends up where you first expect it will go.

Howard Andrew Jones

MASSACRE RIDGE
Lewis Patten
1971

"Adding another level of action to what is already, a satisfying thrill ..."

Massacre Ridge is a fictional account of the real-life 1866 Fetterman Fight between troops and Native Americans in present day Wyoming along the Bozeman Trail. While using the historical figures of the battle, like Colonel Carrington and Colonel Fetterman, the main character is the fictional civilian named Jess Paddock. He's an everyman labourer who assisted in building Fort Phil Kearny despite the constant barrage of Sioux attacks. Along with building the fort, Paddock voluntarily serves Carrington as a scout, reporting on Sioux patterns and strategies.

As the labouring finishes, Paddock realizes the only reason to continue residing at the fort is Molly, a young widow that he's fallen for. The two have plans to marry and as the two talk about the safe passage from the Fort, Paddock is drawn into a dense battle plan to defend the fort from on-going attacks. Carrington's aggressive strategy is to bait the Sioux with a wood cutting detail. When they are attacked, which is normal, Colonel Fetterman and Lieutenant Bingham will ride to their relief and then pursue the Sioux along the typical escape route through two hills and across two valleys. Carrington will lead a flank attack that will catch the Native Americans between Fetterman's force and his own. Paddock disagrees with this approach and advises the Army that the Sioux are much smarter than that and they are simply baiting the troops for a counterattack.

Paddock opposing this battle strategy is a big part of the book. Patten places the character into the battles, both as a scout watching from afar or inserted into the intense action. Western fans will be pleased that Patten creates a villain for Paddock as well. Early in the book, Paddock wins big from Sergeant O'Mara during a night of poker. The ridiculed sergeant fights with Paddock throughout the premise, adding another level of action to what is already, a satisfying thrill.

Massacre Ridge is another outstanding western tale from Lewis B Patten. I couldn't be more pleased with it.

The Paperback Warrior

ONLY ONE MAN UNDERSTOOD THE DEADLY TRAP LAID BY THE SIOUX—BUT COULD HE STOP THE IMPENDING SLAUGHTER?

MASSACRE RIDGE
LEWIS B. PATTEN

GUN THE MAN DOWN
Dudley Dean (Dudley McGaughy)
1971

"A number of secondary characters with clashing motivations and arcs of their own, and they cross and spark masterfully..."

Under his Dudley Dean pseudonym, Dudley McGaughy wrote more than a half dozen westerns for Gold Medal, starting in the '50s, and drafted numerous westerns under that and other names for decades before and after, for numerous publishers. I've enjoyed some of his work for Ace, finding him a capable and sometimes surprising author, with spare and even hardboiled prose and characters. But this novel really made me sit up and take notice, and I'm going to keep my eye out for his work going forward.

A deputy in a small community, Clete Argo's hunting two bank robbers, one of whom is a young man he was trying to steer onto the right path. When he's forced to kill young Billy Seach, Clete Argo suddenly finds himself on the wrong corner of a big parcel of trouble. Billy's conniving partner tells Billy's father a twisted account of his son's death, and Clete suddenly finds himself with a $10,000 bounty on his head, the catch being that Clete has to be shot down while Billy's father is watching, and the death has to look legal and fair.

The plot has further wrinkles, for much of the town distrusts Clete and even questions his account of Billy's murder. Some even wonder if Clete himself kept the missing holdup money. There's the matter of Billy's widow, who's sweet on Clete, and a gunslinger who's an old 'friend' who may or may not be gunning for him, and a small army of gunslingers who are. There are a number of secondary characters with clashing motivations and arcs of their own, and they cross and spark masterfully. And finally, there's the matter of the mano y mano gunfighting itself, which certainly stands among the best I've seen in any western. Highly recommended.

Howard Andrew Jones

 ★ ★ ★ ★ ☆

WITHOUT MERCY (MORGAN KANE 1)
Louis Masterson (Kjell Hallbing)
1971

"Characterized with sullen and dead eyes, and bitterly looking upon the damage done to his gun hand..."

This book is the first in the long running series by Norwegian author Kjell Hallbing. A classic in its homeland where it ran for eighty-three novels, it had limited success in the UK where about half were translated and published. The first entry into this series opens with Texas Ranger Morgan Kane losing nearly every dime he has in a poker game, getting drunk, and hopping hungover on the train the next morning. Sitting across from him is a beauty named Allison that he gets an eye for. Thinking he has a new run of good luck he steps out of the carriage onto the platform where he goes bust – Kane is bushwhacked, shot through the hand and in the gut, and tossed off the rails to be left for dead. He survives this ordeal by some well-placed hardware, spends the rest of the book trying to solve the 'who' and the 'why' of this encounter, so he can (of course) get his revenge.

I was hesitant since the book is translated, but it appears just as if someone were a native writing in (British) English. Kane is a moody and introspective fellow, not wanting to get close to the women that show up in the book, characterized with sullen and dead eyes, and bitterly looking upon the damage done to his gun hand. It's sparse on action till the satisfying

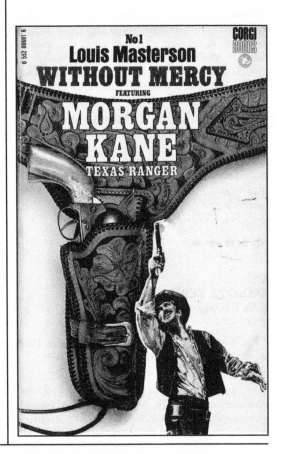

finale, heavier on descriptions like a hardboiled Piccadilly Cowboy. Overall, I liked what I read but was left wanting more. An average start to what's supposedly a good series.

Sean Nodland

★ ★ ☆ ☆ ☆

THE STAR AND THE GUN (MORGAN KANE 3)
Louis Masterson (Kjell Hallbing)
1971

"Leaving the reader as breathless as Kane ..."

Louis Masterson really does come up with the goods here, in both developing Kane's character and in superb storytelling. The reader will find out more about Kane's weaknesses – women and alcohol – and how determined he can be when fuelled by revenge. Masterson also creates two of the most memorable villains in the series, Lonnie Kidd and Claus Winter. Deadly, sadistic, with hinted-at perversions that Kane finds repulsive, these two men are nearly Kane's undoing. It's after a brutal beating by them that Kane's lust for vengeance rises to drive his being and in turn reveals just how deadly the lawman can be.

Towards the end of the story Masterson really does excel himself with some top class writing that sees Kane racing against time, the sense of urgency, the feeling that for all Kane's efforts his frantic ride may be all for nothing, really comes across strongly, leaving the reader as breathless as Kane.

Does Kane manage to save the day and kill the bad guys or is he destined to fail and wallow in more heartache? They are questions I'm not going to answer here, you'll just have to read the book and find out for yourselves and in doing so I'm sure you'll find yourself enjoying this story as much as I did.

Steve Myall

★ ★ ★ ★ ★

DAKOTA TERRITORY
John Benteen (Ben Haas)
1972

"You'll also find historical details that ring true, as well as prose with real pathos and power..."

Haas had a clean, sharp prose style with driving pace and an excellent command of plot and characterization. His work stands head-and-shoulders above most men's action adventure novels because it's far better than it has any right to be. The characters are consistent and well motivated, the plots propulsive, and somehow, he manages variety even while crafting formula work. You can read each of his books just for the surface enjoyment and be well-satisfied, but in addition to the expected action and sex you'll also find historical details that ring true, as well as prose with real pathos and power. Haas's own skills elevated the work so that it remains revered and appreciated by readers and studied by modern writers who want to learn from a true master. And in case it's not clear, his work is simply a lot of fun to read.

Haas created two great series characters for Leisure Books back in the 1970s. Usually it's Haas's globetrotting Fargo who gets all the love, but some of us like his half-Cheyenne Sundance character just as well. This title is among my favourites from the series, throwing Sundance into an explosive situation in the Dakota Territory where there are multiple problems boiling to the surface – there's a money-hungry buffalo hunter after some land that doesn't belong to him. There's General George Armstrong Custer out to fight some Indians and

keep the peace and maybe get a little something for himself, and then there's a revengeful Sioux medicine man who thinks he's got magical powers. Throw in a love interest and you have one pressure cooker of a plot that sees Sundance up against it in multiple ways almost from the very start. I was particularly impressed with Haas's depiction of the medicine man, an antagonist that you can't help liking a little even though he's gone mad with his own power.

Howard Andrew Jones

The big hunter came down from the mountains to paint the town red. It was red when he left —red with blood.

THE GUNHAWKS (CUTLER 2)
John Benteen (Ben Haas)
1972

"It soon misfired with an uneven storyline..."

Who would believe with both **Fargo** and **Sundance** under his belt, Ben Haas's well would run dry with his third western series, **Cutler**, for Belmont/Tower Books? Writing as John Benteen, the author's prose is bone dry, abandoning the character after only two books.

John Cutler had been a federal Marshal in Indian Territory before settling down with a new bride on his Arizona Ranch. But when a rogue grizzly starts killing cattle, it soon moves up to human prey. Escaping our hero's traps by gnawing off its paw, it takes revenge on Cutler's wife before disappearing in the mountains. Five years later, now Cutler is caught in a trap: haunted by the memories of his dead wife, he lives in the bottom of a whiskey bottle. The big raw-boned mountain man now hunts rogue animals and men for a living, still searching for the monster Grizzly that destroyed his life. I had high hopes going into **Cutler #2 The Gunhawks**, but it soon misfired with an uneven storyline. When savage gunmen take over a Mexican village making them slaves in their own silver mine, an old friend barely escapes, writing Cutler for help. Our mountain man answers the call, now stalked by a gunfighter with a chip on his shoulder for Cutler. They join forces to kill a crazed panther and save the villagers before their final showdown. Vernon Hinkle galloped in to write four more Cutler novels under his H V Elkin moniker, but a part-time drunk who hunts animals full-time seemed a waste of time to most western fans.

Dave Karlen

THE LONER (EDGE 1)
George Gilman (Terry Harknett)
1972

"This is a rollicking ride and if you can stomach the violence then you're in for a treat..."

From the opening chapter we are introduced to the violent world that Edge (Josiah Hedges) occupies. After many years fighting in the Civil War, Hedges returns to his farming home in Iowa to find his brother has just been brutally murdered. So begins the greatest revenge novel I think I've ever read. Hedges has a few clues to set him on his way as he is determined to exact his own revenge on the men who killed his family and stole nearly $2,000 that Edge had sent home.

The action is detailed and does not pull any punches. It's quite amusing that virtually every woman who encounters Edge almost immediately falls for him, even when he's been displaying his own version of ultra-violence. It's not all plain sailing though and at times Edge is almost near-death.

Suffice to say this is a rollicking ride and if you can stomach the violence then you're in for a

rides up on Mr Dennis and his daughter Amy traveling by wagon to Stinson County, Oklahoma. Amy explains that her father purchased a ranch called Flying 8 and the two are off to live there and raise pigs. Fugate explains that the trek could be dangerous, and Amy asks him to accompany them. Mr Dennis refuses the offer and Fugate soon rides up on them again, only Mr Dennis has been murdered and Amy is shooting at two killers.

In a rather nonsensical fashion, Constiner attempts to detail a strange transaction between owners of the Flying 8 and the Dennis family. Loosely, Mr Dennis saved $15,000 in gold only to throw it away on a fraudulent letter he received from an unknown source. The letter explained that if he paid some mysterious train passenger the money, he could take over ownership of the ranch and live out his merry life as a pig farmer. It's far-fetched to think this man saved money for half his life only to throw it away so easily. Fugate decides he will lead Amy to the ranch safely and resolve his own suspicions about the Flying 8. Along the way the two meet characters along the road, sleep in various towns and generally just waste the reader's time. Eventually (and painfully), the two discover the

treat. The series, which ran for an incredible sixty-one volumes, doesn't let up. Terry Harknett, perhaps the most prolific of all the UK 'Piccadilly Cowboys' certainly created something special here.

Start with this first volume as the story does progress volume to volume. Also, do try to track down the physical novels rather than the Kindle versions as they are full of grammatical errors and spelling mistakes.

Jules Burt

STEEL-JACKET
Merle Constiner
1972

"Nothing that would quench the thirst of die-hard western fans ..."

The book introduces us to 19-year old Joe Fugate, a roughshod orphan who grew up on the streets. The opening chapter explains that Fugate is passing through Oklahoma after looking for work further south in Arkansas. He

mystery behind the ranch ownership and why killers were after Mr Dennis.

It's easy to recognize Constiner's love for mysteries and detective work. **Steel-Jacket** is really a 'who's who' sort of story but jacketed (pun intended) inside the cloak of western fiction. There's a couple of very quick action sequences but nothing that would quench the thirst of die-hard western fans. Aside from that, the book reads more like a young adult tale with both Fugate and Amy being very young and displaying 'inexperienced' characteristics. It was the author's last work and it's fitting that his closure was this book's rather tidy finish. I won't revisit this one again.

The Paperback Warrior

THE MORTIMER SERIES
Art by Victor de la Fuente
1972 – 1973

"Twelve issues of Stetsons and smut."

Spanish artist and writer Victor de la Fuente was one of the most prolific authors of Euro western comics in the 1970s and early 1980s, with several significant series to his name. In the 1960s he was a regular artist on westerns in British adventure comics (**Blackbow the**

Cheyenne for example, in the **Eagle**) but began working in earnest in the genre in 1969 when he drew the series **Sunday** with writer Victor Mora. Later de la Fuente both wrote and drew **Amargo** for Hachette in France (1974) and provided art for Jean-Michel 'Blueberry' Charlier's **Los Gringos** books. His final western work was for the Italian firm Bonelli, on their long-running cowboy strip, **Tex Willer**.

But back in 1973-74 de la Fuente also drew the erotic-western digest comic, **Mortimer** for Italian fumetti publishers, Ediperiodioci (EP). At the time EP were producing a whole slew of pocket-sized titles, often with an historical or horror element, that featured a healthy dose of soft porn amidst their 100-odd pages per issue. Mostly in black in and white but with some (like **Mortimer** often) in colour, many of these cheap and cheerful adult comics were then republished in France by publishers Elvifrance.

Mortimer is a cold but dedicated bounty hunter, traversing the old West in search of his quarry and usually bedding at least one pretty saloon girl per story along the way. De la Fuente managed twelve issues of Stetsons and smut before moving on to (ironically!) comic book versions of Bible stories amongst other projects. The **Mortimer** books' small size and the tight deadlines the artist was evidently working to didn't allow de la Fuente to deliver his very best art, but the set are intriguing curios and are worth tracking down if you are holidaying in Italy or France.

Jim O'Brien

THE WILD ONE
John Reese
1972
"Absolutely refuses to be predictable..."

Author John Henry Reese was a prolific pulpster in both the western and crime genres, writing in the late 1930s and on through the '40s and '50s and spinning out literally hundreds of short stories for publications like **10 Story Western**, **Ace High**, **Argosy**, **Big Book Western**, **Dime Western Magazine**, and dozens of others. He moved on with the market, graduating to the 'slicks', especially the **Saturday Evening Post**, and then on into a prolific career as a novelist, penning almost fifty of them.

The Wild One is a Fawcett Gold Medal book published in 1972 and is a good representation of Reese's style. It absolutely refuses to be predictable. Protagonist Henry Ely, at 18 years of age, has an unfortunate attraction to his best friend's mother, who falsely leads him on in an attempt to gain stud rights from the Ely family horses. Her family, however, has a different opinion and they put young Henry through a horrendous beating, ultimately forcing him to leave his home and strike out on his own. These events change Henry significantly, and lead him on a series of adventures, close calls, and questionable life decisions. He takes on a new name, 'Jack Neely', with an edgier persona, but manages to leverage both his keen intellect and penchant for hard work. Working as a ranch hand, he latches on to a mentor who combines ranching with other moneymaking business opportunities, proving to be a great move for him. But when that mentor is killed in cold blood by a notorious gunslinger, Jack seeks immediate revenge, proving a faster draw and earning a reputation of his own.

The author is adept at taking western tropes and spinning them in different ways. For example, just when you think young Henry/Jack is finally close to gaining a successful future he gets talked into robbing a bank. Not because he needs or wants the money, but just to see if he can do it and get away with it. I enjoyed the story and was entranced with the main character even though the plot was much like an old Republic movie serial with the hero drifting from one adventure to another. This book isn't often mentioned as one of John Reese's best but it's certainly a worthy introduction and should spur readers to look for more of his work.

Benjamin Thomas

BUCHANAN'S GAMBLE
Jonas Ward
1973
"Marriage is the only thing Buchanan wants to dodge as much as he wants to stay alive ..."

Tom Buchanan is the hero of his own series by Jonas Ward. He's a big, peaceable Texan who just wants to bum around and enjoy life – but where would the stories be if that was ever allowed to happen?

In this entry, he starts by setting up a prize fight in San Francisco, gets swindled out of thousands of dollars and then ends up back in the small Western town he started from and eventually winds up in a very crooked poker game with a town marshal who's an ex-con, a couple of very crooked deputies and a banker who loves to

gamble. Oh, and a couple of his friends get murdered on the way. So, despite his best intentions, Buchanan must buckle on his guns and start pounding some justice into the town.

There are complications, of course. His best friend, black boxer Coco Bean, wants to have a match against Buchanan that Tom is doing his best to dodge (he fakes a Chester Goode-like limp for part of the book), and Flo is after him for a different kind of wrasslin' – in the bonds of reasonably holy matrimony. And marriage is the only thing Buchanan wants to dodge as much as he wants to stay alive.

I first read and enjoyed this series forty years ago – and the passage of those years hasn't eroded my enjoyment for these books (or the Randolph Scott movie based on **Buchanan Rides Alone**). He's still a fun character, constantly getting himself into scrapes that force him to ignore his preference for a quiet life and help his friends out.

John Peel

heat up when a grumpy Edge goes against the Hood gang.

The action is fast and Edge is meaner than a rattlesnake. Shooting Mayer's arm off with a shotgun for an insult is a little bit extreme even for Edge, but nobody at the Paramount loses sleep over it. There are more bad puns per page than in all the previous novels combined, allusions to movies and Hollywood's golden era.

An early must-read of the series. One can only thank the farsightedness of editor Laurence James that he let the series continue in this slightly bizarre direction. It couldn't have been an easy decision to go such a unique way against all genre conventions. On the other hand, how often can you duplicate the Italo-western formula before readers get bored?

Andreas Decker

CALIFORNIA KILLING (EDGE 7)
George G Gilman (Terry Harknett)
1973

"More bad puns per page than in all the previous novels combined, allusions to movies and Hollywood's golden era..."

California Killing is the novel where the series truly arrived. Sure, neither the violence nor the nihilism was new or shocking at this point, but the plot unfolds in what I like to call 'Edgeland', a slightly surreal take on the western-genre which must have purists run screaming for the hills.

The plot is rather straightforward. On the way to Hollywood, Edge's coach gets robbed by sadistic Sam Hood and his killers. The survivors arrive in the 'Town With No Name' which calls itself a boom town. Mr Mayer is the owner of the Metro hotel, but Edge stays in the Paramount, owned by the Warner brothers and run by taciturn bartender Cooper. Grauman's Chinese Restaurant is conserving boot prints of famous people in the mud of the street. Things really

THE COWBOY AND THE COSSACK
Clair Huffaker
1973

"Respect and trust are forged in the molten fire of nature..."

If I could only choose one western novel to recommend, it would be **The Cowboy and the Cossack**. The traditional cattle drive formula is given a refreshing twist when fifteen Montana cowboys sail into Vladivostok, Russia, with a herd of five hundred longhorns. The experienced wranglers are fired up to drive their herd across a thousand miles of Siberian wilderness but are startled to find a band of Cossacks – Russia's elite horsemen and warriors – waiting to act as an unwanted escort. Very quickly, the culture clash between American six-shooters and Russian sabres detonates the action. The sequence in which the cattle are herded off the ship to the shore is one of the greatest of all novel openings. Against the sweeping majesty of a cruel winter in the Russian wilderness, two men – Shad, the leader of the Montana cowboys, and Rostov, the Cossack commander –come into tight focus. Respect and trust are forged in the molten fire of nature fuelled by a ruthless Apache-like Tartar army and powerful men whose only motive is profit. The cowboy code and the Cossack credo measure men differently – but honour and courage will rise when the Wild West rides the plains of the Russian Tsars.

Paul Bishop

HAWK 1
Bret Sanders
1973

"The worst offence is that it was simply boring..."

In the first entry into the **Hawk** series by Bret Sanders (not to be confused with the Piccadilly Cowboy series of the same name), the titular character is saved from hanging at the last minute with the offer to rescue a wealthy landowner's bride, who's been kidnapped and held for ransom by the evil Colonel Spate. Boy, where do I begin with this book? It starts out decently enough but when it took five chapters for someone to die, the warning bells were going off. I was cautioned initially about the general low quality of Award Books' output but decided to power through it anyways. In the author's defence he can string together a sentence well enough, he just lacks power behind any of them.

This book is advertised as 'a brutal western series' but there is little of that on display, mostly minimally described gunshot and blade wounds, with a tame whipping scene in the beginning and an awkward and forced spike torture scene near the end. The characterization of Hawk is also inconsistent and frankly stupid. As one character asks him, 'How can you be so ruthless in one breath, so gentle in another?' Honestly lady, I don't know, and it drove me nuts the whole time. He'll spout some gruff, edgy dialogue that's supposed to make him look like a hardass in one section and then turn into an emotional golden boy western hero in another. You get similar from Colonel Spate, who at first is portrayed as a semi-suave conniving villain, but then turns into a raving bloodthirsty torturer for no good reason. The worst offence, however, is that it was simply boring.

If there was any punch behind the work, I could overlook these discrepancies, but it just dragged with the minimal amount of drive necessary. The overall effect is off-putting and made me resent the last third of the book. I will be hard pressed to follow up on the other two books I've got, this is one I will not recommend to any western reader here.

Sean Nodland

★ ☆ ☆ ☆ ☆

HIGH LONESOME (LASSITER 6)
Jack Slade (Peter McCurtin)
1973

"It wouldn't be a McCurtin without a fistfight..."

The first of the **Lassiter** novels written by the eponymous Peter McCurtin, the setup for this novel is very straightforward. We meet Lassiter in New Mexico Territory as he's riding into the town of McDade, planning to kill a man, for which he was paid $250. The town is filled with gunhawks and killers, which puts him on edge. He knows something is up and learns from a whore what the score is. The town is run by Irish ex-Confederate Major Caulfield, however he's at odds with Colonel Danvers, a New Englander who's in charge of that part of Socorro County. With Lassiter smelling money and opportunity, we have a straight **Yojimbo** setup on our hands. Lassiter is a callous and crafty sonufabitch, not above double-crossing his employer for a better payday.

McCurtin, the ever-lean writer that he is, provides us with a hard, no-frills tale that those who enjoy his work love. The plot is railroad straight and I picked up on it right from the start. There's nothing groundbreaking here but as far as I'm concerned that's just fine.

Now, it wouldn't be a McCurtin without a fistfight, and he includes a rough one. Bullets don't hit as hard as knuckles in one of his books

TOWER 43-250   60¢

HIGH LONESOME

JACK SLADE

Lassiter didn't mind looking for a man he didn't know. Lassiter figured they'd get acquainted when he killed him.

LASSITER #6
A Big T Western

and the hand-to-hand scrap Lassiter gets into in this one is tense and had me wincing at several points.

Light on scenery, heavier on cynicism, these 138 pages follow Lassiter navigating hard gunfighters, loose women and a side-swapping scheme, all with a Cheshire grin on his face. This is a quick evening read that went down well.

Sean Nodland

★ ★ ★ ☆ ☆

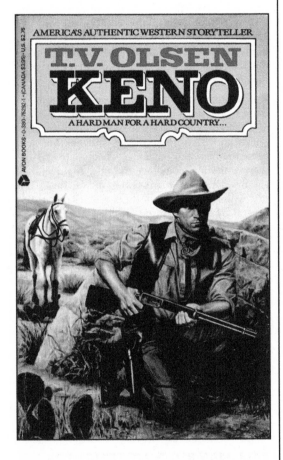

KENO
T V Olsen
1973

"A tough and rugged hero and a likeable cast of supporting characters ..."

'No good deed goes unpunished.' Not only is this a funky little saying, it's also how this fine book, **Keno,** by prolific western writer TV Olsen, begins. Riding through the desert on his way to his next job, cowboy Keno happens across a battered and bloody Mexican man left to die in the unforgiving sands. Not the type of man to ignore a person in need, Keno promptly acts as Good Samaritan and rescues the man from certain death. This good deed sets Keno on a collision course with one Bone Shefflin, a sadistic hunter who was the cause of the Mexican's woes. And that's just the first chapter!

The main storyline is built around a heist that Keno gets involved in to relieve an unscrupulous miner of his ill-gotten gold, but many more minor storylines gradually appear as the tale progresses, stories of love, of friendship – and even a little bit of mystery. Many of the people in the mining operation that Keno is out to steal from seem to recognise him from somewhere, but he has no recollection of ever meeting any of them. Why is that? The reader will likely figure this out long before Keno does, but it's a fun little subplot all the same.

Keno is a fun and engaging western with a tough and rugged hero and a likeable cast of supporting characters. There's plenty of action to be had too, with the author doing a particularly good job of detailing the fist fights that Keno gets himself into. They certainly pack a punch! **Keno** is a quality read for any western fiction fan.

Dan Shanahan

★ ★ ★ ★ ☆

THE LARAMIE RIVER CROSSING
Jack Ehrlich
1973

"Nothing goes as planned, loyalties are tested and broken, and things get brutally violent ..."

After a career as a lawyer, a district attorney and a reporter for Newsday, Jack Ehrlich started writing fiction late in life. Thank God, because **The Laramie River Crossing** is stunning –a lean, mean, hard-edged adult western that left me hungry to read everything by the author. This is a genuinely literary novel that takes the time to craft characters of real depth with myriad shades of grey. Smith (no first name given), and Preacher are bad men with a history of violence and crime.

The first half of the book has a classic 'men on a mission' set-up as Preacher goes about putting their old crime ring back together at the behest of The Limey, their old handler and heist mastermind. Preacher is not above bushwhacking his former colleagues or breaking them out of jail to force their involvement. The plot itself is deceptively simple: The Limey wants to go legit and reunites the old gang to protect his investment as he brings sheep into traditional cattle country. The problem is the local cattle barons are willing to start a full-scale range war to keep the sheep from reaching the former crime boss's property. To give away any more plot would be a disservice to the reader. Suffice to say, nothing goes as planned, loyalties are tested and broken, and things get brutally violent as Smith and Preacher find they possess a previously undiscovered moral compass. Strong language and a frank sexuality are prevalent, though nothing is overtly explicit.

This book deserves to be heralded as a classic. I give it my very highest recommendation!

Steve Carroll

★ ★ ★ ★ ★

STRIKE AT CRIPPLE CREEK
Bob Haning
1973

"Refused to take itself too seriously..."

If you're looking for an obscure western novel, it would be hard to find one further from the beaten path than this one, published in 1973 by Belmont Tower Books. Bob Haning is the name on the cover but whether this is a pseudonym, or he only wrote a few books, is a mystery still to be solved.

The novel revolves around two central plots, both involving Boyd Sinclair, the town of Cripple Creek's assayer. He's also a mining engineer and therefore has a leg up when it comes to finding likely gold deposits. Before the novel opens, we discover that Boyd was hired by Mick Carver and has found a rich deposit on land leased by Carver. The owner of the land believes the find should be his and, naturally, seeks to apply threatening, bullying, and eventually lethal means to get Carver to sign over the lease. However, Boyd happens to be attracted to Carver's pretty daughter, so steps in to defend Carver's rights, mostly via his fists and his six-shooter.

But here the second part of the plot merges in. Turns out Boyd has a past; one that stepped afoul of the law. He's not proud of it but when one of Boyd's former flames and her husband come to town, he's recognized, leading to exposed secrets and a jealous love triangle. A gunshot in the middle of the night barely misses Boyd, but just who is trying to kill him becomes the story's central question, adding an element of mystery to the whole thing.

Reading this novel was a real hoot. Lots of fistfights and gunplay led to some exciting adventure but all the while, it refused to take itself too seriously. A couple of plot holes here and there didn't really distract much from the tale and the descriptive scenes about various aspects of mining techniques were interesting without being overdone. More a 'middle-of-the-road' western than a 'must-read', this one nevertheless proved an enjoyable experience.

Benjamin Thomas

★ ★ ★ ☆ ☆

TALL MAN RIDING (CARMODY 1)
Peter McCurtin
1973

"It lacked some charm and punch ..."

The book opens with our titular character coming to the decision to rob the local bank in Ringgold, Texas before local outlaw Luke Greenwood and his gang get into town. He does so in an efficient manner, however he's not able to get out of town fast enough. After a humiliating and near deadly horse-dragging by a particularly sadistic member of the Greenwood gang, he manages to overcome his assailant before passing out. And so, we get the introduction to a fairly straightforward revenge plot whereby he aims to hunt down every last one and get the money he stole first, fair and square.

I read this book right on the heels of the Lassiter entry and it ended up falling short. There's nothing wrong with McCurtin's no-nonsense writing, Carmody is the mean asshole we're looking for, and there's plenty of violence. What it lacked was some charm and punch; Lassiter was mean and violent but did it all with a shiteating grin that endeared him to the reader, while Carmody is just mean and violent, no other elements adding to his character. The hand-to-hand in Lassiter was legitimately gripping whereas Carmody engages in a more traditional punchout. Lassiter's antagonists and side characters were interesting but with Carmody the only colourful character we see enters the book in the last two chapters.

For fans of McCurtin I would recommend the book as a solid but uneventful entry into his western career, for others I would suggest you pick another entry in his output.

Sean Nodland

THE TIME IT NEVER RAINED
Elmer Kelton
1973

"The characters and dialogue are pitch perfect..."

I didn't know what to expect from this selection since I've always thought of Kelton as a notable writer of formula cowboy type books. This is NOT a cowboy book. **The Time it Never Rained** is an outstanding contemporary novel, telling the story of Charlie Flagg, a self-reliant, stubborn and cantankerous old rancher, and the devastation that occurs from a long Texas drought on his family, workers, friends and neighbours. The novel covers a lot of ground – lost youth, approaching old age, friendship and love. The characters and dialogue are pitch perfect, and the novel does a great job of portraying the lives of Texas ranchers in the mid-20th century, before corporations and factory farms changed the farming and ranching landscapes forever. I'll read this one again someday, and that's high praise for me.

Edwin McBride

CARTRIDGE CREEK
Richard Meade
1974

"An exciting fight on top of a moving train that is breath-taking ..."

This story is about greed for both money and power. Meade creates some terrific characters to battle for these and battle they do in large scale. There are two well-written major gunfights that result in many corpses littering the streets of **Cartridge Creek**.

Violent acts and love cause Leatherman to reconsider what he wants from Cartridge Creek and leads to him facing massive odds. It's the power of persuasion that helps rally the help he needs to take on the small army that stands in his way. As well as vivid descriptions Meade comes up with believable dialogue that makes the speech heavy sections of this story a joy to read.

I mentioned love in the previous paragraph, and that's an element of the story that works well as Leatherman finds himself competing for the affection of the woman in question and also leads

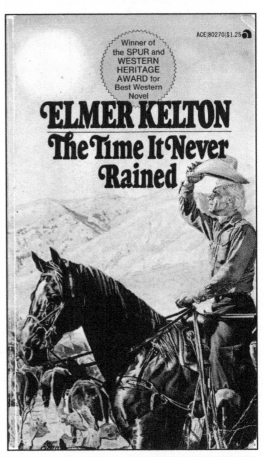

to treachery, hate and an exciting fight on top of a moving train that is breath taking.

Richard Meade is a pseudonym of an author better known for writing westerns as John Benteen. As many will already know, both these pennames were used by Benjamin L Haas and his name ought to be enough of a recommendation for all western fans to grab a copy of this book without me urging you to do so too.

Steve Myall

★ ★ ★ ★ ★

COLORADO KILL (THE LONER 1)
Robert Trimnell
1974

"Even the readers of Edge books, used to savagery- might be taken aback by the violence and the nihilism throughout..."

Titled **The Loner**, one would imagine that the author of this book, Robert Trimnell, was trying to reap a bit of the financial windfall that George G Gilman was enjoying with his hugely popular **Edge** series of books. Gilman's first book was

titled **Edge: The Loner** (Pinnacle Books, 1972). And Trimnell a veteran of the pulps, used the same stark and brutal writing style that endeared the Edge character to millions of readers. Harry Keel was on a mission of vengeance against the men that wronged him. While in the military Captain Murphee and the Indian agent Lashen had conspired to massacre some Sioux and sell their land. When Captain Murphee called for Lieutenant Keel to lead his men against a small company of defenceless Sioux, he and his men refused and were court-martialled. Even Keel's girlfriend Beth Anderson had turned against Keel, adding salt to the wound by marrying Murphee. Some of Lieutenant Keel's men, who followed his orders not to attack the Indians, either escaped from jail or hung. So, after two years of prison hard labour and five years of searching, Keel finally had in his sights the men responsible for his downfall and the death and destruction of the lives of his men.

First off, I will say that this book is not for everyone. Even the readers of George G Gilman's **Edge** books, used to savagery, might be taken aback by the violence and the nihilism throughout **The Loner**. Harry Keel rode into the town where Murphee and Lashen ruled with iron fists and violently dissected it, turning into a bully along the way, almost inhuman in his vengeance. Keel must fight against the whole town, who are either on the payroll of Lashen or are too frightened to stand up against him. But as the book ends and Lashen and his goons annihilated, word comes to Keel that Murphee has escaped to New Mexico, setting up book two, **The Loner #2: New Mexico Massacre**.

The atmosphere throughout the book is heavy; it just never lets up on the brutality and makes for a rather gloomy read. The Harry Keel character has justifiable reasons behind his carnage, but he turns into a killing machine, who comes across at times as a heartless entity who is dead set on vengeance. I enjoyed the book but felt that it could have used a few more instances of light-heartedness. The book put me into a rather dark mood, and I could only read it in increments. While I recommend this book, one must prepare for an onslaught of ugliness and the main character who is as violent as we have seen in a western book and realize that there will be blood and plenty of it. Manor Books released this book as a paperback in 1974, which is the release I read for this review.

Mike Hauss

★ ★ ★ ☆ ☆

SPRINGFIELD .45-70
John Reese
1974

"It packs one hell of an emotional wallop!"

The title refers to the "Springfield .45-70 bolt action rifle that would throw a slug as big as a man's thumb a quarter of a mile with accuracy." John Reese delivers a multi-level story of a country still divided twenty years after the end of the Civil war. The hatred was among not only the sworn enemies but also the men who had served together as officers and enlisted men. When the richest man in the area is robbed and killed by a man named Raitt, the sheriff Casey Oaks decides to track the man down- Raitt blazes a trail of death as he heads out for Mexico. Once Raitt gets his hands on the Springfield .45-70, he takes his pent up hate out on his fellow man, a psychopath dead set on making his way across the border. And Casey Oaks, a former Texas Ranger who was dismissed from their ranks after some money came up missing and is now a sheriff in a small cow town, is on a life or death mission to help bury his past, which ultimately is the basis of this book. All the main male characters in this book have issues in their past that they cannot

escape- In eternal conflict with things that transpired and birthrights.

John Reese delivers a multi-level story of a country still divided twenty years after the end of the Civil war. All the main male characters have issues in their past that they cannot escape. The hatred was not only between the sworn enemies but also amongst the men who had served together as officers and enlisted men.

While I enjoyed this book and it is vibrantly written, I found that it just took too long to get to the points of action. The characters are brought to life, painting a vivid picture of the main characters, but substituting some action for those developments. But I must say that when the ending comes around those character constructions pay dividends as it packs one hell of an emotional wallop!

I quite honestly was a bit let down by this book as I was expecting it to be along the lines of Reese's brilliant series of Jefferson Hewitt's books. To me, the book is uneven, the beginning with the character constructions is intriguing, and the reader hangs on every word by Reese, the middle flounders a bit and is rather talky, but like noted above the ending is well worth any issues that proceeded it. While I am recommending this book, I feel that one must approach it as a character study with a great payoff.

That ending, which I will not reveal, gives two men chances at not only redemption but also rewards them with self-worth and a future. The Springfield .45-70 was made to kill another man, which is the author's point of including it here, and a gun like this in the hands of a psychopath can only bring death and destruction until he is stopped by the only mean necessary, death! But that gun that brought death also gave two men a chance at redemption and, more importantly, a reason to live again!

Mike Hauss

RANGER KIRK
W C Rawford (William Crawford)
1974

"The upside is that it's a blessedly short paperback ..."

The character of Ranger Kirk is Sergeant Tom Kirk, an Old West Texas Ranger with the Frontier Battalion along the Mexican border who approaches his job the way a modern intel officer

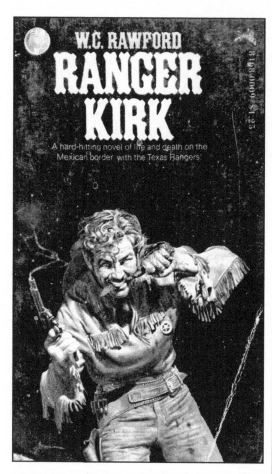

might. He deploys undercover agents into Mexico to gather information about criminal activity. This clandestine approach to law enforcement makes Kirk an oddity among his colleagues who are more of a shoot first and ask questions later bunch of guys. Moreover, Kirk's spy operations have been going poorly and three consecutive operatives are slaughtered and mutilated by the enigmatic Mexican crime lord, Tuerto.

As the reader gets to know our hero, we quickly discover that Kirk is a flaming asshole. He's that friend of yours who starts taking swings at you after he has a few drinks in him. His abhorrent behaviour crosses the line one too many times, and he is forced to give up his Ranger badge. This leads to a clever and unexpected series of events that brings Kirk right into the heart of Tuerto's operational base in Mexico. When Kirk finally meets Tuerto face-to-face, it's a surprising encounter. Once again, the author chooses a plot turn quite unexpected and somewhat more satisfying than the typical western showdown the reader expects. Tuerto is a fascinating character, and Crawford should have done more with him.

Along the way, there are Indian attacks, a damsel in distress, and the eventual redemption of our hero.

Even with all this, **Ranger Kirk** is a pretty lousy novel. The story never really comes together into anything particularly interesting. The action scenes are poorly written, and Kirk never turns the corner fully into a likable character. The upside is that it's a blessedly short paperback at 160 big-font pages with a blank page between each chapter for further padding. In fact, the brevity of the book is the only reason I finished it. Finally, the cover art by George Gross is outstanding, but this paperback isn't worthy of its own packaging. Final assessment: Don't bother.

The Paperback Warrior

★ ☆ ☆ ☆ ☆

SUN MOUNTAIN SLAUGHTER
Clint Reno (Todhunter Ballard)
1974

"It's fast-moving, frothy and I read the first few chapters with a smile on my face..."

The first of a two-book 'Vigilante' series (although the character is always referred to as The Major) which was presumably one of Fawcett Gold Medal's responses to the likes of **The Executioner** as well as the **Edge** westerns. The book has a certain anachronistic vibe, in which it carries a pulp-hero tone more reminiscent of decades prior where heroes are brick-jawed, pure of heart and indestructible (author Ballard was in his 70s when writing this book and had started his career in the 40s pulps) but with off-hand descriptions of bodies being blown to pieces. The Major is a fun enough character, carrying so many weapons that even the author comments it must have been impossible to move and with the nice touch of a customised bandolier full of dynamite sticks. Equally fun is the supporting cast of impossibly loyal and lunk-headed men who join his crusade against a corrupt mine-owner who killed his family. Ballard's professionalism shines through with the grease-lightning plot development and efficient writing. It's fast moving, frothy and I read the first few chapters with a smile on my face, but eventually its lack of sophistication or innovation changed that to a frown. If you dig that old-time religion typified by **Doc Savage** and **The Shadow**, this could be a western duo for you.

Justin Marriott

THE GHOST DANCERS (SUNDANCE 8)
John Benteen (Ben Haas)
1975

"Sundance just wants to settle down, start a ranch, and find peace…"

You know what's hotter than a mid-August Ranger game in Texas? The scorching writing of author John Benteen (Ben Hass) on his **Sundance** Western series from Belmont/Tower Books. So, engrossed in **Sundance #8, The Ghost Dancers,** I never heard someone yell 'foul ball', and woke up on a stretcher with the paramedic reading my copy. But the tale was so exciting, who could put it down!

Riding high on the success of his **Fargo** series, Hass wrote the first sixteen stories, followed by a gang of wordsmiths for its forty-three violent volumes. Jim Sundance had the rugged face of a Cheyenne warrior he inherited from his mother, and the striking golden mane of an English father. His Indian name, Sundance, was given to him after enduring the Sun Dance ritual, but our hero walks a fine line between two cultures at war with each other. A master of the white man's civilized weapons, his Navy Colt, Bowie knife

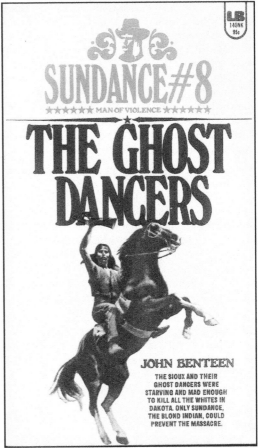

and Henry rifle were always by his side. But when he had to do some serious killing, a primitive tomahawk, longbow and Cheyenne dog soldier shield were just what the medicine man ordered. In this adventure, Sundance just wants to settle down, start a ranch and find peace. But with Indians starving and desperate due to a white man selling bad beef, a red man finds the solution in reviving the Ghost Dancers to go on the warpath. And only one man caught in the middle can stop this massacre, Sundance!

Dave Karlen

★ ★ ★ ★ ☆

GUN RUN (ADAM STEELE 5)
George Gilman (Terry Harknett)
1975

"I'd rather be reading about that heartless bastard Edge…"

Adam Steele is a tough guy. Blissfully, ridiculously, amazingly tough. The character in a nutshell is marked by toughness and dickishness with a dash of ass-kicker. George

Gilman is much more well-known for his **Edge** series, which brought a nasty, dirty, mean Spaghetti western feel to the page. So bloody that the red stuff nearly drips from the pages of the book. Gillman was really Terry Harknett, who did awesome work in both the western and Men's Adventure genres. I particularly like his 70s-set **Crown** Hong Kong Dirty Harry series. In all cases, whether it's Steele, Edge, Crown or even Fortune, Harknett wrote stone-cold guys that you should never mess with.

But of course, they always get messed with or you wouldn't have a book. Steele gets held-up in a stagecoach and his fellow passengers are killed and a stash of gold is stolen. That doesn't rile Steele up too much, but these desperadoes stole his father's rifle. That royally pisses Steele off, enough to go on a rampage to get it back. To do this he rides into the desert with next to nothing to help in his task and mows his way through all the baddies in this rocket-fast tale of revenge.

The only problem with Steele is that he's not Edge. While the book was a lot of terrible fun, Steele always sort of comes off as the B-team, he's marginally a nicer guy then Edge and I think that's my problem with him. I'd rather be reading about that heartless bastard, Edge.

Roy Nugen

★ ★ ★ ★ ☆

HONEYMAKER'S SON
Ray Hogan
1975

"A plot for a half hour TV western barely stretched to novella length ..."

Universally feared yet despised land baron Burl Honeymaker has been bushwhacked, shot in the back by an unknown assassin. Now it's up to his young estranged son, Tom, to find the killer even as he assumes responsibility of the family ranch and with it, inherits an escalating land war with three other powerful landowners who all want his vast acreage. The question for Tom to answer is, which one of them is willing to kill to get it? Overall, this is a pretty straightforward western. There's plenty of gunplay and dastardly potential villains with their personal armies, all ready and willing to take the Honeymaker property by force. Complicating things is an unexpected romance that develops between Tom and the daughter of one of the scheming landowners.

Ray Hogan wrote well over 100 books in his career and has a smooth style, although even at a slim 143 pages, this book feels padded. It's kind of like a plot for a half hour TV western barely stretched to novella length. Plot points are repeated often as Tom muses at length about his predicament, rehashing what the reader has already perfectly grasped. But the action is frequent and well described, the romance angle never gets in the way, and the end is acceptably suspenseful as an all-out range war erupts. This is not an essential western by any means, but it is enjoyable enough to pass the time without regrets.

Steve Carroll

★ ★ ★ ☆ ☆

KILBURN 1
Sam Victor (Morris Hershman)
1975

"A tendency to overcomplicate the plot..."

Kilburn is a black-clad killer for hire and one of the genre's mean and cruel antiheroes. This series showcases "The West in all its violence. If you're strong enough to take it." in a warning label blazoned across the first volume's Berkley

Medallion front cover. The tone is set in the first chapter when a family is savagely raped and beaten to death by a corrupt sheriff and his deputies. Taking a note from the Piccadilly Cowboy westerns of the same period, this one keeps its violence brutal, cruel, and cold-hearted.

Kilburn is hired by the government to get his hands on Carstairs, the sheriff mentioned previously and bring him in, preferably alive (but probably dead). He is presented to us as a cold, calculating character, a loner with a short-tempered fuse who hates towns and elicits a shiver of fear just by being around. Unfortunately, the author is inconsistent in trying to make his character another Edge. The grim descriptors and nonchalance for cruelty are there, but he begins to spoil it in the second half with Kilburn expressing a distaste for killing or feeling sick at the sight of death.

He also has a tendency to overcomplicate the plot; instead of this being a straightforward game of cat and mouse between Kilburn, the sheriff, and his deputies, he introduces a strange cattle rustling scheme and several other townsfolk who nearly take over the narrative from our protagonist. After muddling through this revolving door of unnecessary characters, the author closes with a decent enough shootout in the middle of a steer stampede.

Overall, if this book had its kinks cleared out and unneeded plotlines removed, it would be a solid start to another western series.

Sean Nodland

★ ★ ☆ ☆ ☆

BORDER INCIDENT (BANNERMAN 2)
Jay Flynn
1976

"A James Bond novel in dusty clothes ..."

This book is a bawdy hell-raiser of a paperback. 'Slim' Jim Bannerman is an operative of the Gallows Detective Agency at the turn of the century. On the brink of World War One, the Germans are in Mexico trying to persuade the Mexicans to let them turn their army into a striking force to give hell to America. Mexico would get back the southwest and the Germans figure the United States won't be a problem after a blow like that. It, like all good paperback action-fests, is up to one man: Bannerman.

Border Incident reads a whole lot like a James Bond novel in dusty clothes. There's British spies, including the plucky female love interest,

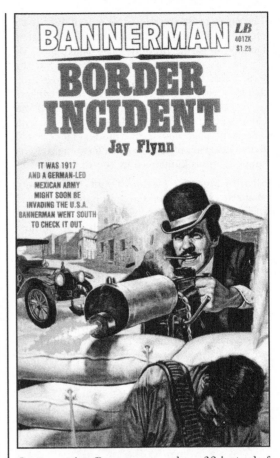

German spies, Bannerman packs a .32 instead of a Colt .45, there's disguises and espionage abound. The Bannerman character is a hard-boiled company man and that's about it, besides his penchant for smoking marijuana, which makes him stand out a bit. I can't think of many paperback heroes that did at the time. Flynn wrote a solid series of contemporary (the 60s) spy novels about McHugh. It halfway reads like Bannerman was a long-lost cousin to McHugh and that's a real good thing. Bannerman had the pulp chops to have a lot more adventures then the two he did have. The book is a nice Saturday afternoon read, nothing life changing but a wild-ride. The spy angle might be off putting to anyone wanting a straightforward western novel, but it worked for me.

Roy Nugen

★ ★ ★ ★ ☆

MAN OUTGUNNED
Lewis Patten
1976

"A master of the craft and one of the better writers of any genre ..."

The novel begins during a Fourth of July town picnic in Placita, Colorado. With its citizens happily preparing fireworks and baked goods by a river, six escaped prisoners arrive to find the local bank barely staffed. In a gut-wrenching display, the prisoners shotgun the bankers (decapitating one) and unmercifully kill an elderly, pleading couple in the streets. During an extremely poor choice of timing, 16-year old Sally Dickerson returns to town for some cooking supplies and is kidnapped by the six outlaws.

Sheriff Morgan McGuire and his deputy Donovan soon learn about the murders and robbery and form a makeshift posse to run the outlaws to ground. Unfortunately, the outlaws are a half-day away and the posse isn't fit for a long, hard ride. With Sally's grieving father in tow, the group gallops their horses to death and lose ground finding new rides. It's here that the narrative really settles in as only McGuire and Donovan are left to run the outlaws down. I won't share an important spoiler here regarding Sally Dickerson...but this is a western and these are six hardened criminals with a 16-yr old girl. Patten doesn't hold back punches.

In a cruel twist of fate, the story loses Donovan, and McGuire is left as the 'man outgunned' against the murderers. There's a couple of good side-stories that develop regarding a Mexican sheriff, an orphaned boy and a grieving widow. Patten threads these elements into the novel's road trip, focusing on McGuire's date with destiny while attempting to build even the weakest of alliances to fight the overwhelming odds.

If you love westerns, this is a mandatory read. Patten is absolutely a master of the craft and one of the better writers of any genre. **Man Outgunned** is one of the best books I've read of late and another fine entry in what has become a treasured author. Buy everything the man has written. It's worth every cent.

The Paperback Warrior

TEN TOMBSTONES (EDGE 18)
George G Gilman (Terry Harknett)
1976

"Highlights the cold and cool characterization of Edge ..."

Another entry in the bitter Western series chronicling the adventures of the Loner, this book follows Edge as he escorts two women and a massive albino stud to Texas, where the bull is worth $50,000. However, these women are being hounded by a cattle rancher named Evans and his nine hands, who killed the husband and brother of the two women, and lay claim to the bull and its price tag. These women aren't just on the run with this stud and they've brought more than just feed and supplies. They have vengeance in their hearts and **Ten Tombstones**, one for each man to be killed. Overall, this was a pretty fun Edge novel, it shows a lot of the character's ambivalence and mercenary nature, which I really like. You see, he's not there to kill these men and take part in justice or vengeance. He wants to do the job he's hired to do: get the bull to Texas for that sweet payday. And when the girls put his life in danger or threaten the safety of the bull? His price goes up. A standalone entry in the series, this book highlights the cold and cool characterization of Edge. Less continuously violent than earlier entries in the series, I enjoyed the focus on the tensions between Edge and the women during the race south. Harknett keeps the action, when it does occur, tight and fast, which complements the chase aspect of the plot very well. Overall, a great entry point into the series if unacquainted and a refreshingly well-done chapter to those already familiar.

Sean Nodland ★ ★ ★ ★ ☆

TRAIL OF LOST SKULLS
Nelson Nye
1976

"How about dinosaurs?"

Gunfighters? Check. Indians? Check. Lost-in-the-desert-without-a-horse-or-water? Check. Treasure? Double check? So what more could **Trail of Lost Skulls** by Nelson Nye throw in?

How about dinosaurs?

No, I'm not talking about cowboys roping prehistoric creatures, as in **Valley of Gwangi** – I don't mean real, live dinosaurs – I mean real DEAD dinosaurs.

The novel is based on a real incident in the 1880s, when two professors working for the Natural History Museum in New York City competed with each other to get the most – and biggest! – dinosaur skeletons, and thus to get

their names on the front pages of the newspapers of the day. They were not above a bit of chicanery to achieve their goals, and they had teams of excavators out in the Deadlands hunting up bones.

And here we have one Yavapai Jones (probably some lesser-known cousin of the better publicized Indiana) – Indian scout, failed prospector and incredibly lucky finder-of-skulls – helping one professor (and his voluptuous daughter) head into Indian country and ward off the machinations of his main rival. He soon discovers that daughter Francie is a self-centred, conniving bitch and pines for Hester, his hash-slinging girlfriend...only to find that Hester has discovered her inner diva and is now a musical hall singer named Maisee Devereaux who is enjoying her new-found celebrity. Will Yavapai achieve his twin goals of marrying Hester/Maisee and getting filthy rich? Will Maisee/Hester ever come to her senses? (Or has she already?) And who knew there was so much skulduggery in digging skulls?

John Peel

★ ★ ★ ★ ☆

WHITE DEATH (HERNE THE HUNTER 1)
John McLaglen (Laurence James)
1976

"Crazy, comic book action and timeless otherworldliness..."

If you've not read the **Herne the Hunter books**, you're in for a treat. The first entry in the violent series is a prime example of western fair, and a solid sampling of the Piccadilly Cowboy subgenre. What is the Piccadilly Cowboy subgenre, you say? Well, in short, it was a movement in the Seventies and Eighties of several British authors, the joke of which was that none of them had ever been west of Piccadilly. The **Herne the Hunter** series was attributed to John McLagen, the nom de plume of the writing team of Laurence James and John Harvey. It seems the duo tag-teamed, each writing every other volume.

The thing that strikes me about the Piccadilly Cowboy westerns is their stilted take on the genre. They are not unlike the spaghetti westerns of Sergio Leone . . . over the top, violent; an interpretation of what the old west might have been like, viewed through the special lens of European sensibilities. But that crazy, comic book action and timeless otherworldliness is exactly what I love about these books.

Herne fits a standard story mode of an anti-hero born out of tragedy. In short, it's a tale of cold revenge. But the most fun thing about this volume is the Easter eggs. Yep. There are at least four references to other genre favourites tucked into the pages. The cover itself borrows from the movie poster of Clint Eastwood's **High Plains Drifter**. Then you have the reference in dialogue: 'That was the greatest shot ever,' and the line of, 'It was the worst. I was aiming for the horse.'— riffing on **The Magnificent Seven**. There is even a reference to a hotel clerk named Terry Harknett, who some will recognize as the creator of the **Edge** series.

Have yourself a high time picking out all the Easter eggs. They're as much fun discovering as the story itself!

S Clayton Rhodes

EVIL BREED (THE LAWMEN 1)
J B Dancer (Angus Wells)
1977

"Scenes play out cinematographically, emphasizing the natural environment, sounds, and imagery..."

This series, written alternatingly by Angus Wells and John Harvey, is one whose paperback editions are extremely hard to find in the wild or online. I myself only have five of the six titles after close to a decade of collecting. The first entry in the series follows Lee Fisher, a laconic gunslinger, as he works for the Mid-Western Detective Agency out of St Louis. He operates with Brad McGarry, the man who hired him, as they hunt down the Stillwell family, a gang of train robbers operating in the territory.

The first thing I noticed about the writing style is how cinematic it is, a familiar aspect of Wells' style. Scenes play out cinematographically, emphasizing the natural environment, sounds, and imagery, snapping and tracking to other characters and events. I loved this style, it allowed the novel to play in my head like the spaghetti westerns that they were influenced by. The gunplay is fast and brutal, although the body count is relatively low (for a Piccadilly Cowboy western). Fisher has little in the way of deep character development; some details about his past are brought up but only to reaffirm his cool emotionlessness. The secondary characters are more interesting, especially a strong female

agent and a couple of family members' relations with each other. The plot moves along briskly and brutally, climaxing with a gory lynching and a hunt of the remaining family members.

This will obviously appeal to any Piccadilly Cowboy fan, however I think the tight plotting and interesting style and characters will lend itself well to plenty of western readers.

Sean Nodland

FLESH – BOOK 1
2000AD Progs 1-19, 1977
Written by Pat Mills, Ken Armstrong, Kelvin Gosnell and Studio Giolitti
Drawn by Boix, Ramon Sola and Felix Carrion

"A fine adventure and a neat satire on western greed..."

What do you get if you mix Ray Bradbury's 1952 T Rex and time travel yarn 'A Sound of Thunder' and Ray Harryhausen's 1969 cowboys-versus-dinosaurs romp **The Valley of Gwangi** with – in no particular order – the Yul Brynner robot from **West World**, a western town complete with an old time saloon sat beneath a perspex safety dome, and a large dash of anti-establishment polemic? Why, **Flesh** of course... and lots of it.

The 23rd century. With many of the world's animals now extinct, profit hungry multinational corporations send 'rangers' back in time to round up vast herds of plant-eating dinosaurs so that their flesh can be served up to the starving millions. These rangers (lead by flinty old hand Earl Reagan) dress as cowboys and for the most part corral the dinosaurs on horseback so that the world depicted in the strip is very much the wild west of the 1880s. Except with dinosaurs. As the herd makes its way towards the rangers' base/slaughterhouse they are harried and attacked by T Rexs, the Apaches or Sioux if you will to the rangers' cowboys and the plant chewing dinos' buffalo. Pat Mills' strip functions as a fine adventure and a neat satire on western greed and the indomitable will of the Indian/T Rex underdog not to be dispossessed of what is rightfully theirs. To push the message home, the 1978 **2000AD Annual** had Reagan and fellow ranger 'Claw' Carver (shades of the **Klaw** western series by W L Fieldhouse and the **Claw** books by Matthew Kirk here – Carver has a dinosaur's claw in place of a right hand) time travel back to the western plains in 1821 to bring back buffalo meat instead of Styracosaurus steaks for a change!

UK weekly comics of the period are generally episodic in nature, but **Flesh** holds up well as a complete narrative and the art (particularly that of Ramon Sola) is great.

Jim O'Brien

★★★☆☆

UN NOMMÉ MAC COY (MAC COY 2)
Jean-Pierre Gourmelen and Antonio Hernandez Palacios
1977

"Making the series one of the longest-running westerns in European comics..."

French author Gourmelen and Spanish artist Palacios created their top-notch western adventure series Mac Coy for the French comics market in the early 1970s. Originally serialised in the magazines **Pilote** and **Spirou**, individual story arcs were later collected and published as hardback albums by Dargaud. Gourmelen and

Palacios produced twenty-one volumes all told between 1974 and 1998, making the series one of the longest-running westerns in European comics. Lieutenant Alexis Mac Coy is a Confederate soldier struggling to make sense of his life following the defeat of the South in the Civil War. This second volume in the saga opens with Mac still languishing in a Northern jail, until he and buddy Charlie offer to undertake a dangerous mission into Mexico in search of renegade Northern officer, Captain Saint-Croix, who has absconded southwards with a fat pile of cash. But the mission across the border is made all the more delicate by the presence in Mexico of French troops stationed there to defeat Juarez and his rebel army. In no time Mac and Charlie are playing both sides off against the middle in their attempts to track down Saint Croix and regain the North's lost gold. Palacios modelled Mac Coy's appearance on Robert Redford who, following **Butch Cassidy and the Sundance Kid** (1969) and **Jeremiah Johnson** (1972), was very much an established western 'face'. More than either of these two films though, **A Man Called Mac Coy** recalls some aspects of Peckinpah's 1965 film **Major Dundee** in its plot and settings. Palacios could draw like a dream and lavished his talents for western strips not just on Mac Coy but also on the slightly earlier series, **Manos Kelly**. Both are well worth seeking out.

Jim O'Brien

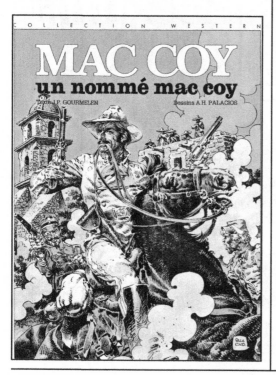

THE FIRST SHOT (CALEB THORN 1)
L. J Coburn (Laurence James)
1977

"Goes out of his way to make his hero as vile as possible ..."

On the eve of the Civil War Caleb Thorn kills young Lieutenant Janson in a duel. Thorn is 21 and one of the idle and depraved rich of the North. He has an unnatural affection for his mother and has murdered his brute of a father. At the battle of Bull Run the mother is killed and Thorn now has a mission; kill as many Rebs as possible. But fate intervenes. Janson's vengeful father is his new commanding officer, and he will send Thorn with a group of court-martialled deserters and killers on suicide missions into the South.

How do you top your own achievements in the most violent westerns ever? You try to make your anti-heroes even more vicious. Caleb Thorn gets high marks in this category. A sociopath with an incestuous relationship with his mother, gruesome killings and tons of gore. Laurence James, who did the series with John Harvey, sure goes out of his way to make his hero as vile as possible but fails to make him interesting. While the predicament to be sent on suicide missions by his vengeful superior is a darkly humorous twist, the rest of the concept is an unoriginal rehash of **Edge** and his posse of uniformed killer's adventures in the Civil War, a highlight of the Gilman series. The exploitation here is a bit too calculated, and, what is worse, boring. With only five novels in two years this was the first misfire of the Piccadilly Cowboys, and it is not hard to see why.

Andreas Decker

★ ★ ☆ ☆ ☆

OLIVIA WAS THE MOST BEAUTIFUL WOMAN SLOCUM HAD EVER SEEN—AND THE MOST DEADLY.

RIDE FOR REVENGE (SLOCUM 11)
Jake Logan (Martin Cruz Smith)
1977

"Nicely realised characters and a clever plot round it out..."

Whilst on the trail of the killers of his bank-robbing partner, loose cannon Slocum is drawn to a strange ranch which is overseen by an alluring yet deadly girl and disciplined by two sadistic henchmen, one of whom has a link with Slocum's past. An early entry to what would become a long-running adult western series with future bestseller Martin Cruz Smith behind the Jake Logan house-name, this is a superior example of the genre.

Its set-up reminded me of **The Name of the Game is Death,** the classic Dan J Marlowe hardboiled crime novel of the previous decade, with its lead characters being bank-robbers agreeing to split up to avoid capture, and one later summoned by a mysterious letter from the other. If you're going to riff on anyone, why not the best? There's still plenty of originality to savour though, such as the book's opening sequence with Slocum and partner trapped in a bank following a raid gone wrong, with the building literally being shot to bits by a small army of Pinkerton detectives. There are also inventive set pieces involving windmills and hot-air balloons which are unusual for a western setting. Plus, a flashback to a prison scene, which is always welcome. Nicely realised characters and a clever plot round it out. Although restricted by the conventions of the adult western genre – which is why ultimately it falls short of a four to five-star rating – this is a super book.

Justin Marriott

★ ★ ★ ☆ ☆

THE HIDER
Loren D Estleman
1978

"It's bittersweet when Estleman shows the old ways butting up against the new ones..."

I enjoyed Estleman's Holmes pastiche **Sherlock Holmes vs Dracula** and one of his P I Amos Walker books, **Angel Eyes**, so I thought I'd give one this western a go. It's a great coming-of-age tale set in the dying days of the Wild West. Jeff Curry is left a rundown farm plot after the death of his drunken father. He is contemplating a sale, when a rangy stranger shows up dusty and thirsty from the trail.

Jack (no last name) is a remnant of the Old West and claims to have served under Teddy Roosevelt and is the last of the buffalo hunters. He has been searching for one last great beast for several years. Intrigued by the tales, Jeff decides to join him on this last hunt. They later are joined by the outlaw Indian Logan, running from a wrongful accusation of murder.

Through detours and subplots, Jack always gets back on the track of his last buffalo. He is an interesting character: a walking anachronism, a teller of tall tales, a crack 50-cal rifle shot, and the biggest fan of mules this side of the Mississippi. He thinks the mule is the superior riding and pack animal for long journeys. It's bittersweet when Estleman shows the old ways butting up against the new ones, when the trio come to a bustling town.

Jeff is the first-person narrator, who is book smart, but not too bright sometimes in the ways of life. Logan is....well... Logan. We're sometimes not too sure where he's coming from. The three make quite a team and the last portion of the book has some great suspense. I really enjoyed this tale.

Scott Ranalli

★ ★ ★ ★ ☆

THE INDIAN INCIDENT (BLADE 1)
Matt Chisholm (Peter Watts)
1978

"His pacing is excellent, his characters are tough, his plots gripping..."

At the beginning of the story we find Joe Blade shoeless, horseless and without weapons, all these having been stolen from him. Blade is hunting down those responsible for his current predicament and it's whilst doing this he stumbles onto the site of a massacre of Indians and discovers the only survivor and the action never lets up from there.

Chisholm introduces a whole load of terrific characters such as Crazy Annie, someone I don't think any of us will forget quickly. Then there's the half-breed, George McMasters, and a great selection of outlaws. The story switches between the various groups before they all come together for a prolonged final showdown that offers a number of twists and surprises along with a variety of deadly situations that will have you wondering how anyone can possibly escape with their lives, never mind the gold they are all hunting for.

If you've never read any of Matt Chisholm's books, then this is a great place to introduce yourself to his work. His pacing is excellent, his characters are tough, his plots gripping, his action vivid without being too graphic and he doesn't include explicit sex scenes while bad language is used sparingly.

I will also add that to get the best enjoyment from the Blade series you should try to read them in order as several characters appear in more than one book.

Top entertainment from yesteryear that more than matches anything being written today.

Steve Myall

★ ★ ★ ★ ★

THE LAST BOUNTY HUNTER
DC Presents 16 – Jonah Hex Spectacular
1978

"Can't think of another story which gave such a cruel yet powerful ending to its character ..."

Breaking ground and hearts, this is a comic book story that has never received its rightful recognition as such, presumably because it featured a western character rather than a super-hero. Jonah Hex was DC's longest-running western character, 'The Man with no Name' amped up to eleven with a hideously scarred face and seemingly indestructible. At the time of this story, Hex is seventy and needs glasses, but his refusal to leave behind frontier justice marks him out as an anachronism in the early twentieth century, and a young reporter attaches himself to Hex to document the Old West before it dies out. And die it does, when the half-blind and unsuspecting Hex is shot-gunned in the back as he is polishing his spectacles during a poker game. To compound their vengeance, his killers embalm the corpse and sell it to a travelling carnival to be displayed as a morbid curiosity piece and burn his wife alive to steal it. The story ends six decades later, with a gum-chewing kid viewing the tatty and rotting Hex and enquiring to his mother whether it was ever a real person.

I can't think of another story which gave such a cruel and powerful ending to its character. It is similar to the themes of Peckinpah's **The Wild Bunch** in its depiction of the passing of an era and the people that carved it out. But unlike **The Wild Bunch**, Hex didn't get his chance to go out all guns blazing. That the most feared gunman in the West would later be dismissed by bored tourists as a figment of the imagination of a huckster carny, is deeply subversive. This achingly cruel finale was penned by long-time Hex scribe Michael Fleisher, who had never been a life-long comics fan in the way that many in the industry were (and who once sued Harlan Ellison for describing him as 'bugfuck crazy') which is perhaps why he wasn't constrained by convention when imagining such a bleak end. Artist Russ Heath, someone who is undoubtedly underappreciated as he didn't produce superhero comics, provided his normal crystal clear and realistic graphics to reinforce the harsh and brutal reality of the script. You really haven't ever read a western comic like this one.

Justin Marriott

★ ★ ★ ★ ★

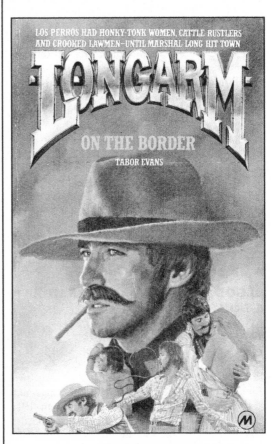

LONGARM ON THE BORDER
Tabor Evans (Melvin Marshall)
1978

"Little of the spark and fizz of his typical narrative..."

Longarm is a US Deputy Marshall in the late nineteenth century, based out of Colorado but sent across the South on trouble-shooting missions. In this book's mission he is asked to track down three apparent deserters from the cavalry who were originally cattle rustler-busting. Longarm's trail takes him from a frontier town run by a sadistic sheriff and his brutish henchmen, over the border to Mexico where he is imprisoned by the Federales who sees Longarm as a prize worthy of a ransom from the US government. This was my first Longarm book and based on my high expectations for one of the longest-running adult western series and one

that was originated by one of my favourite western authors, Lou Cameron, I was very disappointed. It had all the expected ingredients of an adult western and some of the trademarks of Cameron's plotting, but little of the spark and fizz of his typical narrative. Subsequently I discovered that despite being only the second entry to the series, it was written by Melvin Marshall and not Cameron. The alliterative Marshall may sound like a pseudonym but is a name that appears on many other westerns, so is presumably a different author to Cameron. I assume that Cameron produced a bible for other writers to follow, and he may have even developed the plots in the early books for other writers to complete, so I will return to Longarm but with more of an eye on the writer behind the Tabor Evans pseudonym, ensuring that it is definitely Cameron or one of the three penned by Harry Whittington.

Justin Marriott

★★☆☆☆

BLOOD, SWEAT AND GOLD (RAIDER & DOC 2)
J D Hardin
1979

"A bit episodic and paint-by-numbers..."

Raider (Rade) and Doc Weatherbee are two Pinkerton detectives. As you may or may not know, Pinkertons were much more than PIs; they could be called upon to be bodyguards, bounty hunters, or – as in this case – security experts for an unprecedented quantity of gold bullion to be shipped via rail. The gold disappears and Pinkerton and our two heroes are on the hook for $12 million and they have ten days to retrieve it!!

It seems Doc and Raider were intended to be a Brains and Brawn team, but it's not that cut and dry. They bicker constantly, but there's lots of true respect between the two – much like Monk and Ham, for you Doc Savage fans. And like Ham, Doc is quite the slave to fashion and fastidious and calculating; unlike Ham, he is a stickler for the rules, especially Allan Pinkerton's. Raider is a less defined character, but he is not brawn without a brain; in fact, he displays a good bit more 'street smarts' than Doc.

I do not know anything about the authors using the Hardin 'house' name (Donald Bain, Victor Milán, Neal Barrett Jr, etc), so I couldn't guess which one wrote this. The writing is not horrible,

and the sex scenes were thankfully brief, but it just didn't grab me. It all seemed a bit episodic and paint-by-numbers to me. Maybe the series fleshes out and gets better later? I just don't see myself checking any more of these out.

Scott Ranalli

★★☆☆☆

FORT DESPAIR (ADAM STEELE 23)
George G Gilman (Terry Harknett)
1979

"Even the hero reflects that this is the sixth time he somehow ends up in a fort..."

As a character, Adam Steele always was a bit more relatable than Edge, in the best novels of the series he had an aura of true melancholy and loss. But then he had to be different to be interesting. This one is a bit of a slow burner, though. After meeting a deserter, Steele gets entangled in the affairs of Fort Benedict, where Major McCoy has established a draconian regime and is hated by everyone, even the civilians. Unfortunately, the Major has pushed the Sioux too far; when they attack, the settlers seek a safe place in the fort. Which is bad, as the troopers finally start a mutiny and put their commander into jail.

Siege stories can be suspenseful, but this is mostly about the internal conflicts of the besieged. The rebelling soldiers start fighting with each other and Steele and the civilians are caught in the middle. While there are some nice ideas and tense scenes, the plot leaves not much room for the Virginian to do something. The attack finally happens in the last two chapters, and while the action is plenty and bloody, it is also rather by the numbers. This is kind of understandable, as the basic scenario is nothing new. Even the hero reflects that this is the sixth time he somehow ends in a fort, which is not a signpost for originality.

So, while some of the conflicts in the fort are entertaining in the usual cynical Gilman way, it must be said that this is not the best entry in the series. But also, not the worst.

Andreas Decker

★ ★ ★ ☆ ☆

THE FRISCO KID
Robert Grossbach
1979

"A rugged, delightful tale of an odd couple out West..."

The year is 1850 and a Jewish congregation in San Francisco want a Rabbi from Europe. The one they are sent is Avram Mutz – who knows very little about the world but means well. On arriving in America, he's swindled and forced to team up with a bank-and-train robber to cross the country. But, boy, what a journey it is.

Based on the film starring Gene Wilder and Harrison Ford, this is a rugged, delightful tale of an odd couple out West. They face every possible disaster – from crossing a burning desert to being hunted by the conmen who stole Avram's money. Indians, railroads, wagon trains... all lie in their path. And Avram must suffer it all while keeping kosher...

It's well-written and filled with background details (though I did discover one mistake – somebody is surprised not to see the Statue of Liberty when they arrive in America; I'm not, since it wouldn't be constructed for another forty years...). There are delightful, screwy characters, lots of silly repartee, all the clichés you can imagine and a Jewish horse. But my favourite part is when Avram and his outlaw friend Tommy are escaping from a murderous posse... but it's the Shabbat, and Avram isn't allowed to ride a horse...

Enjoy!

John Peel

★ ★ ★ ★ ☆

GUNS ACROSS THE RIVER (GRINGOS 1)
J D Sandon
1979

"Pushes the limits of being a western ..."

The **Gringos** series was another Piccadilly Cowboy series popular in the UK during the late 70s that are now extremely hard to find. Written alternately by Angus Wells and John Harvey, these tales follow a misfit group of gunrunning mercenaries through Revolutionary Mexico, in the mould of Peckinpah's **The Wild Bunch**. Ex-Army Major Cade Onslow, our main protagonist, is joined by three others – Jonas Strong, a tough black ex-Sergeant who rose through the ranks under Onslow and crossed the border with him;

close and personal as you would expect, moving at a smooth clip.

With the time period being the early 20th century, it pushes the limits of being a western. There's more than just Peacemakers and Winchesters on display here: Onslow's sporting a Mauser pistol with attachable stock and Strong a Browning shotgun, not to mention the proliferation of machine guns and modern explosives. However, there's enough grime, grit, and gore to satisfy the bleak tastes of **Edge** and **Steele** fans out there.

Sean Nodland

★ ★ ★ ☆ ☆

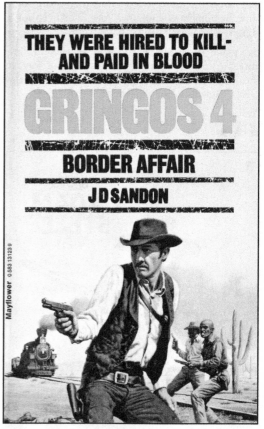

Jamie Durham, a demolitions expert and morphine addict ever since half his face was accidentally blown away, and Yates McCloud, a sadistic and bigoted (but well-connected) Southern 'gentleman' on the run for rape and murder.

Following his marriage to Linda Hoyos, the daughter of a wealthy Mexican landowner, the need to defend against Pancho Villa and the revolution arises. With this crew, Onslow manages to negotiate arms deals across the southwestern US, however the plan is for naught. Onslow's wife is killed by Major Montoya of the Mexican Army during the siege of Hoyos' ranch, massacred with the Villistas holed up there. Vowing revenge and with enough guns to outfit an army, they proceed to do just that – and then some. The novel follows their gun sales and further acquisitions of hardware from the US, which include some great shootouts and the unique bombing of a railway station. While the book lagged a bit in the first third with setup and introduction to the crew, Wells makes up for it in the last two. He changes points of view regularly and keeps up the action, which is as up

BORDER AFFAIR (GRINGOS 4)
J D Sandon
1979

"The wild and lawless setting of revolutionary Mexico is so ripe for adventure stories. And the mash-up of the western genre colliding with the introduction of more modern weaponry is irresistible to me."

It's 1913 and a quartet of outlaws travel south

of the border to fight for the highest bidder in the bloody Mexican revolution. They make a deal to run some guns down to Pancho Villa's arms-starved army but are betrayed and ambushed at the El Paso crossing. One of the gang is taken prisoner in the shoot-out and facing a date with the hangman and it's up to his three compadres to come to his rescue with bullets and explosives.

I'm a sucker for stories set in this place and time. The wild and lawless setting of revolutionary Mexico is so ripe for adventure stories. And the mash-up of the western genre colliding with the introduction of more modern weaponry is irresistible to me. I'm not alone as so many movies and books have covered this territory. This series, in particular, is beholding to **The Wild Bunch** for its inspiration as is more and obvious from the cover imagery of a character who is dressed much like Pike Bishop (as played by William Holden) from that film. Each cover prominently features this same figure in an effort to recall the Peckinpah flick. I suppose **The Professionals** could also play a part here as the stories feature a quartet of weapons experts doing business south of the Rio Grande.

The story is fun, and the author moves things along. There's a bit of a 'one damn thing after another" feel to it. And there isn't a whole lot of story beyond the initial set-up. I started with the fourth book in the series and I suppose, if I had begun at the beginning, the four leads would have been more distinguishable to me. I can only assume that, in the first entry, we learned more of their backstories as well as being given more cause to give a damn about them. There's not a lot of character building here but I suppose anyone reading these in order wouldn't need that by book four.

The writing is muscular but, as I find in many Piccadilly westerns, there's something amiss. Perhaps a level of authority that's not aided by the occasional Briticism that slips into the writing. Nothing outrageous, mind you (you won't find Pancho Villa crying, 'Blimey!') but there are subtleties to the wording now and then to remind the reader that these were written by someone who never travelled farther west than Swindon.

But, as I said, I love this period and setting so I'll be heading back to book one to re-start my reading properly.

Chuck Dixon

THE HANGED MAN (THE LAWMEN 5)
J B Dancer (John Harvey)
1979

"Everything is kind of subdued, the story is dull..."

There is gold in Montana. While in the east the Civil War rages, bandits are robbing wagon trains. Things get so bad that a vigilante committee hangs the sheriff of Virginia City who also was the leader of the largest gang. Bankers hire the detective firm of The Lawman. Emma Wright goes undercover as a faro dealer. While Bradford McGarry gets elected as the next sheriff, gun man Lee Fisher infiltrates the gang and tries to find their informant.

The Lawman was one of the few misfires the Piccadilly Cowboys created. John Harvey and Angus Wells did six novels, then it was cancelled. The idea was a team book with a historical hook: beautiful Emma Wright, dark clad gun man Lee Fisher and soft-spoken Bradford McGarry operating in the west while having a kind of developing love-triangle. The concept was sound, as it is a bit different than the other series and the stories are more grounded in actual history. Still, this novel is John Harvey on autopilot.

Everything is kind of subdued, the story is dull. The villains are not particularly interesting, basically it is a lot of running around. The woman of the group gets the best scenes, maybe because such a character was a rarity in the PC canon. But the guys are basic, as far as British western characters are concerned.

At the end it sadly just doesn't come together and remains a bland novel.

Andreas Decker

★ ☆ ☆ ☆ ☆

HIGH HELL (BODIE THE STALKER 3)
Neil Hunter
1979

"A great deal of blood has spattered High Grade's main street before the novel ends..."

To date, veteran pulp paperback writer Michael R Linaker has published eleven Bodie westerns under the pseudonym Neil Hunter. The first six of these came out at Star in short order across 1979 and 1980, with the subsequent set of books only appearing after 2015. Post Bodie,

Linaker subsequently wrote twelve volumes in the Brand western series, as well as several standalone western novels.

Bodie is the Stalker, a tough former lawman turned bounty hunter, and each entry in the series functions as a pretty much self-contained yarn for the high plains drifter, with only minimal references back to earlier adventures. In **High Hell** our (anti?) hero finds himself helping attractive young mine owner Angela Crowne to see off her enemies in the town of High Grade – said enemies being (a) ruthless fellow mine owner Jonas Randall, who wants to muscle in on the Crowne mining business, and (b) scheming local whore Beth Ayling – who wants pretty much the same thing, and is more than happy to bed Angela's lust-struck and duplicitous brother Raymond to get closer to it. Needless to say, Bodie and his Colt get in the way of both plans, and a great deal of blood has spattered High Grade's main street before the novel ends.

There are several good 'westerns' names in amongst the cast of characters: Jonas Randall recalls long running western comic series **Randall the Killer** (drawn by the great Arturo del Castillo), while the Stalker takes on one Tom Benteen no less as a hired gun in High Grade. Bodie itself as a name no doubt sounded as-hard-as in 1979, given the high profile of Lewis Collins' character in LWTs then current hit, **The Professionals**. There is plenty of hot flesh to go with the hot lead, with softcore shenanigans every twenty pages or so to leaven the killing and laconic one-liners. I haven't yet been able to identify the cover artist for the early Bodies – but they are all very good.

Jim O'Brien

★ ★ ★ ☆ ☆

PREY FOR THE WOLF
Cary Bates and Brian Lewis
Vampirella 82, 1979

"The whole thing looks magnificent..."

Perhaps not surprisingly, Warren Magazines' 1970s black and white horror comic **Vampirella** very rarely featured westerns, but Cary Bates and Brian Lewis's 'Prey for the Wolf' is a tautly written and beautifully drawn if unusual excursion into 'weird western' territory. Jeb Dolan, Indian hating owner of the Circle J ranch, leads a posse out into mesa country in search of stolen steers, only to discover on his return that his mail order bride Jenny has been beaten and raped, supposedly by Indian medicine man Wolf-in-the-Throat and four other braves. Ranch foreman Tom suspects the three surly white men who discovered the naked Jenny know more than they are saying and, when one of the men shoots Wolf-in-the-Throat dead before he can proclaim his innocence, Tom is determined to see the old Indian off with due ceremony. He lays his corpse on a burial platform from which the medicine man's body mysteriously disappears in the night. A solitary set of wolf tracks can be seen leading away from the platform...

I won't spoil the denouement but, needless to say, in death Wolf-in-the-Throat more than lives up to his name when it comes to dealing out justice from beyond the grave to the defilers of Jenny Dolan. In many ways a revisionist western, 'Prey for the Wolf' is a story very much of its time: white man Tom and redskin Wolf-in-the-Throat are friends of old, with the decent Tom respecting the Indian's culture and values far more than he does those of his boss Dolan or the brutal bounty hunters who chance upon Dolan's wife.

Under Brian Lewis's pen the whole thing looks magnificent and it's a great shame that the artist, who died shortly before the story was published, never did any other western strip work.

Jim O'Brien

★★★★☆

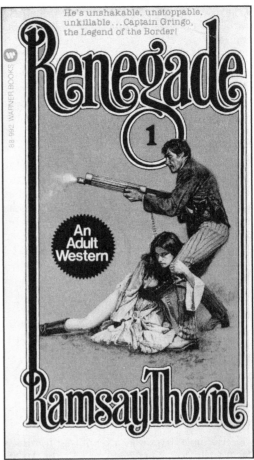

RENEGADE (RENEGADE 1)
Ramsay Thorne (Lou Cameron)
1979

"There is a definite pulpy, almost episodic feel to this novel..."

The cover proudly announces that this is 'An Adult Western' and they are not wrong! The series gets off to an action-packed start as we are introduced to Dick Walker, AKA Captain Gringo. He's due to be executed by the US Army as he allowed a bunch of condemned prisoners to escape. By sheer good fortune he is himself able to escape execution and extract some revenge on his sadistic jailers.

He soon hooks up with the local madam and a sweet relationship forms. This is where the 'adult western' pops up and the entire section of the book is filled with XXX action. It does fit into the story but here the author dwells on the action rather than it being a part of the story.

He soon meets up with a mainstay of the series, a well-drawn character called Gaston Verrier. A middle-age soldier of fortune who came into

Mexico with the Foreign Legion. Together, the two of them raise hell and beat the odds time and again.

Cameron is known for his historical accuracy, with the surroundings where the action is taking place down to the machinery of the period. Obviously, he was an expert, and this is employed in his novels. The mention of a water-cooled machine gun early in the story is an example of this.

There is a definite pulpy, almost episodic feel to this novel, and it leads directly into book two which appears to have been written even before book one was published. I'm currently up to number nine in the series and I'm still enjoying them although some scenes do tend to repeat themselves again and again (the sex). Whether I make it to the final book in the series, number thirty-six, remains to be seen.

Jules Burt

★ ★ ★ ☆ ☆

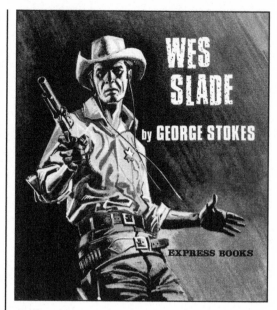

WES SLADE
Scripts and art George Stokes
1979

"Possibly too clear and clean a White Hat to resonate with today's readers..."

Western comic strips were a significant feature of the British newspaper landscape in the 1950s and 1960s, the genre's 'Big Three' being **Matt Marriott** (reviewed elsewhere in this issue) by Jim Edgar and Tony Weare from the **London Evening News**, **Gun Law** by Harry Bishop in the **Daily Express** – and this review's focus, **Wes Slade** by George Stokes in the **Sunday Express**.

This small, square reprint volume from 1979 is a good introduction to Wes and his world, featuring as it does the strip's first three (linked) stories: 'The Living Dead', 'Fast Guns in Carrizal' and 'Ambush at Ochoa Springs'. In fact, 'Ambush' is presented in a heavily edited-down form and all three stories are (very successfully in my opinion) reformatted so that they look more like pages from a standard comic book than just a collection of three-panel newspaper strips.

Stokes's art is not as strong as Tony Weare's on **Matt Marriott**, but his story telling across the saga is good: Wes Slade is Deputy Marshall of Silver City and the archetypal good man – Stokes draws him as part Gary Cooper, part Rod Taylor – in a generally pretty bad world, who roams far and wide across the old West in the course of the

strip's life, righting wrongs and standing up for the underdog. Possibly too clear and clean a White Hat to resonate with today's readers, **Wes Slade** is very obviously a product of its times.

Sex and violence are kept to a minimum and the cussing is endearingly quaint ('You're goldarned right it is!'). The historical detail seems bang on though, and the Indian characters are treated with a degree more sensitivity than many movies of the period provided. Overall, however, the strip now feels old-fashioned and wooden.

Jim O'Brien

★ ★ ☆ ☆ ☆

WORSE THAN DEATH (CROW 2)
James W Marvin (Laurence James)
1979

"An overall air of nihilism that permeates the entire affair prior to a decidedly downbeat ending..."

Under a variety of house names, Laurence James was a mainstay of the UK-based Piccadilly Cowboy stable of writers and penned the **Crow** series, as well as contributing to the **Apache**, **Gunslinger**, **Herne the Hunter**, and **Caleb Thorn** series. Following a short prelude, **Worse than Death** introduces readers to a wagon train made up of Cavalry officers' wives and a small detachment of soldiers escorting them through the blizzard-ridden Dakota Territories and into the sights of renegade Shoshone chief, Many Knives, who is on the warpath against whites. After an initial attack on the wagon train decimates the ranks and leaves the travellers stranded, our anti-hero, Crow, enters the scene and assists what's left of the soldiers and the women. Lest this sound like an altruistic bit of heroism, it's made clear that Crow is only looking out for Crow and how he can best survive the situation. Much mayhem ensues as a series of attacks are repelled in some fierce, well-paced action described in gruesome detail. The combined threat of the Indians and the extreme severity of the elements make for a gruelling but intense read. Yet Crow still finds time to engage in a jaw-droppingly left-field ménage à trois that includes the 16-year old virginal daughter of one of the lieutenants, who has very recently been tortured to death within her sight. There's also cannibalism, dead infants, butchered animals and an overall air of nihilism that permeates the entire affair prior to a decidedly downbeat ending. While not exactly my personal cup of tea, I can't deny that it was well done; I read the entire book in two days and was never bored. But traditional fun it was not.

Steve Carroll

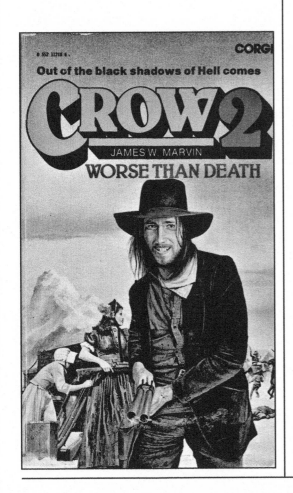

1980- 1989

The decade of the series character.

By the middle of the decade the Piccadilly Cowboys had reduced to self-parody and died out.

The Adult Western continued to thrive, with the number of new series increasing each year.

New takes on the genre were emerging, including the use of western tropes in SF, horror, kung fu and Sasquatch.

THE ANGEL GANG
Writers: John Wagner and Alan Grant
2000 AD
1980 onwards

"The writer's conception of... the future USA was often purest wild, wild west."

Wild western Texas City outlaws the Angel Gang were for a brief but glorious time in the early 1980s prominent antagonists of stony-faced lawman of the future Judge Dredd in the UK boys' sci-fi comic, **2000AD**. Although Dredd's writers John Wagner and Alan Grant were seeking to portray life in the 2180s rather than the 1880s, the pair's conception of the irradiated wastes and mutie-infested badlands that made up the 'Cursed Earth' interior of the future USA was often purest wild, wild west, and certainly the Angel family (to wit, venal patriarch Pa Angel and his no darn good sons, Fink, Junior, Link and Mean Machine) looked and sounded more like characters from a Sergio Leone spaghetti western than anything more science fictional. Well, maybe a Leone filmed crossed with elements of **The Hill Have Eyes** or **The Texas Chainsaw Massacre**, but a western nonetheless. Even when the Angel Gang went 'off-world' as they did occasionally in long running quest saga 'The Judge Child', the planets the outlaws ended up on still managed to look as they'd been modelled on mining towns in the Dakotas around the time of the Battle of the Little Big Horn. Several artists had a hand in visualizing the Angel Gang's seminal first appearances (poor benighted Ma Angel was also

to feature briefly in flashback) but the most significant of these by some way was Mick MacMahon, whose chunky, earthy drawing style suited the 'western' aspects of the Angels perfectly. Various members of the family still reappear from time to time in the pages of **2000AD** or the **Judge Dredd Megazine**, but to appreciate the gang in all their hillbilly glory you need to head back to the aforementioned 'Judge Child Saga' from Progs 156-181 and follow-up story 'The Fink' in Progs 193-196.

Jim O'Brien

★ ★ ★ ☆ ☆

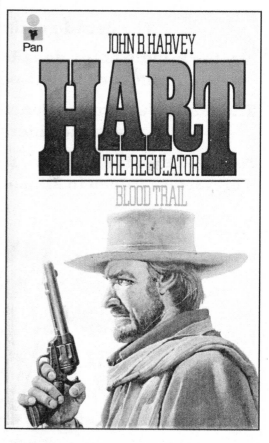

BLOOD TRAIL (HART 2)
John B Harvey
1980

"His lean, crime noir-influenced style makes Hart a bit of a dull character..."

Wes Hart – ex-soldier, ex-Texas Ranger, ex-rider with Billy the Kid. The Regulator. This one was created by John Harvey, who later became one of the important crime writers of Britain. Hart is for once a character with no gimmick attached. He has no crippled hand, no claw for a hand and is no older guy. His roots are in western history.

Hart is looking for a job. Rancher Fredericks wants to build an empire, before the Indian Territory gets to be a part of the state. Soon the yearly cattle herds will be driven over his land, for which he charges, and rustlers will be crawling out of the woodwork. The Cheyenne are on the rampage, killing settlers with brand-new Winchesters. Hart takes the job as a regulator, as there is no law about, even if he dislikes the man and his shady dealings. It doesn't end well after he discovers that Fredericks is stirring trouble with the Indians.

Here Harvey takes a more traditional approach to the western, so this hasn't the trademark OTT elements of Laurence James or the ultraviolence of Angus Wells. And while he may be the best stylist of the PC Cowboys with his lean, crime noir-influenced style, it makes Hart a bit of a dull character. The second novel of a ten-book run, it's perfectly okay and has plenty of action, it is just not very interesting.

Andreas Decker

HOT AS A PISTOL (SADDLER 3)
Gene Curry (Peter McCurtin)
1980

"Decent read with plenty of action and just the right pace…"

Adult western that was trying to catch the wave of the big guns (**Lone Star**, **Longarm** and others). The main character is Jim Saddler and he is on his way south to Mexico until he helps out an old friend in Arizona. Mix in the gun fighting and the two luscious ladies and you have an adult western. Decent read with plenty of action and just the right pace.

Scott Kime

KLAW (KLAW 1)
L A Fieldhouse
1980

"Focusing on themes of white-hot vengeance and fighting back against The Man…"

John Klawson is a veteran of the Civil War, who returns from the war to find his home controlled by evil banker Warren T Jennings, who is using a combination of financial threats and staged Indian raids to tighten his iron grip on the local townspeople. When Klawson's own parents are killed during one such counterfeit attack, his initial attempts at revenge result in the loss of his right hand. Finding a group of allies, including a blacksmith who fashions two sharp prongs to replace his missing hand, Klawson goes about raiding the banker's fortress.

The **Klaw** trilogy, to which this is the first entry, has gained something of a reputation over the last few years, and although I don't think they are outstanding, they do carry a twisted charm and a gritty tone which I vibed on. Fieldhouse is a no-nonsense and gritty storyteller, wasting little in the way of word-count as he propels his story forward, focusing on themes of white-hot vengeance and fighting back against The Man. He excels with his portrayal of scumbag low-lives (which he takes to the next level in follow-up, **Town of Blood**) and I like his anti-capitalist sub-text and use of Klawson as an everyman under-dog. If this is your thing, then **Klaw** *really* is your thing.

Justin Marriott

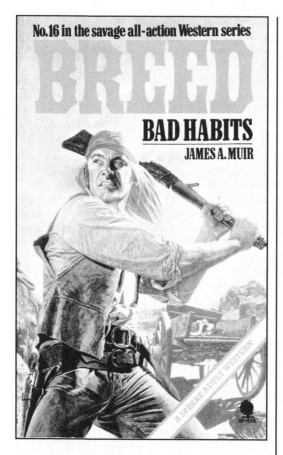

BREED

BAD HABITS

JAMES A. MUIR

plots of **Edge**. Just an Italo western imitating episode of blood-soaked western carnage and a high body count. At that Wells did excel. Like most books of the series, **Bad Habits** is a fast, entertaining read, but only in small doses, as the formula never changes.

Andreas Decker

★ ★ ★ ☆ ☆

BAD HABITS (BREED 16)
James A Muir (Angus Wells)
1981

"Must have had an anatomy textbook, so lovingly detailed are his descriptions of the many killings…"

Matthew Gunn, also known as Breed and Azul, is part-white, part-Apache and all killer – as the blurb on book one proclaimed. Created and written by Angus Wells, with twenty-two novels in eight years, **Breed** is one of the success stories of the Piccadilly Cowboys. In this novel, three nuns hire Breed as a guard for the voyage to their convent in Mexico. But the beautiful women are not what they seem, they work for some banditos, who leave Azul lashed on a cross to die. Bad idea. The 'Adult Western' tag on the front cover is not for the non-existent sex but the ultra-violence. Right next to some **Guns of the West** reference manual, Wells must have had an anatomy textbook, so lovingly detailed are his descriptions of the many killings, which frankly gets a bit wearisome at the end. This is Wells imitating the early **Edge**, right down to the bad puns, which mostly are a bit forced. Nuns – bad habits. Get it? But without the characterisation or the wacky

Captain Gringo—free and fighting No man can stop him No woman can hold him

WARNER BOOKS 94-293 $1.75

RENEGADE 4

DEATH HUNTER

An Adult Western

Ramsay Thorne

DEATH HUNTER (RENEGADE 4)
Ramsay Thorne (Lou Cameron)
1981

"Oodles of earthy sex and humour, often combined…"

By the fourth volume of his excellent south-of-the-border men's adventure/western series, author Cameron was hitting his stride, and this is a stellar example of the type of labyrinthine plot and double-crossing that characterise the better entries. Lead character Gringo is the soldier-of-fortune who is caught between the manipulative British spy Greystoke, who would become a recurring character in the series, and the Germans, whom Greystoke believes are building a submarine base in Costa Rica which will give them strategic control of the Panama Canal.

The plot's complexities only become explained in the final chapter, so this is a book that undoubtedly requires your concentration, and if you are a 'skimmer' (guilty as charged), you may well find yourself scratching your head and re-reading the closing sections to make sense of it all. There's oodles of earthy sex and humour, often combined, with Gringo over-powered by the frustrated and big-boned fraulein who lives with a German plantation owner, and a mother and daughter who show Gringo you can get too much of a good thing. There's a great vignette where Gringo is drilling the rag-tag team of mercenaries and drunks he has frantically assembled to sail down the Panama Canal on their mission. When one of the new recruits shows insubordination, Gringo's sidekick Gaston jumps on his head and delivers a deadly stomping. Soon after, Gaston is seen paying the 'dead man' who was a plant to help Gringo make his brutal point about the need for discipline.

An unusual setting, complex plot, constant intrigue, great dialogue, plentiful sex and violence – this is a superior example of a superior series.

Justin Marriott

★ ★ ★ ★ ☆

THE LEGEND OF THE LONE RANGER
Gary McCarthy
1981

"A really weak and clichéd script..."

The movie this book was based on was legendary mostly for how bad it was. The book keeps firmly to this tradition. Almost every Western fan knows that the Lone Ranger was the sole survivor of a troop of rangers wiped out by the Butch Cavendish gang. This version drags out the origin (usually the first ten minutes of other versions) so much that the Lone Ranger doesn't even appear until page 111 of 188. Instead, we're treated to page after page of very PC writing about noble Indians being badly mistreated (off-page) by whites, and how Tonto wants revenge – which he cheerfully reneges on when Kemo Sabe needs a hand to rescue President Grant, the author of the policies that Tonto hates so much.

Adding to a really weak and clichéd script, the novel is also poorly proofread. One character's name actually changes from Whitliff to Westlake halfway down a page! My favourite mistake is 'Wiatt and his deputy glanced up from their newspaper." Apparently, they couldn't afford one each...

Fran Striker (story-editor for the old radio show) wrote some far, far better novels back in the Fifties, and they've been reprinted more recently. If you want some thrilling tales of yesteryear, pick those instead of this turkey.

John Peel

★ ☆ ☆ ☆ ☆

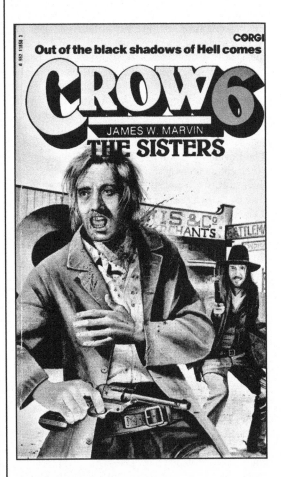

THE SISTERS (CROW 6)
James Marvin
1981

"How far can you escalate the gore and sadism before it becomes parody?"

This penultimate entry to the **Crow** series was towards the tail-end of the Piccadilly Cowboy cycle of books which amped the violence to unheralded levels in the western genre. And it shows why that cycle was coming to an end, as the small group of writers producing such a large volume of books in a short period of time were inevitably running out of ideas and energy. And how far can you escalate the gore and sadism before it becomes parody? Certainly, **The Sisters** is beyond that tipping point, and in deference to the brilliant Laurence James who wrote this as James Marvin, he would have had has his tongue firmly in cheek with this outrageous gothic-western. 'Shootist' Crow rides into a small-town where he is immediately confronted by a lynch mob who blame him for a series of murders plaguing them. The hanging party is interrupted by an unidentified shooter, who randomly picks off the fleeing crowd. Crow is hired to flush the shooter out from a church-steeple which sets in train a series of events resulting in Crow facing the deadly pair of the title. With a thin page-count and an even thinner plot, the only characteristics worthy of note are the outrageous violence and in-jokes. When attacked by a wounded grizzly, Crow first uses his sabre to defend himself before resorting to biting the sensitive jowls of the bear! Leonard Di Caprio in **The Revenant** take note. There are references to other characters in the Piccadilly westerns and their authors, a nod to infamous school-shooter Brenda Spencer as well as callouts to the likes of **The Exorcist** and H P Lovecraft. But it didn't add up to much, and even with my predilection towards the PC westerns and Laurence James, there was scant reward in this book.

Justin Marriott

SIX GUN SAMURAI
Patrick Lee (Mark Roberts)
1981

"Repugnantly violent, especially toward children ..."

As was the case with many men's adventure series, **Six Gun Samurai** was actually authored by three different writers all working under the house name of Patrick Lee; this first book's copyright is attributed to Mark Roberts. Even though I have always had a strong affinity for martial arts-related adventure fiction, I did not enjoy this book and had to repeatedly force myself to keep slogging through to finish it. The first book in this short-lived, eight-book series introduces us to Tommy Fletcher, son of American missionaries to Japan in the mid-1800s. After a massacre leaves him orphaned,

Fletcher is taken in by a samurai and trained in the art of Bushido, learning not only karate, but many different weapons forms, including of course, mastery of the katana sword. However, years later word reaches Fletcher that his Savannah, GA home has been attacked and ransacked by deserted Yankee marauders who raped, defiled, and butchered his entire family (a recurring theme). The remainder of the book is Fletcher, or Tanaka Tom as he is called, seeking vengeance (multiple decapitations) against those responsible as he scours the American West. It is simple, poorly plotted, and goes exactly where you expect at every turn. It is also repugnantly violent, especially toward children, who are not spared in any sense, including rape. In this regard it shares some commonalities with the Piccadilly Westerns, but without the better literary qualities most of those possessed. This is simply bad, which disappoints me no end, since I spent years and much effort collecting them.

Steve Carrol

THE GREAT GAME (RENEGADE 10)
Ramsay Thorne (Lou Cameron)
1981

"An old-pro of blood-and-guts fiction..."

On the first page of **The Great Game** two words sit boldly, standing out in a class all by themselves. What are those words? 'Crocodile fart'. I think it's there to tell you that you are in for a damned good time and you damned sure are.

Captain Gringo is the title renegade, also known as Dick Walker. He's a turn-of-the-century mercenary who likes shootin' folks and an enjoying spicy time with the ladies. So, it's good that he exists in an Adult Western world of nasties to shoot and beautiful women to bed. He travels with his sidekick Gaston looking for cash to fight for people. Plenty of opportunity for the sex and the gunfire. Gringo steps into danger involving the brink of a mini-war between the US and England in Venezuela, nearly being duped by a woman named Bubbles!

Renegade takes some cues from John Benteen's utterly badass **Fargo** series, with its turn-of-the-century setting and a cowboy as mercenary lead, but **Renegade** is a bit lighter in tone and the sex is MUCH more frequent. Ramsay Thorne is really Lou Cameron and a he was an old-pro of blood-and-guts fiction when he started writing **Renegade** and it shows. The pace never drags and rolls along smoothly. It's all well thought out as Gringo and Gaston bicker and blast their way through American and British spies, gets accused of murder, bandits, armies, beds old flames and nuns (sorta) and generally causes hell. It's a hoot of a book.

Roy Nugen

★★★★☆

HUNT THE BEAST DOWN (SPECTROS 2)
Logan Winters (Paul Lederer)
1981

"It all culminates in a battle between Spectros and —wait for it—Bigfoot!"

The second book in the **Spectros** series, focusing on a master magician in the old west. Over the course of the series, the aged Spectros is continually chasing down the evil Blackshuster, a rival wizard who has kept our main character's lifelong love, Kristin, in suspended animation in a crystal coffin for decades. In this addition to the series, Spectros has tracked Blackshuster to the Oregon coast. Here the evil magician plans to loot a shipwreck, hoping to obtain the silver he needs to maintain Kristin's comatose state. Spectros arrives with his cohorts – dashingly handsome gunslinger Ray Featherskill, the ageless Moor, Inkada, and Montak, a mute hulking giant. Mixed into all of this is a female ranch owner being forced off her land for our villain and his entourage to have unfettered access to the shipwreck. Our heroes decide to help this lovely lady, not realizing that her plight ties directly into their hunt for Blackshuster. The highlight of the book comes when Spectros uses his wizardry to transform into the legendary master gunfighter Kid Soledad, a character that seems to ride right out of an RKO Radio Saturday matinee serial. It all culminates in a battle between Spectros, in the form of Kid Soledad, and Blackshuster, who transforms into – wait for it –Bigfoot! This is a wild and fanciful ride with one foot firmly planted in the cinematic West of Saturday serials from the 40s and the other foot in the fantasy realm. In that respect it qualifies as Weird West, but in an overall tame environment.

Steve Carroll

★★☆☆☆

THE GUNSLINGER: THE DARK TOWER PART I
Stephen King
1982

"For those eager to test the waters of a different type of six-gun fiction..."

So, you say you'd like to read a different kind of western, something not so same-old, same-old? Well, allow me to direct you to Stephen King's **Dark Tower** series, which starts off with **The Gunslinger**.

Written as an eight-book collection, with an additional volume sort of tacked on, the series follows the adventures of Roland Deschain, a man on a quest for (you guessed it) the Dark Tower. As you might expect from King, this is not a straight up western, as it relies heavily on the supernatural, the otherworldly, and the fantastic. We are treated to events taking place in an alternate universe, which coincides, at times, with our own.

The first volume – and the point of our focus here – is one-part Arthurian legend, one part **The Good, The Bad, and the Ugly**, and a dash of **Lord of the Rings** thrown in for good measure. Actually, the thing the book reminds me of most is Michael Moorcock's **Elric** series. It has a similar indefinable timelessness, as well as a certain stylistic attention to language I find endearing.

A little history... Roland's story was first inspired by Robert Browning's poem, 'Child Roland to the Dark Tower Came.' According to King, he first started his work in 1970. Five stories saw print between 1978 and 1981 in **The Magazine of Fantasy and Science Fiction**. These stories were collected and fleshed out into a novel, published in a limited edition by Donald M Grant in 1982. Yet an additional revised and expanded version of the novel was issued in 2003, which apparently resolved some inconsistencies with later books in the series. So ultimately, in a sense, the book in its final version took some thirty-three years to come to complete fruition!

Honestly, **The Gunslinger** isn't indispensable to the average western genre aficionado. Nor do I believe the first volume in the series is necessary for those interested in the works of Mr King (though many say the series represents some of his finest writing). But the book has great merit, successfully melding an unlikely mix of genres. For those eager to test the waters of a different type of six-gun fiction, I suggest you try this one on for size, and you can consider the rich illustrations by renowned fantasy artist, Michael Whelan, a bonus.

S. Clayton Rhodes

★ ★ ★ ☆ ☆

HARVEST OF DEATH (RENEGADE 14)
Ramsey Thorne (Lou Cameron)
1982

"The plot has to flow and it was not happening here..."

This was the first of the series that I read, and I did not get into the book. Captain Gringo blasts his way through mayhem and the lusty ladies. I do not mind third person, but the plot has to flow, and it was not happening here. The action was OK, but for some reason I could not get into it. I gave up on the series after this title and went back reading mysteries.

Scott Kime

★ ★ ★ ☆ ☆

THE LADY RUSTLER (BRAD SPEAR 10)
By Chad Calhoun (Ron Goulart)
1982

"The big problem with the books is that there's simply too much of it. ..."

Brad Spear is your regular adult western hero with a private eye veneer: a tough Civil War Vet who gets into working for Pinkertons, eyeing to avoid lumberjacking. He's suitably roguish with a quick gun-hand and an eye for the ladies. The Lady Rustler is not surprisingly about a woman rustler who is a quasi-Robin Hood named Nita. She's a swell-looking woman with revenge on her mind. She mostly wants to kill Big Jim; owner of a ranch called the 'Circle BJ', which I'll cop to laughing out loud about. Big Jim and his cronies hate Brad so naturally Nita and Brad team up. Hell raising ensues.

The big problem with the books is that there's simply too much of it. There's easily a hundred pages too many. At times it seemed to just be hitting its marks, spending too much time with the baddies and taking too long to get to the sexy Lady Rustler we were promised. Goulart is a solid pulp writer whose work I love but this seemed to be Goulart with the brakes on, never going at full speed. The humour that peppers his novels did work its way into Brad's voice and the opening of the book, which is the highlight. Brad and a famous singer's bedroom time gets interrupted by a train robbery and he thwarts it clad in his underwear with the help of the singer's bare chest. Sadly, it never catches this fire again but Goulart's flair and humour kept the book readable.

Roy Nugen

★★★☆☆

MACKLIN'S WOMEN (GUNSMITH 1)
J R Robert (Robert Randisi)
1982

"Still a nice series to follow…"

This was the very first western I actually liked. First person (check) plenty of action (check), smooth flow of the story (check), no over the top sex scenes (check). I like this first story that I had at one time collected and read the first one hundred or so. It was sad when the series went to third person, but still a nice series to follow.

Scott Kime ★★★☆☆

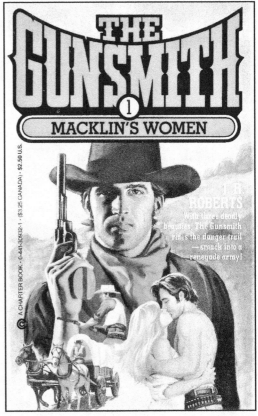

ON THE TREACHERY TRAIL (LONE STAR 1)
Wesley Ellis
1982

"I had expected a lot of karate and canoodling and only the sketchiest of western yarns crackling along in the background…"

I picked up this first entry in the long-running **Lone Star** series primarily because of the intriguing 'east meets west' element of the series. As a fan of the early 70s TV series **Kung Fu**, I have always enjoyed yarns that mash up the western with a touch of eastern mysticism and martial artistry. In **Lone Star**'s case the latter is supplied by American-Japanese fighting master, Ki, who accompanies 'young western beauty' Jessica Starbuck on her journeys of vengeance across the west. Using jujitsu and other combat skills (along with a vast array of weapons concealed about his person), Ki defends Jessie without question.

Mind you, both have time for some good ol' western loving along the way. Aside from its martial arts content, I also knew that **Lone Star** books were prime adult western material. And sure enough there are three (and a half) or so tastefully described sex scenes positioned amidst

WESLEY ELLIS

UNDER THE SINISTER SHADOW OF THE LARAMIES, JESSIE & KI FLUSH OUT A LAND-RUSTLING CONSPIRACY!

LONE★STAR

ON THE TREACHERY TRAIL

First in the new series from the creators of LONGARM

the fights and the accounts of ranching in Wyoming. And in fact that was the big surprise for me about **On the Treachery Trail**: where I had expected a lot of karate and canoodling and only the sketchiest of western yarns crackling along in the background, what I actually got was a solid story of cattle farming and financial skulduggery. Indeed perhaps a little *too* solid: 'Wesley Ellis' (in reality, author Jeffrey M Wallman) certainly knows his western stuff, but some of the passages in which he shows off his knowledge of, for example, western wagons types, or the minutiae of stocking densities on ranches, can feel a little ponderous. Generally however, things do feel authentic, and the only moment I felt I was reading something set in the 1980s rather than the 1880s came when in one scene where Jessie changed her clothes...into a pair of jeans and a denim jacket. This is probably totally 'correct', but it made me feel as if I was reading an '80s Brat Pack movie script rather than a western for a moment.

Jim O'Brien

★ ★ ☆ ☆ ☆

TWO FOR TEXAS
James Lee Burke
1982

"Anyone who appreciates Burke's elegies for the lost Eden of an older America, or who savours his tough yet poetic prose, will enjoy Two for Texas."

Readers may cry foul at finding **Two for Texas** here. Set in the mid 1830s during the war between Texas and Mexico, James Lee Burke's novel admittedly falls a little outside the commonly-accepted late nineteenth century time frame for westerns, although in many respects it features characters and plot lines that readers would recognise as being pretty typical of the genre. Son Holland and Hugh Allison bust out of a Louisiana penal camp where they have been persistently brutalized by their guards and make a break for freedom. Sheltering briefly in a Tonkawa Indian village, Son and Hugh hitch up with a squaw named Sana before they head towards Texas. Their footsteps are dogged at every turn by Emile Landry, vengeful brother of the prison guard the pair killed during their breakout. And Son and Hugh's troubles don't end there: having taken part in a Tonkawa horse-stealing raid on a Mexican army corral, the men are also wanted by the Federales. Ultimately they find sanctuary with Sam Houston's Texian army and pledge themselves to the fight against Mexico, with the prospect of an army pension and 640 sweet Texas acres each if they survive the battle.

The majority of James Lee Burke's novels are set in modern day Louisiana, Montana or Texas but the presence of the nineteenth century past in the lives of his heroes and villains is a common thread in his writing. **Two for Texas** is more openly an 'historical novel' than most of his books, but anyone who appreciates Burke's elegies for the lost Eden of an older, rural America, or who savours his tough yet poetic prose, will enjoy **Two for Texas** every bit as much as his better known Dave Robicheaux crime novels.

Jim O'Brien

★ ★ ★ ☆ ☆

DAY OF FURY (CLAW 1)
Matthew Kirk (Angus Wells)
1983
"Could always be relied upon for his outrageous depictions of violence ..."

Blacksmith Tyler Wyatt joins the ranks of gunfighters with mutilated hands when he tries some side-work as a bank-guard in the employ of his rich father-in-law. A cutthroat gang raid the bank, kill his family and use his blacksmith tools to pulp his hand over the course of several eye-watering pages. Of course, they let him live, so he can attach a razor-sharp metal claw to the stump and track them down, one-by-one over the period of six books with diminishing returns.

There is little doubt that Angus Wells was a talented writer, regarded by the tight-knit bunch of authors that made up the Piccadilly Cowboys as their best, but there is little evidence of that in the **Claw** series. Wells could always be relied upon for his outrageous depictions of violence, with anyone dying either shitting or coming in their pants, and **Day of Fury** doesn't deviate from this, but it carries little impact when you are beyond caring about the characters. Written on autopilot, with a cookie-cutter plot and zero originality, all stretched out to reach the minimum acceptable page-count.

It is little wonder that the western market in the UK soon collapsed.

Bloody (cl)awful.

Justin Marriott

★ ☆ ☆ ☆ ☆

FINGERS (LUCKY LUKE 52)
Morris (art) and Lo Hartog van Banda (script)
1983

"Pitched fair and square at a very young audience, the series is of only passing interest to this jaundiced old reader..."

Belgian comic strip artist and writer Morris began his western series **Lucky Luke** in 1946, and he continued to draw the stories (with a variety of other writers including Rene Goscinny and – as here – Lo Hartog van Banda) up until his death in 1977. Now steered by other hands, the strip continues to this day. An amiable comedy romp through the old West, **Lucky Luke** looks and feels very much like the **Asterix** books (of which Goscinny of course was the co-creator) – a cartoony art style, lots of visual and verbal gags and an ensemble cast of zany characters who feature regularly across the series. Chief amongst these are Luke's trusty steed Jolly Jumper, ex prison guard dog Rantanplan and all round, no darn good crims the Dalton brothers. A bit like the aforementioned **Asterix** books and the **Tintin** series, Lucky Luke has seen a good many of his adventures translated into English. Pitched fair and square at a very young audience, the series is of only passing interest to this jaundiced old reader, although its sheer longevity alone certainly makes it worth at least a glance.

Jim O'Brien

★ ★ ☆ ☆ ☆

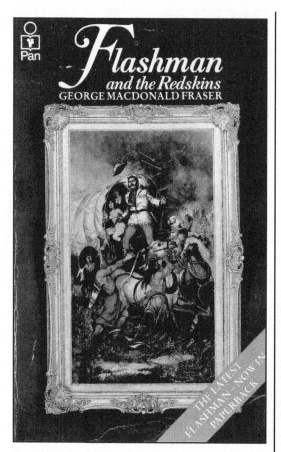

FLASHMAN AND THE REDSKINS

George Macdonald Fraser
1983

"The entry in the series that can most properly be called a 'western Flashman'..."

For anyone not familiar with George Macdonald Fraser's **Flashman** books (published between 1969 and 2005), the series' central premise ran something like this: Harry Flashman, the notorious school bully from Victorian novel **Tom Browne's Schooldays**, is kicked out of Rugby for cruelty and subsequently joins the army just in time to help turn the world map pink with British imperial possessions. A womanizer, scoundrel and all round rogue, Flashman is rarely far from trouble or beautiful women throughout his subsequently long and unjustly illustrious career, and Fraser cunningly makes sure that Flashman is on hand for just about every major international incident and battle from the 1840s up to the early 1900s. Several of the novels feature Flashman's adventures in America but this is the entry in the series that can most properly be called a 'western Flashman'. In fact, **Redskins** is two books really, rather than one: the novel's first half follows our

anti-hero as he escorts a wagon train of whores from New Orleans to California just as the '49 gold rush gets under way, while the second section deals with the wily Brit's later involvement with General Custer at the Battle of the Little Bighorn. Fraser was a stickler for historical accuracy and the book comes complete with scholarly footnotes explaining who was who and what was what in the old West. Fraser also writes about the 'redskins' in question with genuine respect and knowledge although he pushes back against snowflake notions of American Indians as simply peaceful nomads in touch with nature and living lightly on the land.

Jim O'Brien

★ ★ ★ ☆ ☆

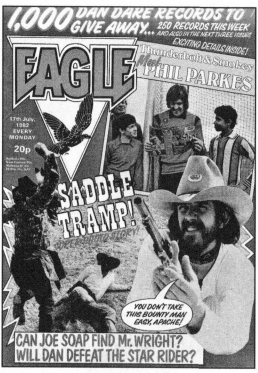

SADDLE TRAMP

Gerry Finley-Day and Howard Payton
Eagle, June to October 1983

"Howard Payton's photography is really dynamic, often looking more like a series of freeze-frames pulled from a western movie."

When IPC Magazines decided to relaunch veteran boys' adventure comic the **Eagle** in 1982, the editorial team opted to use photo strips alongside traditional drawn comics, the idea being no doubt that hip photo stories would seem more 'modern' than old style pen and ink art work. Not surprisingly, stories set in contemporary Britain therefore featured prominently in the Eagle's pages: a day's photo shoot in a municipal park or shopping centre with whatever the kids were wearing at that time and you were done. Not so easy to mount a fully-fledged, 1870s-set western you'd have thought. **Eagle** editor Dave Hunt and veteran comics writer Gerry Finley-Day were both keen to run a western photo story, but couldn't see a way to do it credibly until experienced photographer Howard Payton (who had cut his teeth on 70s romance photo strips for IPC) saved the day. Payton had shot an historical romance photo story at Littlecote House in Wiltshire and knew that there was a western re-enactment 'town' called Frontier City operating as a tourist attraction at the house. Thus was born **Saddle Tramp**, the story of bounty hunter Trampas and his search for justice in the Old West. By shooting Frontier City from every conceivable angle and making maximum use of the vast range of props and costumes assembled by the re-enactors, Payton was able to make the story's various western towns look pretty damned authentic. Judiciously chosen Berkshire sand pits then stood in for the scrub and desert of the Tex-Mex borderlands. Having come from a background in film making, Payton's photography is really dynamic, often looking more like a series of freeze-frames pulled from a western movie rather than a set of static, posed shots. Look out especially for **Eagle's** issue from 21 August 1982, where the photographer himself makes a brief guest-appearance as Barbo the killer, gunned down by Trampas in a deadly desert shoot out.

Jim O'Brien

ABILENE (STAGECOACH 10)
Hank Mitchum
1984

"Some rather sad and even tragic events for a couple of the main characters..."

The **Stagecoach Station** series of novels were published under Lyle Kenyon Engel's Book Creations, Inc. and comprised fifty-two books during their run from 1982 to 1991. A variety of authors were behind the Hank Mitchum house name including James Reasoner, DB Newton, Will C Knott, and others. For the most part they are standalone stories involving four or five main characters thrust together by a stagecoach journey and destination, with intertwined

subplots and almost always with a romance between a couple of them.

Abilene, Kansas with its rarely matched reputation for violent drunken revelry by cattle drovers coming in and letting off steam serves as an excellent backdrop for a western yarn. Several of the book's main characters are historical, not the least of which is 'Wild Bill' Hickok, who was marshal for a brief time. Also of note is the presence of his deputy Mike Williams, and gambler Phil Coe. These historical characters are rounded out by a handful of fictional characters including a newspaper editor, a recent widow from back East, and a slimy gunslinger intent on revenge.

A prominent part of the plot is the infamous Bulls' Head Saloon incident wherein the proprietors had playfully painted a large risqué picture of an 'excited' bull on the side of their establishment. The scenes where Hickok handled the near riot that occurred, and the final resolution were a hoot. The novel also details some rather sad and even tragic events for a couple of the main characters but balances this out with happy endings for others.

The quality of the individual **Stagecoach Station** books is a bit spotty but for the most part they are enjoyable reads. This book was penned by the prolific Will C Knott, who also wrote several **Longarm**, **Trailsman**, and **Slocum** entries. While still a standalone novel, this one does tie into the next in the series as we pick up several years later with Hickok at station #11 in Deadwood, South Dakota. We all know what's coming there...

Benjamin Thomas

BOWDRIE AND BOWDRIE'S LAW
Louis L'Amour
1984

"Just the mention of his name 'causes the most hardened gunman to break out in a cold sweat!'"

As a fat man that wears both a belt and suspenders to cover his bets, I like to get my money's worth at the all-you-can-eat buffet down on the corner. I relish getting a little bit of everything on my plate rather than on my tie when I sit down to lunch. So, I was delighted to find out one of America's most beloved storytellers, Louis L'Amour, had written eighteen short stories about a tough Texas Ranger named Chick Bowdrie. Created in 1946 for the pulp magazine **Popular Western**, these terrific Texas tales ran until 1952. The first

STORIES BY THE WORLD'S BESTSELLING FRONTIER WRITER

LOUIS L'AMOUR
BOWDRIE'S LAW

FIRST TIME IN PAPERBACK

collected volume entitled **Bowdrie** has eight stories, but I would suggest starting with the second volume **Bowdrie's Law**, that contains ten bone-crunching tomes including his first adventure, **A Job for a Ranger**. Just the mention of his name 'causes the most hardened gunman to break out in a cold sweat!'

Equally as fast with his fists as his six guns the Rangers decided to recruit this hard case before he wound up on the wrong side of the law and they had to fight against him. Raised by Comanches after his parents were murdered, Bowdrie looked more like an Indian than a white man, but he learned how to hunt, track, and survive on the frontier. Returned to 'civilization' when he was 12, he got mixed up with the wrong crowd by 21, survived a shootout caring three slugs in him, before being sworn in and started riding for the law. A smart Ranger who spoke five languages, he was also part detective as some of his adventures felt like a **CSI:Larado** of 1885.

Lawman, Manhunter, Peacemaker...Bowdrie.

Dave Karlen

★ ★ ★ ★ ★

ROCKWELL
Peter McCurtin
1984

"The swift, no-frills pace that McCurtin brings keeps the novel moving faster than it would in other hands."

Considered one of his best works, and actually by the man himself (not always the case as McCurtin employed ghost-writers), **Rockwell** follows the life and exploits of Orrin Porter Rockwell, a Mormon sheriff in the Utah territory during the early 1860s. The novel is written through the perspective of William Forbes, a reporter for the **New York Sun** who covered the on-going civil war until suffering a gunshot wound to the chest. On the excuse that the climate will do his injured lungs good, they send him to write up an account of the man that isn't wildly biased against the secretive sect – but will also sell papers. Upon arriving and making the acquaintance of Rockwell, he learns quickly why the man has the reputation that he does.

Rockwell is an imposing, uncompromising figure. Devoted wholly to his faith and people, he is willing and able to do anything to protect them from outsiders, Americans and anybody else that is a threat to the Mormon community. Forbes makes for a very good narrator because his opinions towards all that is going on are difficult to pin down at first. He tries hard to keep an objective view of the conflicts while still coming across as a human being affected by the events before his eyes.

It was a little strange to read McCurtin's writing style in this kind of a book, one that focuses less on the hard-hitting action and more on the characters, how they interact and what they think of each other over time. Not entirely a western, at least in a traditional sense, the novel had a solid amount of gunplay and violence suitable for one. More than double the size of a typical western paperback, the swift, no-frills pace that McCurtin brings keeps the novel moving faster than it would in other hands.

I couldn't safely call this McCurtin's best work, or even his best western; I think his style works better with shorter page counts. However, it is a great novel and I would recommend it to those who aren't even familiar with his work.

Sean Nodland

★ ★ ★ ☆ ☆

EURA EDITORIALE

LAGGIU NELL 'OVEST
Ray Collins and Arturo del Castillo
Skorpio, 1984

"The black and white artwork is beautiful – often quite simple, but with great use of zipatone and displaying some quirky panel shapes..."

Skorpio was an Argentinian comics anthology title than ran from 1974 to 1996. The magazine regularly featured westerns including, in its early days, **El Cobra** (written by veteran comics writer Hector German Osterheld, who was 'disappeared' by the Argentinian military junta in the late 1970s), and **Loco Sexton** (penned by 'Ray Collins', real name Eugenio Zapietro). Both were drawn by the outstandingly talented Chilean-born artist, Arturo del Castillo. Del Castillo was responsible for the art on many other western series besides, both in the UK – where he was a contributor of cowboy strips to various boys' adventure titles – and in Argentina, where his stories were regularly syndicated for republication overseas, particularly in Spain and Italy.

And it was in Italy that **Skorpio** had its second lease of life, being published there in a standalone Italian edition from 1977 onwards. The Italian version of the magazine took plenty of material from its Argentine forbear and added in new strips of its own. One wheeze the new **Skor-**pio had was to publish a long running serial as an 'insert' that could be pulled from the centre of the comic and then, when the story was complete, bound up in a set of hardcovers that could be bought from the publishers. And so, a long run of Del Castillo and Collins' **Loco Sexton** stories re-emerged as the insert collection **Laggiu Nell'Ovest** – literally, **Over there in the West.**

I won't pretend I have read all these stories: even with the admirable assistance of Señor Google Translate, working through comics in an unfamiliar language is hard going. But the black and white artwork is beautiful – often quite simple, but with great use of zipatone and displaying some quirky panel shapes. Second-hand comic shops in Italy often seem to have teetering piles of old *Skorpio*s in a dusty corner, and the ones with Del Castillo's westerns in them are really worth seeking out, if only to look at.

Jim O'Brien

★ ★ ★ ☆ ☆

DEAD IN THE WEST
Joe R Lansdale
1983
"This is one of the earliest—and best—examples of the weird western..."

I'd have to say Joe Lansdale is the king of genre mashups. He regularly blends horror and sci-fi, suspense, mystery, men's adventure, steampunk and fantasy. I submit that no one bends genres more frequently or more successfully than Joe Lansdale. One only has to look at his Ned the Seal books (starting with **Zepplins West**) to see an example of him at the top of his game. And **Dead in the West** is no exception to the body of varied work.

Written in 1983, the book was published in a time when zombies weren't so much of a standard trope, and certainly they were never thrown into a western. The premise: an old Indian medicine man is lynched and throws a curse onto the good townsfolk of Mud Creek, Texas. Enter the Reverend Jedidiah Mercer, a gun-toting ex-emissary of God, who must either renew his faith or face certain doom (and death by zombies). What could go wrong, right?

This is a gritty, gory and fun romp through the woolly west, and while a far cry from Zane Grey, it's an extremely enjoyable read. Is it indispensable for the western reading aficionado? I kind of think so, yeah. This is one of the earliest – and best –examples of the weird western, and Mr L mixes the diverse plot

elements so deftly, you'll find yourself wanting more of his unique blend of fiction. Speaking of which, if you are looking for this novel, I suggest you go ahead and splurge for **Deadman's Road**, which contains this novel, along with further adventures of the Reverend Mercer. Check it out. I suspect you'll be glad you did.

S Clayton Rhodes

★ ★ ★ ★ ★

LE BOUT DE LA PISTE (BLUEBERRY 22)
Script: Jean Michel Charlier. Art: Jean Giraud. 1986

"Even the early books I at one time scornfully dismissed are more than worth having on your shelves..."

All the books in the long-running **Blueberry** series are justly renowned for their historical accuracy and complex plotting. Charlier and Giraud first developed the character of Lieutenant Mike Blueberry in 1963 and, many albums later, the series is still going strong despite the deaths of both original creators. Epic in the States and Titan in Britain have put out English translations of a few volumes over the years. In this entry, Blueberry and partners 'Red

Neck' Wooley and Jimmy McLure find themselves protecting US President Grant from an assassination attempt whilst simultaneously attempting to prove Blueberry's innocence in the matter of stolen Confederate gold. Story wise, the book is as solid an entry in the series as a reader could wish for. But there is another reason I picked **Le Bout de la Piste** (basically, 'the end of the trail') particularly to review – although, to be honest, I am not sure it says much about my artistic judgment! Before I discovered **Blueberry**, I knew Giraud not as Giraud but as his pseudonym, 'Moebius'. Moebius was responsible for a seminal series of groundbreaking 70s sci-fi comic strips, all of which were tightly drawn and often astonishingly coloured. I found Giraud's art in the first Blueberry albums I read disappointingly scrappy by comparison with his science fiction work, with more cartoonish figure drawing, dodgy hand lettering and slapdash and strident colouring. However, Janet Gale's colouring for **Le Bout de Piste** is superlative and makes the book really stand out from some of its predecessors. My tastes have improved over time and I can see that even the early books I at one time scornfully dismissed are more than worth having on your shelves – but this still seems one of the best of the lot!

Jim O'Brien

★ ★ ★ ☆ ☆

HANGMEN'S TRAIL
Jim Bowden
1986

"Harkens back to the classic western tales of old..."

You'll need to have your wits about you when starting this book as it begins by dropping us immediately into a scene of sheer bedlam. A convoy of Union soldiers transporting a huge amount of money is attacked by Confederate troops. Bullets whiz by and smack into bodies as the reader is left trying to get their bearings. It's a hell of a way for the adventure to begin!

Things settle down a shade by the second chapter when we are introduced to our main character, a drifter by the name of Cap Millet. He is quickly set upon by a gang of outlaws who frame him for horse theft and lynch him from the nearest tree. Much like in the Clint Eastwood classic **Hang Em High**, these fellas made one big mistake. They didn't finish the job. It's thus left up to Millet to hunt these men down and figure out why they set out to murder him in the first place, and how it ties into the mystery of the stolen Union money.

Hangmen's Trail is a fun and breezy western tale. There's a nice sense of innocence about it as, despite the occasional bout of violence, it harkens back to the classic western tales of old. The good guys are good, and the bad guys are bad. It's a short book, which may not be to everyone's liking, but it's a perfect way to while away a lazy afternoon and get caught up in an adventure.

Dan Shanahan

★ ★ ☆ ☆ ☆

KANSAS BLOOD
Jay Mitchell (Jennifer Robertson)
1986

"An unusual and eloquently written book..."

Lonnie Ryan is a 17-year-old orphan who works her family's farm alone – until the day she stumbles across a badly wounded young man, Toby. She nurses him back to health, only to find that the notorious Barstow Gang are hunting him. His testimony got one of them hung, and the survivors want him dead. Part of the story progresses pretty much as you'd expect – Toby falls for Lonnie, but she's lost everyone she ever loved once, and she's in no hurry to repeat the experience. And then the Barstows show up, still hunting Toby, and everything changes. One of the gang likes to rape and murder women, and he's decided that Lonnie will be his next victim.

This is an unusual and eloquently written book. The only slight hitch is that part of the resolution takes place off the pages, and we hear about it only afterwards. The main thrust of the story is how Lonnie grows and changes, and that's all here. The reason that this story belongs to Lonnie is that the author – 'Jay Mitchell' – is actually Jennifer Roberson. Her publisher thought that nobody would buy a Western novel written by a woman, so she was forced to adopt the rather androgynous penname to sell the book. And I, for one, am glad she sold it, because it's a delightful read.

John Peel

★ ★ ★ ★ ☆

SHERFF JORY
Milton R Bass
1987

"The prose is peppered with Jory's colourful use of language and wordsmithing..."

The third entry in the Jory series of books and another worthy effort from Bass as the titular young gunfighter returns to Barron County, the setting of the first book (**Jory**, 1969) and takes on the job of sheriff. It's a big job for the eighteen-year who soon finds that's there's more to keeping the peace than a fast gun, especially as he's dedicated to being the ''howdy and a smile' brand of civil servant. Jory is soon embroiled in a conflict with a local ranch owner and his crew of bad apples. Complicating things are the attentions of the attractive widow of the former sheriff and the young wife of the villainous ranch owner. Adding to Jory's troubles with gals is his scandalous hiring of a female deputy!

This is standard shoot-em-up stuff plot-wise but made special through the first-person account as told by the lead character. This same point of view is what sets these novels apart. In the first book, Jory's origin for all intents, we learn that he was raised by lawyer father and can read and write though is not particularly well read. That all plays into how Jory describes his world to us. He's often at a loss for the words to express his experiences and this is where most of the fun of

these stories lies. Bass has created a unique voice for his lead character and the prose is peppered with Jory's colourful use of language and wordsmithing. I vividly recall a scene in the first novel in which Jory is challenged by a bad guy who, too late, realizes he's up against a gun faster than him. Jory envisions the man's panic by describing him as opening and closing doors in his mind in search for a way out of his predicament. 'Nope, not that one.'

Much of these unique turns of phrase are humorous as Jory is quite candid in his reactions yet genteel even when describing things scatological or sexual. I admire the inventiveness and consistency of the way Bass has his character express himself in a way that never seems contrived or strained. That's a narrow line to walk and the author makes it look easy and young Jory really comes to life through his own words.

Chuck Dixon

★ ★ ★ ★ ★

THE IMPOSTER (THE BADGE 7)
Bill Reno
1988

"Gripping storylines that twist and turn..."

The Badge is a series of twenty-four books that are linked only by the fact that their heroes wear a badge of some kind, although I believe one or two characters do appear in more than one story. Each book, therefore, is a standalone tale.

Bill Reno is a pseudonym used by Lew A Lacy, and he is an author that knows how to write page turners that capture the reader's imagination easily through excellent characterization, visual descriptions of both landscape and action and gripping storylines that twist and turn and offer surprising outcomes for some of his characters, both good and bad.

The Impostor has as its main theme the desire for revenge and this drives several different people, including Suzanne Lane, whose need for vengeance is as just as that of Johnny Valentine's. When Valentine takes on the identity of a dead lawman it isn't long before he's riding alongside the unsuspecting Suzanne, and the story builds to the moment Suzanne discovers his deception superbly. The need to find out how she reacts to this discovery, especially as she's falling in love with this fake lawman, the man she's vowed to kill, is what makes this book so hard to put down.

FROM THE CREATORS OF
WAGONS WEST AND STAGECOACH

THE BADGE

SEVENTH IN THE BOLD SERIES
OF THE OLD WEST

THE
IMPOSTOR
BILL RENO

The **Badge** books are hard-hitting, action-packed and often quite dark in tone. You can never be sure who will be left alive at the end either. All this adds up to compelling reading that leaves me eager to pick up the next in the series straight away.

Steve Myall

ZUNI GOLD (GATLING 1)
Jack Slade (Peter McCurtin)
1989

"The carnage is thrilling and satisfying in equal measure. ..."

It was the cover that drew me to it. A wonderfully colourful and vibrant image of the main character brandishing a mean looking machine gun, while the Indiana Jones style font giving the book's title above him hinted at promises of action and adventure in the pages within. The book set itself a high bar from the outset. Thankfully, it lived up to the expectations.

Zuni Gold, the first in Jack Slade's **Gatling** series, is the story of John Gatling, a man who was left orphaned following an Apache attack in his youth, who was then taken in and raised by the peaceful Zuni tribe. Now an adult and under the employ of the Maxim Company, manufacturer of all kinds of deadly firearms, Gatling's job is to find opportunities that will give him the chance to test the company's latest creations. What better place for him to do this than on the evil Copper Trust, an organisation dead set on driving his beloved Zunis off their native land so they can mine for gold there.

The book's cover proudly states that all weapons mentioned within its pages are authentic and historically accurate. They are the stars of the show here, as we bear witness to machine guns ripping through bodies and sniper rifles blowing heads apart from a thousand yards. The carnage is thrilling and satisfying in equal measure.

Zuni Gold is a fun read with a likeable enough main character and plenty of action-packed scenes for him to shoot his way through. I'll be on the lookout for the other books in the series. So should you.

Dan Shanahan

OUTLAW EMPIRE (GATLING 2)
Jack Slade
1989

"A pretty sublime set-up for a series of action epics especially if you prefer your body counts neat..."

A gimmick series that never strays far from the gimmick. The premise is a gun-loving vigilante with a real hatred for evil-doers and a real love for experimental firearms gets the greatest dream job since Li'l Abner got hired to test mattresses. He's employed by Hiram Maxim who wants the self-named Gatling to field test automatic and self-loading weaponry in real combat situations. Maxim shells out a bounty and pays all expenses for Gatling to hunt down and murder criminals with new-to-the-market pistols, machine guns and cannons. This doesn't make Gatling many friends in the underworld and so he often finds himself shooting his way out of one tight corner after another.

In this outing, Gatling's hunt for a gangster boss with grandiose plans to build a kind of nation-wide criminal cooperative, takes him from San Francisco to the bayous of Louisiana in a bloody

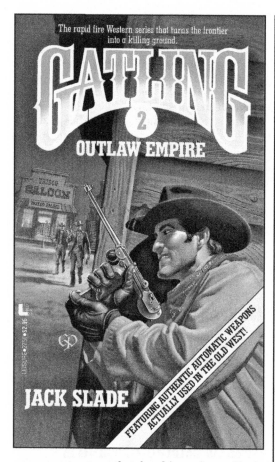

The rapid fire Western series that turns the frontier into a killing ground.

GATLING
2
OUTLAW EMPIRE

FEATURING AUTHENTIC AUTOMATIC WEAPONS ACTUALLY USED IN THE OLD WEST!

JACK SLADE

assertions are here but that's where the authority comes in, right? It sure sounds right when he asserts it.

My only problem with the series is that Gatling's characterization doesn't go much beyond him being a big, tough bastard who's good with any gun you hand him. He's not driven by revenge or a sense of right and wrong. The guy just loves guns and using them on anyone he decides derives being shot full of holes. And I'm okay with that, I really am. But there's little reason to actually care about the guy beyond some references to a tribe of Zuni Indians that he owes an allegiance to and helps support with generous payments from Maxim. His back stories with the Zunis was dealt with in the first book of the series and all they do from there on out is provide a back story told through some exposition sequences in which Gatling recalls them. Other than that, these folks that are so important to him remain faceless and nameless.

Chuck Dixon

RAZORED SADDLES
Edited by Joe Lansdale and Pat LoBrutto
1989

"Much to applaud in the unpredictability of where each story might go.."

I so wanted to like this seventeen-story 'cowpunk' anthology as I am both an admirer of co-editor Lansdale's fiction and a fan of the weird western genre, but it took me two attempts to work through it, with a gap of several years. Few of the stories made an impression which endured or made me wish to recommend them. Robert McCammon's opening story **Black Boots** is stylistically the most impressive, drenched with dark psychedelia as a gunfighter is relentlessly pursued by one of his victims. **Thirteen Days of Glory** was the most outrageous, with its diary format account of how certain America icons besieged in Fort Alamo took a Spartan-like approach to bonding. I was most entertained by Richard Laymon's typically bad-taste and snickering account of a yarn-spinning cowboy with a lecherous eye on his friend's gal and what lurked in **Dinker's Pond**. I also smirked at F Paul Wilson's humorous **The Tenth Toe** which carried a twist worthy of the horror comics of 50s. I was most surprised by the eco-western **Empty Places** by Gary L Raisor, which combined the surprisingly touching last journey of a railroad hobo and the decimation of the

cross-country tour that has him using a Skoda machine gun, a Borchardt autoloading pistol, Lee-Enfield rifle and a Hotchkiss cannon. Along the way, immigrant hoods die by the bushel load until we get to a quite harrowing extended chase through the swamps of the Mississippi delta where Gatling faces dying of fever, exhaustion, snakebite or gators before he can reach his intended quarry.

It's an adult western in that it doesn't watch its language and deals with some bluntly described skeevy subject matter including a floating pedo-brothel that Gatling blows up with dynamite on the kid's night off! But there's none of the sex scenes that are standard in series like this. At least in this entry anyway. And the descriptions of violence don't go too far over the top. Gatling, like any of our favourite gun-toting vigilantes, is not a sadist. He just likes blowing baddies up real good when he's not pumping them full of lead.

It's all a pretty sublime set-up for a series of action epics especially if you prefer your body counts neat. And Slade writes with a real authority about locales, history and, of course, weapons. Not sure how accurate any of his

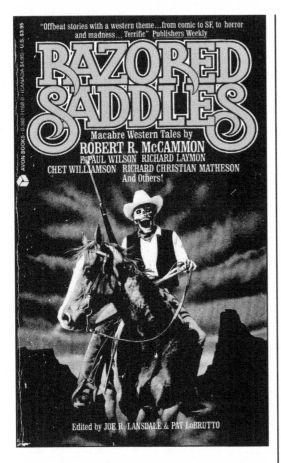

"Offbeat stories with a western theme...from comic to SF, to horror and madness... Terrific" Publishers Weekly

RAZORED SADDLES

Macabre Western Tales by
ROBERT R. McCAMMON
F. PAUL WILSON RICHARD LAYMON
CHET WILLIAMSON RICHARD CHRISTIAN MATHESON
And Others!

Edited by JOE R. LANSDALE & PAT LoBRUTTO

American buffalo. Adding to the wild mix are SF-westerns, one of which provides the anthology's title, modern-day gunslingers such as Joe Lansdale's pair of amoral hitmen in **The Job**, and even pirates in Lewis Shiner's **Gold**. **Razored Saddles** is brave in the eclecticism of its selection, and there is much to applaud in the unpredictability of what territory each story explores. Ultimately, its ambition and innovation are not matched by the quality of the stories and **Razored Saddles** is something of a failure, albeit a glorious one.

Justin Marriott

★ ★ ☆ ☆ ☆

WHITE WATER DEATH (QUINN'S RAIDERS 5)
J D Bodine (Charley Pelberg?)
1989

"A dispiriting read with each page becoming heavier to turn as the plot unravelled..."

In a slam-bang opening sequence, the titular Raiders, a rag-tag group of Confederate rebels who have gone rogue rather than surrender, discover a buzzard-pecked pile of corpses and a stash of gold. Before they can claim the loot, a rival team of bullion-bandits gallop in for a firefight, which is then interrupted by an attack from hostile Cheyenne. By the time the smoke has cleared, the gold and the rival gang has vamoosed. Quinn and co decide to track it down, following the gold-trail to a nearby frontier town and from here the story flows.

This is the fifth entry in a six-book series, copyrighted by book packaging company Jeffrey Weiss Inc with a thanks to Charley Pelberg which was a typical way of book packagers to credit the actual author. Whomever the author, they are a real professional, as this is a lean and mean narrative, which rattles along at a goodly pace and consistently delivers bursts of intense action. Little attempt is made to develop the potential of the ensemble cast, specifically Quinn whom I assumed would be portrayed as a Robin Hood-style, anti-establishment figure, but ultimately is a self-serving robber and murderer. This lack of connection with the titular bandits combined with the generally sleazy tone and mean-spiritedness of the supporting characters, made this is a dispiriting read with each page becoming heavier to turn as the plot unravelled.

Despite the slick writing, this lack of heart means it's little surprise that **Quinn's Raiders** soon disbanded.

Justin Marriott

★ ★ ☆ ☆ ☆

1990- now

The western genre endures, surviving the implosion of the publishing market and many genres with it.

A number of authors perhaps better known in other genres show their love for the western.

Series characters continue to thrive and authors such as David Robbins, Ralph Cotton and James Reasoner keep the readers fed and watered.

But there is also a new breed of meticulously researched novels with highlights including the Lonesome Dove saga and The Stone Garden.

There's still room for an African-American cowboy who fights the KKK and dinosaurs.

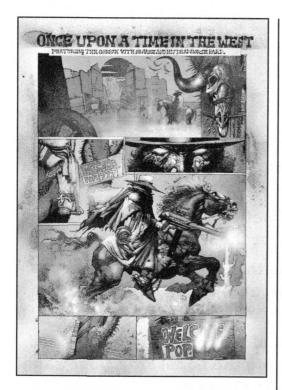

ONCE UPON A TIME IN THE WEST
Script: Alan Grant, Art: Simon Bisley
Toxic! 1
1991

"A great piece of western ultraviolence, courtesy of writer Alan Grant and artist Simon Bisley."

Toxic! was a relatively short-lived early 90s UK comics anthology, aimed by editor Pat Mills and his co-creators at a slightly more mature audience than many newsstand titles of the period catered to. Predominantly sci-fi oriented, issue 1 nevertheless featured this great piece of western ultraviolence, courtesy of writer Alan Grant and artist Simon Bisley. A grizzled, gun-toting Stranger rides into the town of Welcome, and death is his business. Seven pages and a whole mess of bodies later, said Stranger comes to realise that he may not have been *quite* where he intended to be... Grant brings to proceedings the mordant wit he had honed over the previous decade working on, amongst other things, the Judge Dredd strip in **2000AD**. Indeed the Stranger here, with his big gun, stony face and Stetson pulled down almost over his eyes, is in many ways a western antecedent to Joe Dredd. Simon Bisley had established himself as a comics' megastar in the late 80s, when he perfected a painted art style that was part Richard Corben, part Frank Frazetta and part heavy metal (the music as much as the magazine) splatter. Bisley

renders the story's cactus strewn landscapes and western buildings wonderfully, and makes great use of western fonts for some of his sound effects.

Jim O'Brien

★★★☆☆

FEMMES DE L'OUEST
1991
Paolo Eleuteri Serpieri (art); Rafael Ambrosio (scripts)

"In some ways the comic equivalents of the adult westerns that were beginning to see publication at roughly the same time..."

In the decade before 1986 when long-running saga **Druuna** made his name as an erotic sci-fi artist, Paolo Serpieri had spent many years producing a whole series of outstanding westerns for the Italian market, many of them with scriptwriter Rafael Ambrosio. The three tales in this 1991 French collection are reprints from Serpieri's late 1970s western heyday in magazines **Skorpio** and **Lanciostory**. All three feature a fair amount of female nudity, along with plenty of violence, making them in some ways the comic equivalents of the adult westerns that were beginning to see publication at roughly the same time.

In 'The Woman Who Wouldn't Touch Guns' a white girl leaves behind the stultifying conformity of her Quaker home and goes to live with a Lakotah brave, Yellow Face. Many years later she is found by bounty hunter Travers, who rapes her before killing and scalping Yellow Face. The girl must decide whether to stand by her pacifist Quaker morals or avenge the murder of her husband... 'The Act of Courage' finds coarse and indolent pony soldiers Cotty and Renifleur recounting tales of their past misdemeanours to attentive mountain man, Brad. They carelessly regale Brad with the tale of their rape of a Kiowa squaw, Shona, unaware that Brad discovered her body and has tracked the men, seeking revenge... In 'The Convoy of Women', a wagon crossing the Prairies is ambushed and one of the women it is carrying is raped (you may be getting a sense of a repeating pattern by now!). The slovenly wagon master Archew is all for leaving the girl behind as 'spoilt goods' but the remaining girls aboard his wagon have other ideas... All three are solidly told stories with excellent drawing, the best of the bunch being the painted art on 'The Woman Who Wouldn't Touch Guns'.

Jim O'Brien

★ ★ ★ ☆ ☆

THE RANGER
Dan Mason
1992

"Does suffer from thin characters and a predictable plot ..."

An eight-book series featuring the adventures of Texas Ranger Lex Cranshaw. McDade wrote several westerns but also dabbled in other genres including more than a dozen of the Mack Bolan **Executioner** series.

The novel opens with Lex Cranshaw escorting a captured prisoner back to town to stand justice. While en route, he comes across a black man by the name of James Lincoln, an ex-slave who now owns and operates a nearby ranch. Unfortunately, Lincoln has a huge chip on his shoulder due to unequal treatment by the other ranchers. No sooner does Cranshaw arrive in town, criminal in tow, than news arrives of the murder of a prominent rancher, shot in the back. Of course, the black man, James Lincoln, is fingered as the culprit and Cranshaw is pulled in to assist the sheriff in keeping the rapidly forming lynch mob at bay. To make matters worse, Lincoln goes on the run, making him look guilty and forcing Cranshaw to chase him down.

The story is told in a hard-boiled style with lots of witty dialogue. Plenty of action here as Cranshaw faces down assorted bullies, ranch hands, and townspeople, mostly with his accurate gunplay. A mystery element is woven in as Cranshaw tries to determine the identity of the real murderer but unfortunately, this part of the plot is entirely predictable. As the story unfolds, Cranshaw begins to like Lincoln more and more, but he remains unsure of his guilt or innocence until near the end.

This is a fast moving read but does suffer from thin characters and a predictable plot. While I enjoyed it, I won't be going out of my way to seek another in the series.

Benjamin Thomas

★ ★ ☆ ☆ ☆

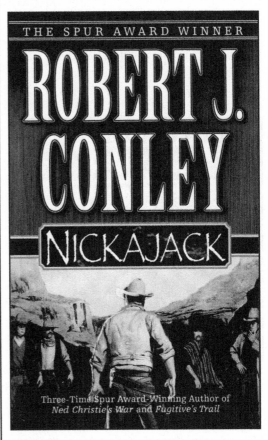

NICKAJACK
Robert J Conley
1992

"A hard-hitting tale of suffering and betrayal based around true events ..."

This is a powerful read. A book that deals with tragedy, that which befalls Nickajack himself and that of his tribe caught up in a political struggle based on corruption and the treatment of minority groups.

Robert J Conley tells this story in prose that will be long remembered, his tale tears at the heart in its sadness. Much of the story is told in reflection as Nickajack remembers the events that have torn through the Cherokee Nation and swept him up in them, which have ultimately seen him on trial for murder. Make no mistake this is a hard-hitting tale of suffering and betrayal based around true events. The tone, as you'd expect, is dark and is beautifully paced as it builds up to its inevitable ending.

Robert J Conley won a Spur Award for this novel and it's easy to see why. It seems such a shame to me that very few readers of westerns mention him when discussing the genre. Conley seems to be a very overlooked writer, and on the strength of this book I'd say that many people have been missing out on some terrific reading. To those I say try this, I'm sure you'll be impressed.

Steve Myall

★ ★ ★ ★ ★

A MAN CALLED HORACE VOL 2
Scripts: Roger Kettle, Art: Andrew Christine
1993

"No-nonsense, straight-up three-panel gag strip with plenty of cowboy puns and groan-inducing jokes…"

Roger Kettle and Andrew Christine are probably better known as the creators of the long running French Foreign Legion-based humour strip, **Beau Peep**, which ran in UK tabloid the **Daily Star** from 1978 up until 2016. Rival tabloid the

Daily Mirror wooed Kettle and Christine over to their side of Fleet Street in 1989 in an attempt to pull away some of the **Star**'s many readers, and **A Man called Horace** certainly plays very much like a Western version of **Beau Peep**. Each daily is a no-nonsense, straight-up three-panel gag strip with plenty of cowboy puns and groan-inducing jokes. Here in Volume 2 for example, Kettle seems to have been in the grip of a mild obsession with the hokey-cokey dance, which forms the basis of much of the humour. I really like Andrew Christine's art (the colour Sunday strips are especially nice) but prefer the strip when it sticks to the human characters (the hapless Horace himself, the cowboy's patently-much-more intelligent-than-Horace Injun sidekick, etc.), rather than the to my mind very much less entertaining talking western animals. Too many stories for comfort feature an insufferable lisping rattlesnake and a hibernating bear, excited to realise that the mating season is close at hand…

Jim O'Brien

★ ☆ ☆ ☆ ☆

THE GUN FIGHT
Richard Matheson
1993

"I got to see the same story by the same author play out two different ways …"

Richard Matheson's story of a lawman wrongly, and innocently – at first – accused of misconduct with a local girl takes off well. During a three-day span, rumours about ex-Texas Ranger John Benton and sixteen-year-old Louisa Harper go from schoolgirl fantasy to idle town gossip to outright accusations. Robby Cole, Louisa's boyfriend, knows he must defend his woman's honour. Under the psychotic manipulations of his father, Robby is forced into a gunfight with the older lawman, a mismatch he can't hope to win.

Robby challenges Benton. Benton thinks the situation is ludicrous, that reason will prevail. At the urging of the local preacher, he agrees to talk to the kids' parents. After being rebuffed by Louisa's mother and Robby's father, he blows the whole thing off. Staying on his ranch, he ignores the nonsense in town. Of course, everyone begins to believe the worst.

Louisa admits nothing happened between her and Benton, it's all been an elaborate fairy tale, but too late. The grown-ups want blood. In a last-ditch effort, Robby tries to bow out, but his father forces the confrontation.

Up until this point, the story reads much like Matheson's 1955 short story, **Too Proud to Die**, but with more characters and a little less introspection from our hero. That's when the older, more seasoned writer sets a new course and makes new inroads into what's gone before with another satisfying conclusion.

It was basically by chance that I got to see the same story by the same author play out two different ways – a rare treat. Someone could probably run a personality profile on you by which story you prefer, but they both have an abundance of character development and deal with real life societal themes we have yet to resolve.

Richard Prosch

This is definitely one weird Western... Billijohn Finley is the Indian agent for a band of Apaches, and they have finally agreed to a treaty after ten years of sporadic fighting. No sooner is the treaty signed, however, than two of the locals from Picture City are found brutally murdered. Boutelle, a political representative from Washington, is certain that the Apaches have broken the treaty, but Finley has a different suspect – one that isn't human...

Matheson provides his usual level of authentic background mixed with vivid characters. Add in an Apache legend, a greedy medicine man and a slightly demented man of science, and you end up with a horror-laced Western. Have the Apaches broken the treaty? For some whites, the answer doesn't matter – the only good Indian... But who is the mysterious stranger who has arrived in Picture City? And why are the Apaches so terrified of him? And is he joking when he claims that somebody once tried – and failed - to stop him by cutting off his head?

Have fun!

John Peel

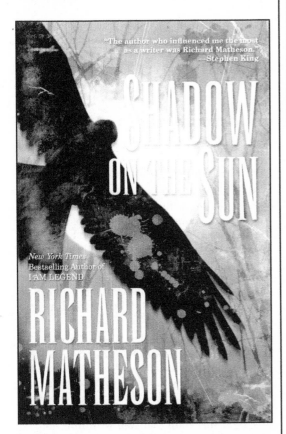

SHADOW ON THE SUN
Richard Matheson
1994

"Provides his usual level of authentic background mixed with vivid characters..."

SIERRA
Richard S Wheeler
1996

"A tale of love; love for a woman, for gold, for a future…"

Richard S Wheeler was one of the great writers of historical western novels. He authored more than eighty titles — westerns, novels of historical fiction, even some detective novels. Accolades have been heaped upon him including six Spur Awards and the 2001 Owen Wister Award for lifetime achievement and a 2015 induction into its Hall of Fame. His stories focus on the history of the West rather than two-fisted action; the real West as opposed to the mythic West.

This novel is a perfect example of that approach. The California Gold Rush affected people in a variety of ways, but it was always with deep passion. Here, we follow two different men who approached the gold fields differently. In 1847, Stephen Jarvis, lately discharged from the US Army after the Mexican war, stumbles upon the very beginnings of the gold find but intuitively realizes the best way to make his fortune is by supplying tools and equipment to the miners themselves. His entrepreneurial spirit triumphs. Meanwhile, Ulysses McQueen, a farmer in Ohio doesn't make his move until 1849, choosing to leave his farm and young pregnant wife and set out across the country to seek his fortune. He's a hard-working man, but the world seems arrayed against him as he struggles to survive with his 'gold fever'.

It's a tale of two disparate men and how they approach their lives. But this is also a tale of love; love for a woman, for gold, for a future. Both men are driven by what they hope awaits them. Their stories are emotional and moving and the book kept me turning the pages. Fans of the authentic West will want to give this one a try.

Benjamin Thomas

★ ★ ★ ★ ☆

THE MEMOIRS OF WILD BILL HICKOK
Richard Matheson
1996

"What if Wild Bill wasn't the grim, efficient gunman we've all been led to think, but a total jerk?"

I would never have imagined I would ever need to write these words about a Richard Matheson story: Avoid this. Throw it from you. Give it to someone you detest. Yes, the author of **I Am Legend**, **The Incredible Shrinking Man** and **Nightmare at 20,000 Feet** for **The Twilight Zone** has done a Casey – and struck out.

It's a one-joke concept: What if Wild Bill wasn't the grim, efficient gunman we've all been led to think but a total jerk? What if, like F Troop star Ken Berry, he was a klutz who stumbles his way to fame? (Only without the earnest goodness and likeability of Captain Parmenter?) Revisionist history can be fun at times, if handled properly – but this isn't. The book goes through Wild Bill's career, demolishing his achievements, demeaning his dignity and filled with belches and puking (when he's not whoring or trying to run away from fights). Over and over again. And with the same, constant refrain of, 'I don't know if anyone will ever read this, but…', before launching into further debased tales. He repeats that line every dozen or so pages like a song's chorus or some haunting spectre warning people off.

Listen to that refrain and obey it. I suspect even Matheson realized he'd penned an absolute stinker with this one.

John Peel

☆ ☆ ☆ ☆ ☆

THE GALLOWSMAN
Will Cade (Cameron Judd)
1998

"Deviates from the traditional western yarn…"

Will Cade is not exactly a household name among Western writers. But if this novel serves as an example of his work, he should be. He wrote just a handful of books, all published by Leisure Books in the late 1990s to early 2000s. His work generally deviates from the traditional western yarn in that he adds a great deal of mystery and suspense to his stories rather than a bunch of flying lead and fisticuffs. Often there is a sense of defending the rights of innocents.

This novel opens with Ben Woolard arriving in the small mining town of Ferguson, Colorado, ready to start his life anew. We soon uncover his backstory, his job as a Union spy during the Civil War, infiltrating Bushwhackers (Confederate guerrillas), and feeding intel to his brother. It was a job that didn't sit well with him, forcing him to lie and turn his back on people who thought him loyal. However, his critical testimony at the trial of murderer Henry Champion led to a successful conviction and hanging. In addition, we also unfortunately learn of the terrible loss of Ben's wife and children to the dreaded measles at about that same time resulting in his nosedive into heavy drinking.

But now Ben has joined his successful brother in Ferguson and been grubstaked for a silver mine. All was well until the rumours started. Henry Champion had been seen alive, right there in Ferguson. That couldn't be true, of course – they'd seen him hang. But then some of Champion's gang was spotted and Ben's brother's business is set afire. How could this be? Ben would have to solve the mystery while juggling his mining concern, look out for his new friends, and avoid the bottle.

This one really kept me turning the pages. Cade writes in a smooth, campfire-story-telling style and Ben Woolard makes for a relatable, sympathetic hero. A side plot involving a pretty girl who disguises herself as a grubby man in order to avoid her abusive/killer brother was a bonus. Mysterious deaths, mistaken identities, kidnappings and colourful characters all combine to make a fun read with a satisfying (and not at all predictable) finish. I want to read more from Will Cade.

Benjamin Thomas

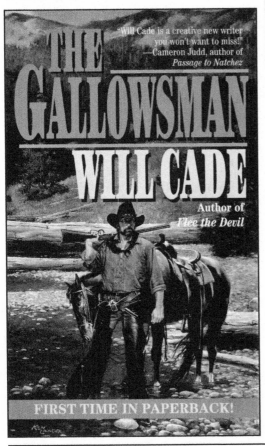

THE TONTO WOMAN AND OTHER WESTERN STORIES
Elmore Leonard
1998

"Outsiders who take a moral stand against the corruption and brutality of men of higher social status..."

The nineteen short stories that make up this collection of Leonard's western yarns come from the period 1952 to 1994, with the bulk of them drawn from '50s western digests such as **Dime Western**, **Western Magazine** and **Gunsmoke**. Some are better known than others ('Three-Ten to Yuma' for example, filmed first in 1957 and then again in 2007) and some run a little longer than their amigos (Rough Rider-themed 'Hurrah for Captain Early' is just a compact 13 pages long, while – at nearly 50 pages – 1955 tale 'The Captives' pretty much qualifies as a novella) but all of the stories here gleam as brightly and tantalizingly as the barrel of a Colt amidst the leaves of the sage brush. A goodly proportion of the stories feature elements and preoccupations that recur regularly in Elmore Leonard's books – western and otherwise. Many focus on outsiders (by virtue of their ethnicity, chiefly) who, whilst hardly being angels themselves, take a moral stand against the corruption and brutality of men of higher social status. In 'The Tonto Woman' itself it is Mexican Ruben Vega who faces up to wealthy landowner Mr Isham. In 'Hurrah for Captain Early' it is African American ex-serviceman Bo Catlett who duels (verbally at first, then literally) with the small-town racists who hassle him as he awaits the arrival of his former commanding officer. As with all of Leonard's books the period detail is authentic but unobtrusive and the prose is clean, sharp and almost poetic in its simplicity. I recommend these stories wholeheartedly.

Jim O'Brien

★ ★ ★ ★ ★

GENEVIEVE OF TOMBSTONE
John Duncklee
1999

"Told from Genevieve's first-person perspective, filled with simplistic yet colourful phrasing..."

John Duncklee was a cowboy, a cattleman and a quarter horse breeder. All are good qualifications

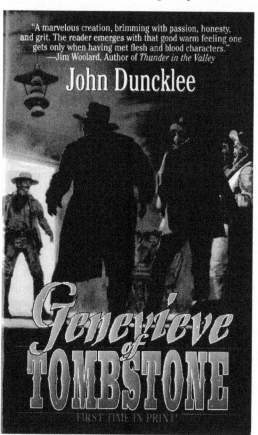

"A marvelous creation, brimming with passion, honesty, and grit. The reader emerges with that good warm feeling one gets only when having met flesh and blood characters."
—Jim Woolard, Author of *Thunder in the Valley*

John Duncklee

Genevieve of TOMBSTONE

FIRST TIME IN PRINT

for writing authentic western fiction and he puts them on display here in this novel. From the title, I was expecting another take on the events of Tombstone, Arizona in the 1880s involving the Earps, Morgans, Doc Holliday, Curly Bill and the rest, but this was only briefly mentioned in the text. Instead, I found myself reading of the extraordinary life of Genevieve Ames, a widow who takes over her husband's cattle ranch just outside of Tombstone.

The novel opens with Genevieve's husband having just been shot in the back, making her a widow. A flashback sequence tells of her backstory, including how she came west and became a whore in Tombstone before marrying one of her clients and buying a cattle ranch. Most of the story takes place over the next few years as Genevieve works her ranch, hires people to assist her, organizes roundups and sells off cattle annually. She's a more than capable woman and, of course, this aggravates most of the men who compete with her, becoming a major source of conflict in the novel. She also has a penchant for befriending people that the rest of the community frowns on, especially some Apaches as well as a Buffalo Soldier deserter. But Genevieve doesn't back down from anybody.

The story takes place over nearly twenty years in the 1880s-90s. Genevieve must face threats from neighbouring ranchers, droughts, con men, bullies – and even the US Government over grazing rights. But she is a feisty and shrewd character, which makes this novel a fun one to read. The story is told from Genevieve's first-person perspective, filled with simplistic yet colourful phrasing reminiscent of Huckleberry Finn like, 'We commenced to palavering about the little feller.'

If you're looking for lots of gunfights or two-fisted western action, then you'll need to look elsewhere. Genevieve, as a character, is a genuine and caring person, facing adversity on all fronts yet standing her ground. Based on this book, I would enjoy another opportunity to sample John Duncklee's work.

Benjamin Thomas

★ ★ ★ ★ ☆

dynamism to the imagery that is befitting of the lightning-paced plot. This will undoubtedly be a divisive book, and even avid fans of Lansdale's fiction and comics might find it too freewheeling and anarchic. I have revisited it several times and each time enjoyed the sheer just-for-the-hell-of-it tone.

Justin Marriott

★★★☆☆

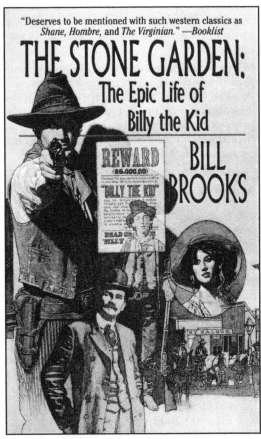

RED RANGE

Written by Joe Lansdale and illustrated Sam Glanzman
1999

"Even avid fans of Lansdale's fiction and comics might find it too free-wheeling and anarchic..."

This 80-page black-and-white graphic novel from long-term collaborators Lansdale and Glanzman is something of an oddity. Its cover subverts the N C Wyeth painting 'Cowboy Watering his Horse' by reimagining the central figure as an African American, which sums up the racial themes at the core of this and so much of Lansdale's work. However, I didn't recognise the reference, and I can't imagine such a sedate image would have pulled in comic fans. It certainly doesn't reflect the high-octane 'weird western' contained inside. Plot spoiler warning, but what starts out as a very grim and violent story of a black cowboy's war with the KKK that slaughtered his family, turns very Edgar Rice Burroughs/Pellucidar about halfway through. It's archetypal Lansdale comics work, and the sick humour, oddball characters, plentiful gore and excessive use of the 'n-word' means you'll likely love or hate it. The art from Glanzman looks rushed, but that brings a fluidity and

THE STONE GARDEN: THE EPIC LIFE OF BILLY THE KID

Bill Brooks
2001

"Filled with many reflections on dying, on depression, on sadness, and the dead ..."

Bill Brooks has written this book in the first person, the story told through the voice of Billy the Kid for the main part, although later he tells part of the tale as Manuella, whom it has been oft-speculated by historians to have been his lover which makes for some fascinating different points-of-view of events in the story.

The story also moves from its present to the past and back again at regular intervals; one minute you are reading memories of a dead person, the next they are alive. You'd have thought all this jumping around in time would make for confusing reading, but it doesn't, it helps add interest as you don't know where the story will take you next.

The whole book has a very dark tone as it's filled with many reflections on dying, on depression, on sadness and on the dead. Having said that, Bill Brooks does insert many moments of humour too, such as the river that washes away graves to send coffins and their contents to new resting places.

In **The Stone Garden** Bill Brooks has really come up with a very memorable and moving book and in doing so has added to the many myths surrounding Billy the Kid and his death at the hands of Pat Garrett. This is a book that will stick in the mind for a long time, for not only being entertaining but thought provoking too.

Steve Myall

RAVEN SPRINGS
John D Nesbitt
2002

"Creepy characters and oddball settings make this one a lot of fun..."

The author has other books about Jimmy Clevis, but this was my first experience with the young adventurer: a fanciful mystery that's still anchored in reality.

When one of his Mexican friends goes missing somewhere in south central Wyoming, Jimmy leaves Colorado to find out what happened. Raven Springs is an unassuming town with two spooky hotels and an ominous secret. Creepy characters and oddball settings (taxidermy, anyone?) make this one a lot of fun without lapsing into camp.

Nesbitt is again at his best along the Snowy Range of Wyoming, exploring the wide-open spaces where (as the cliché goes) danger hides in plain sight. One thing I always find interesting in Nesbitt novels, and it owes a lot to the continuing isolation of the Wyoming wilderness, is that the stories are timeless in the sense that they could be happening in 1870 or 1970 or 2020. Highly recommended.

Richard Prosch

COYOTE'S TRAIL
Edward M Erdelac
2003

"You can almost taste the dirt and blood ..."

Ever since reading Edward M Erdelac's previous western, **Buff Tea**, I've been looking forward to his next, and what a superb novel it's turned out to be. The three main characters are each fascinating in their own rights, each having their own personalities and agendas, each ready to work with and/or use the others to achieve their aims. Edward M Erdelac's west is a harsh place where savage violence is only a heartbeat away. He tells his tale in vivid prose that paints dramatic and lasting imagery within the minds' eye. You can almost taste the dirt and blood, feel the heat and share the anguish and pain as his lead characters Chiricahua boy Na-e-te-nay and broken young Mexican woman America struggle to avenge the wrongs done to them. **Coyote's Trail** is a tough, and brutal, story that grabbed my attention from the first page and refused to loosen its grip even after I'd reached the end. The final scene is moving and will stay in my memory for a very long time.

Steve Myall ★ ★ ★ ★ ★

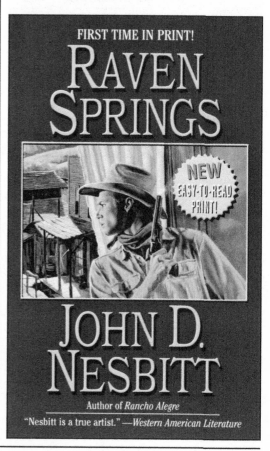

FIRST TIME IN PRINT!

RAVEN SPRINGS

NEW EASY-TO-READ PRINT!

JOHN D. NESBITT

Author of *Rancho Alegre*

"Nesbitt is a true artist." —*Western American Literature*

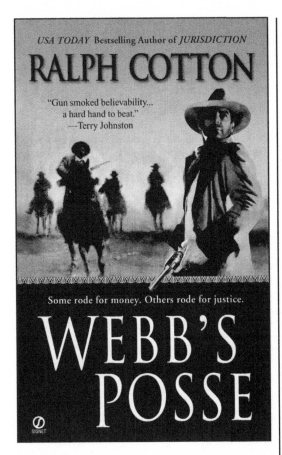

WEBB'S POSSE
Ralph Cotton
2003

"You can never be sure who he'll kill off, and when..."

Ralph Cotton has created a superb bunch of characters for this extremely fast-moving story that barely takes a breath between each savage bout of gunplay. As well as having to deal with the outlaws, soldiers, gunrunners, scalp hunters and Federales, the posse has its own internal conflicts for Webb to tackle – he himself being one of the problems for one of the posse members which sees hate and jealousy rise viciously.

Then there's the suspicions about the horse trader, Will Summers: just what is his angle? And what of the schoolteacher, Sherman Dahl, just why would a schoolmaster be so proficient with a gun and cool under fire? Can either of them be trusted? As the posse begins to face the brutal reality of their task some die, some leave and other people join them, including some who won't think twice about double-crossing the posse.

As the chase takes all sides into Mexico, all these groups find themselves fighting for possession of a Gatling gun and no one is safe from death. That's one of the traits I like about Ralph Cotton's writing, the fact that you can never be sure who he'll kill off, and when.

If you like hard-hitting, action-packed westerns that offer surprises, twists and engaging characters then **Webb's Posse** is a book you should consider tracking down. I don't think I'll be spoiling anything by adding that this book saw five sequels featuring two of the survivors of the hunt to bring the Peltry gang to justice, and I'm certainly going to be reading them very soon.

Steve Myall

THE WESTERNERS
Zane Grey
2003

"It's easy to see why they were unpublished..."

Zane Grey is possibly the best-known name in western fiction – so, naturally, I'd never read him before picking up this collection of his shorter fiction. There are eight of his stories (one of which isn't in any way a Western as it's about whaling in Australia) and a short article by his son Loren about the latter story. The tales cover a wide spectrum – from a Texas Ranger looking for an abducted woman to an early Hollywood stuntman doing a dangerous piece of filming. They show Grey's eye for detail, and his knowledge of Western life.

Some of them are early, unpublished works – and it's easy to see why they were unpublished, as he shows a tendency to over-write. People don't talk, they 'soliloquize' or 'ejaculate'. And he seems quite obsessed with describing the sage. Well, his most famous work is **Riders of The Purple Sage**, so maybe that's why.

The quality of the stories (the published ones date from 1910 to 1929) varies a lot, too. He has a tendency towards the sentimental ('The Camp Robber' and 'Monty Price's Nightingale'), which is not necessarily a bad thing. The longest story in the book (and the title of the book) is terribly absurd, however. It was originally called 'Loose Bridles' (something of a vague pun), and tells the tale of two mothers who head to Reno to get quickie divorces. Each one (one from New York, the other from California) is followed by an unmarried child, with predictable results. They plot to stop their mothers, and the story drags on...

Overall, though, the other tales in the collection make up for this misfire.

John Peel

★ ★ ★ ☆ ☆

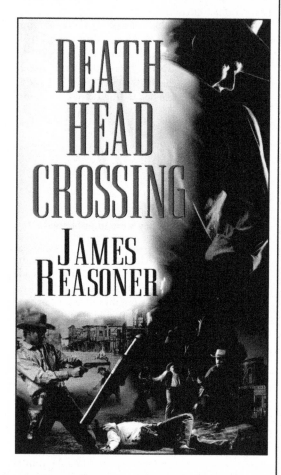

DEATH HEAD CROSSING
James Reasoner
2007

"All kinds of red-herrings and twists to the tale which in turn draw the reader deeper into the story..."

James Reasoner has written a gripping novel in **Death Head Crossing**. A book that is as much a murder mystery as it is a western. The burnt off faces of the victims making for horrific deaths, which hook the reader with wanting to discover how this happens and why. Gunslinger Hell Jackson and cub reporter Everett Sidney Howard make for an unlikely detective partnership but work very well as a team as they start to compile a list of suspects whilst the body count grows.

The discovery that the killer calls himself 'The Hand of God leading to all kinds of possibilities. And as the hunt of the killer escalates the reader begins to wonder as to the identity of Hell Jackson. All this allows James Reasoner to plant all kinds of red herrings and twists to the tale which in turn draw the reader deeper into the story. **Death Head Crossing** is one of the best westerns I've read by James Reasoner and I'd urge all fans of westerns – and mystery murders – to give this one a try. I'm sure you won't be disappointed.

Steve Myall

★ ★ ★ ★ ★

'Fresh, fast and sure... The work of a master craftsman'
Washington Post

RESOLUTION
Robert B Parker
2008

"I was soon swept up in the storyline ..."

Robert B Parker is perhaps better known for his **Spenser** novels than his western work. **Resolution** is the sequel to **Appaloosa**, which was made into the successful film of the same name starring Ed Harris and Viggo Mortensen. **Resolution** starts shortly after the end of that story. This is the first book I've read by Parker and was taken by surprise by the fact it is written in a minimalistic style. There's very little in the way of descriptions and when anyone speaks it is only described as the person having said something. It took a little while to get used to this method of writing but once I did, I was soon swept up in the storyline and really enjoyed the conversations between itinerant lawman Everett Hitch and his friend Vigil Cole, their matter-of-fact observations about life, killing, and solving problems being one of the highlights of the book.

When a greedy mine owner threatens the local ranchers, Hitch's scheming boss Amos Woolfson ends up at the centre of a makeshift war. Hitch knows only too well how to protect himself, but with the bloodshed mounting, he's relieved when Cole rides into town. In a place where justice and order don't yet exist, Cole and Hitch must lay down the law – without violating their codes of honour, duty and friendship.

The story is told through Hitch in the first person as he sides with a man he will only come to detest. With the arrival of Cole, he leaves Woolfson's employ and they both find themselves on the opposite side, facing Woolfson's replacement guns. Cole is a terrific character and sees nothing wrong in eliminating someone who gets in his way if this is the easiest way to solve a problem. In fact, Cole has no reservations about taking on superior odds in a face-to-face situation, something that happens in this book in a very memorable scene. When I finished reading this book, I found myself wondering how this author had slipped by me and have decided I must do something about catching up with his other western work, least of all those other tales starring Cole and Hitch.

Steve Myall

THE GUNS OF SAPINERO
Frank Leslie
2009

"A well-told, fast moving, violent, story ..."

The gruesome, and very visual, descriptions of a man crucified in a wagon bed being feasted upon by vultures whilst still alive, sets the tone for this book beautifully. The story is packed with savage (and bloody) killings and brandings, but it's not just the violence that hits hard, so do the emotions that fuel Colter Farrow's quest for vengeance against his stepfather's killers. Seeing him change from being a carefree cowhand to questioning his abilities to track down his prey,

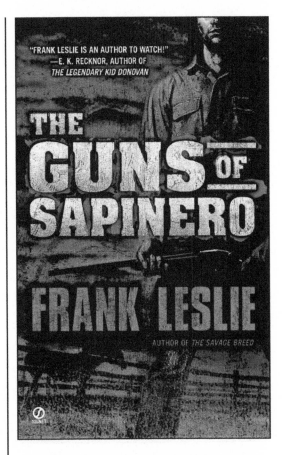

struggling with his inexperience with killing and surviving in this brutal land, fearing how to tell his stepmother the truth about her husband, all make for fascinating and gripping reading.

Of course, it's no secret to western fans that Frank Leslie is a pseudonym used by Peter Brandvold and this book lives up to our expectations of his work. There's even a brief guest appearance by one of Peter Brandvold's other heroes, Lou Prophet, that has a lasting impact on Farrow. **The Guns of Sapinero** is a well-told, fast moving, violent story that is a terrific introduction to the Colter Farrow series.

Steve Myall

THE RATTLESNAKE SEASON
Larry Sweazy
2009

"Excels at blending history into his story without lengthy info dumps or tiresome backstories..."

I picked up the first **Josiah Wolfe, Texas Ranger** title after winning the third one, **The Badger's**

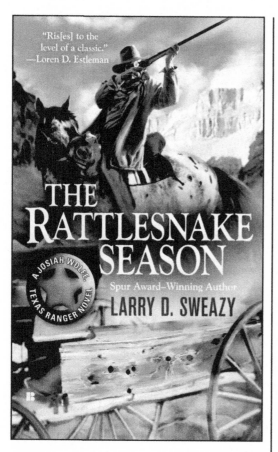

"Ris[es] to the level of a classic."
—Loren D. Estleman

THE RATTLESNAKE SEASON

A JOSIAH WOLFE, TEXAS RANGER NOVEL

Spur Award–Winning Author
LARRY D. SWEAZY

Revenge, in a draw on Larry's blog. In response to my note of appreciation, Larry wrote that **The Rattlesnake Season** was his first published novel and he had used everything he had learned up until that time in writing it. That's a neat comment, because I learned a lot reading it.

Larry excels at blending history into his story without lengthy info dumps or tiresome backstories. This tale takes place in 1874, a year after the disbanding of the Texas State Police and the recommissioning of the Rangers by Governor Coke. Now, Wolfe, a widower with a young son, could become one of the agency's best.

Sweazy is at his best drawing a landscape filled with political wrangling and leaders jockeying for position. That's not to say there isn't plenty of action along the way. I liked this one a lot and will continue to follow the series with **The Scorpion's Trail**.

Richard Prosch

★ ★ ★ ★ ☆

THE OUTCAST (WILDERNESS 60)
David Thompson (David Robbins)
2009

"A violent and emotionally moving ending ..."

When the titular outcast decides to take a wife by any means necessary, he makes the mistake of kidnapping Lou who is the betrothed of mountain man Zach King, who will stop at nothing to return her to his side. Once again, David Thompson creates a strong, powerful – yet tragic – character in **The Outcast**, a man who will long remain in this reader's mind. David Thompson doesn't reveal why this character is an outcast straight away but keeps hinting at his backstory, thus adding an intriguing hook that ensured this reader would find this book difficult to put down. Once the reason for him being cast out of his tribe is revealed it helps explain why he kidnaps Lou instead of killing her as he first intends.

There are many humorous moments and comments to balance the more savage and heart-rending aspects of this story, such as the struggle for man and woman to understand each other's way of thinking. The strength of love, and the lengths that someone will go to in order to protect their loved ones is a strong element of this book – indeed the entire **Wilderness** series – and it isn't just Zach who is affected with the abduction of Lou. Shakespeare is shocked by the near death of Blue Water Woman, and David Thompson writes some very moving scenes as Shakespeare resists the urge to accompany Zach in his search for Lou, and stay behind to tend to his wife.

The book is brim full of action too, as Zach attempts to track the Outcast and free his wife. The life-threatening traps he must avoid, the superbly described slide down the mountainside due to having to traverse treacherous talus. And if the battle of wits between Zach and the Outcast isn't enough, unbeknown to either of them death stalks them both in the form of another group of revenge-seeking Indians that will cause further complications that have a savage and exciting part to play in the struggle to regain Lou's freedom. Does Zach manage to free Lou from her captor? That's something I'm not prepared to reveal here, all I will say is the book has a violent and emotionally moving ending that may come as a surprise.

Steve Myall

★ ★ ★ ★ ★

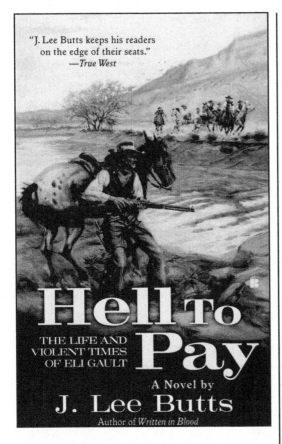

HELL TO PAY
The Life and Violent Times of Eli Gault
J. Lee Butts
2009

"Fills the story with colourful and engaging characters ..."

A story of a young man who, through unfortunate circumstances finds himself forced to kill time and again, something he discovers he's very good at. J Lee Butts writes extremely well, and his style makes this a difficult book to put down. He fills the story with colourful and engaging characters. The book has plenty of tough and brutal action as we follow Gault's attempts to settle down, even taking on a job as a deputy at one point, but each time he finds himself having to kill again and once more having to go on the run. Butts also includes plenty of humorous observations, often commenting on human nature. Eli Gault is the young man learning from legendary killer and expert gun-hand Cutter Sharpe, a likeable enough character but you can't help thinking it can't end well, especially as the opening scenes see Gault sitting in jail awaiting the hangman. The main part of the story being told as a long flashback with the end of the book being powerful and memorable.

Steve Myall

OUTLAW TRAIN
Cameron Judd
2010

"A very fast moving and difficult to put down story..."

Cameron Judd fills this book with a fascinating bunch of characters, many of whom are involved in enterprises that don't turn up that often in westerns. People such as the man with the tattooed ears who owns the Outlaw Train – a rolling museum of dead outlaws and weapons used to kill others. Then there's the stunning Katrina Haus who claims she can communicate with the dead – a woman who some suspect of being the missing killer, Kate Bender. There's the mysterious man who lives in seclusion above the Emporium, never venturing outside. My favourite is the ex-drunk, Dewitt Stamps, who has now got religion in a big way and is employed as the jailer. And it's not just people that cause problems for Deputy Luke Cable; what of the severed leg found near the railway tracks?

Cameron Judd combines all these elements, and more, in a very fast moving and difficult to put down story that fuels the imagination. As all his characters come together in the town of Wiles, Kansas, the author has another surprise waiting for the reader which resolves all his storylines in a dramatic and violent conclusion. I also liked the fact that Cameron Judd included a real person in the story – Kate Bender. Is she the person pretending to be Katrina Haus? That's something you'll have to find out for yourself, and hopefully you'll be as entertained as I was with this book whilst finding out the answer.

Steve Myall

SILENT HILL: PAST LIFE
IDW Comics, 2010
Story: Tom Waltz
Art: Menton 3

"The art... lifts a fairly average slice of weird western up into a different category altogether."

Silent Hill is a 1999 US/Japanese horror-survival computer game in which distressed father Harry Mason searches the Lovecraftian

town of Silent Hill for his missing daughter, Cheryl... and is in absolutely no way is a western. But subsequent comic book prequel **Silent Hill: Past Life** most certainly is, and a mighty fine-looking example of the genre it is too.

1867, the Dakotas. In the recent past Jebediah Foster has been a drunk, a womaniser and a thug for hire, slaughtering Indians and runaway negroes without pity. So fearsome was his reputation that he became known as the Hellrider. Now married to the godly Esther, Foster and his heavily pregnant wife are bound for the town of Silent Hill, there to start a new life and raise a family in peace and solitude.

Yet Silent Hill is not the haven of tranquillity the couple hope for. The town's postmaster is an elderly black man who seems to know more of Jebediah's past than the latter cares for, and no sooner are the Fosters ensconced in their new home than a strange Indian woman appears, showing an unnatural interest in Esther's baby-to-be. When Foster gets stuck into the busthead whiskey once again and begins sleeping with a married woman in town, it seems initially as if he will face no greater fallout than his puritanical wife telling him off for cussing. But in Silent Hill, a man's past will eventually catch up with him...

I said at the top that this is a fine-looking western, and so it is. Menton 3 (real name Menton J Matthews III) paints and draws a sombre, shadow-filled Silent Hill and its characters with an exceptional skill and talent that lifts what is at the end of the day a fairly average slice of weird western up into a different category altogether.

Jim O'Brien

DEAD MAN'S REVENGE
Colby Jackson (Bill Crider)
2011

"Their daughters aren't going to sit around waiting for dad to save them..."

Dead Man's Revenge is a short, action-packed sequel to the first Rancho Diablo title, **Shooter's Cross**. This time, family man Sam Blaylock is pitted against his first and worst enemy. The western action explodes as Blaylock fights to save Rancho Diablo against a dead man who has returned to take unrighteous revenge. I liked the way the Blaylock women were portrayed in the opening scene and later during an attack on the ranch. Sam's wife, Jenny, is no timid stereotype, but a fully imagined partner to her husband. Likewise, their daughters—especially redheaded Miriam—aren't going to sit around waiting for dad to save them.

Favourite points go to ferry driver Eustace Kendall who serves as comic relief after Blaylock gets down to the business of killing and Eustace gets to hauling the dead men across the water to the undertaker in Shooter's Cross.

Dead Man's Revenge is a gem of a tale, and I'm looking forward to reading deeper into the series.

Richard Prosch

REDEMPTION, KANSAS
James Reasoner
2011

"Puts familiar characters into new, uniquely dangerous, and suspense filled situations ..."

I've never been disappointed by a book written by James Reasoner because the characters, setting and plot always ring true. Dialogue and action are well balanced. The narrative, clear and straightforward. It's all there in **Redemption, Kansas**, the first in the **Redemption** series.

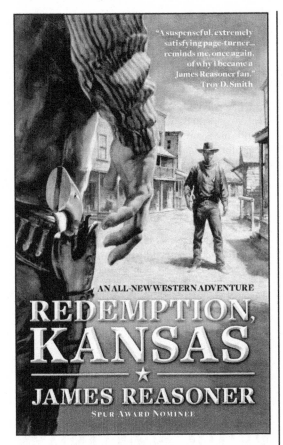

"A suspenseful, extremely satisfying page-turner... reminds me, once again, of why I became a James Reasoner fan."
Troy D. Smith

AN ALL-NEW WESTERN ADVENTURE

REDEMPTION, KANSAS

★

JAMES REASONER
SPUR AWARD NOMINEE

It was my pleasure to discover the title on a rack at my local HyVee grocery store. Unlike so much of what I read, I didn't learn about this title on the web before seeing it for sale. Instead, I just happened upon it – just like in the old days. A surprise that brought back one of the great joys of buying physical books in a pre-Internet world.

After an exceptionally hard week at work, I read the book in three sittings before bed. The house was quiet, the weather was good, and Reasoner's slick prose reminded me why reading is my favourite pastime.

None of that would matter though if the story, a traditional western, didn't rise above the typical formula. It does, because Reasoner puts familiar characters into new, uniquely dangerous, and suspense filled situations.

Injured Texan Bill Harvey, laid up in a Kansas town controlled by back-shooters Marshal Frank Porter and Deputy Zach Norris, is a stranger in a strange land. Not only did I immediately identify with Harvey, I also recognized the sheer improbability of his winning the day.

To paraphrase Lester Dent's guidelines for pulp fiction – Reasoner piles the trouble on Bill – and

just when you think he's had enough, another load comes down. It's great stuff that carried me through to a satisfying conclusion. Highly recommended.

Richard Prosch

★ ★ ★ ★ ★

NOT A HOPE IN HELL
Hank J Kirby (Keith Hetherington)
2012
"A hero that doesn't come out of gunfights and fistfights unscathed..."

Hank J Kirby is one of the pseudonyms used by Keith Hetherington, a writer who has fast become one of my favourite western authors. Each book of his I've read has left me eagerly waiting for his next and this story continues that desire.

Not a Hope in Hell is filled with great characters and in Clay Emory has a hero that doesn't come out of gunfights and fistfights unscathed, in fact for most of the book, Emory is walking wounded.

The plot at first seems fairly straightforward but it isn't long before there are questions that need answers and then the story moves through a couple of twists and turns and the reader is left wondering just which side of the law Emory now works on. Of course, everything is eventually explained and resolved in a spectacular gunfight.

I've been a bit vague with the plot on purpose so as not to give anything away and spoil the storyline for those intending to read this book. I'll finish by saying if you have yet to try any of Keith Hetherington's work then this could well be the perfect place to start.

Steve Myall

★ ★ ★ ★ ★

JAKE MORAN: DEAD MAN'S CROSSING
Robert Broomall
2012

"Creates a great sense of the dangers the desert crossing presents ..."

I like the idea that author Robert Broomall decided to make lead Jake Moran a reluctant hero, a man whose reputation has been built up by others when in reality he didn't do anything heroic, in fact fears facing an enemy and calls himself a coward. Circumstances see Jake having to stand-up for himself and chance sees that heroic reputation grow.

In this case a lengthy desert crossing battling thirst, cholera, and Comanche raids. Broomall creates a great sense of the dangers the desert crossing presents. I really felt the heat along with his characters and found myself in need of water too. As the wagon train is reduced in size due to loss of animals and people, I soon began to wonder how many, if any, would reach safety.

Including disease as one of the threats, one they can't see coming, adds an extra element to the story that plays on their minds, filling them with dread, urging them on to escape the desert whilst promising doom as the hopelessness of their quest takes hold.

There's lots of action as Moran must lead the emigrants in defending themselves against the Comanches. The fights are savage and tense. If that isn't enough Moran is constantly looking over his shoulder at the ex-leader of the train, and his men, as they would like nothing better than to see him dead. As the dangers of the trail take their toll these hatreds must be put on hold as all must pull together if any of them are to survive.

The book builds extremely well to the final confrontation that sees the last few travellers trapped, out of water and ammunition, surrounded by Comanches.

Steve Myall

★ ★ ★ ★ ☆

TOWN TAMERS
David Robbins
2013

"Displays a talent for making a wildly over-the-top adventure seem perfectly logical..."

This novel opens with Asa Delaware, well-known town tamer, about to take on his latest project. Ludlow, Texas is being run by a group of rowdy and violent cowhands, but the town has hired Asa and his sawed-off shotgun to 'resolve' the problem. Together with his son, a poetry loving strategic thinker, and his daughter, a danger loving crack-shot, they rapidly 'fix' the problem, leaving no baddie alive. There is enough action and well-written gunplay here to satisfactorily fill most standard western novels, but all this comprises only the first third of the book.

The bulk of the novel is taken with the trio's operations in the fictional town of Ordville, Colorado, having been hired by a victim instead of the town council. This is a different situation than they've faced before. No violent power-wielding thugs or shoot-outs in the streets here, but rather a peaceful, and amazingly prosperous town that the citizens love. Digging deeper though, Asa discovers a hidden puppet master who controls the town's wealth and the local law, and has anybody who gets in his way brutally beaten or killed. Worse, the three town tamers would have no protection from authorities to cover for their typically lethal methods. What unfolds is a masterful display of strategy, cunning and unfolding tension.

Asa Delaware is a fascinating character and the author does an excellent job of balancing the bits and pieces of his backstory and characterization with edge-of-your-seat action. Robbins displays a talent for making a wildly over-the-top adventure seem perfectly logical and for keeping the reader completely engaged from the first chapter through the last. It's no surprise that this book rests easily in the high-quality pantheon of David Robbin's portfolio.

Benjamin Thomas

★ ★ ★ ★ ★

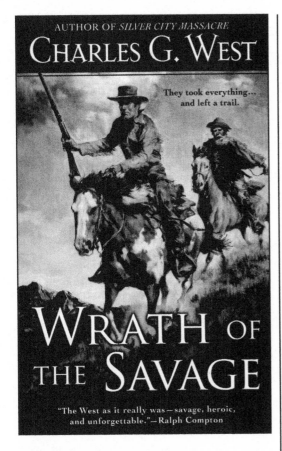

AUTHOR OF *SILVER CITY MASSACRE*

CHARLES G. WEST

They took everything...
and left a trail.

WRATH OF THE SAVAGE

"The West as it really was—savage, heroic, and unforgettable."—Ralph Compton

WRATH OF THE SAVAGE
Charles G West
2014

"Thoughts of suicide, terror at every shadow, and the joy of hope..."

Charles G West paints his landscapes with such vivid descriptive prose that you'll find yourself right there with this book's heroes, Hollister and Coldiron. You'll share their despair at finding two missing women believed kidnapped by a vicious band of Blackfeet Indians in such a vast land. The hunt is frustrating and slow but eventually the clues to their whereabouts begin to reveal the trail they must follow, and in doing so the two men will become hunted themselves.

There is plenty of action scenes within this story but it's more the study of emotions and how people deal with the feelings of anger, hate, despair, fear and elation that comes across so well. Witness thoughts of suicide, terror at every shadow, and the joy of hope of a new life that makes this book such a satisfying read.

Charles G West has a large back catalogue and many of these books sit on my shelves and after

reading this one I've realised that I've read far too few of them and must rectify this as soon as possible.

Steve Myall

SHADOW OF THE HAWK
Ron Honthaner
2015

"How easily this story paints visual imagery in the mind-eye..."

Ron Honthaner is a film and TV veteran whose first script for **Gunsmoke** landed him a job on the series, going on to write other scripts for the show, then working as post-production supervisor and later, associate producer. He was the recipient of two Cowboy Hall of Fame awards for his work on the **Gunsmoke** production team.

The first half of this fast-moving tale includes many flashback sequences to explain the relationship between the three main characters, although much of the emphasis is on McCloskey's life working on flatboats and steamboats. Most of the books other characters have their backstories explained too as a group of very different people find themselves riding in a posse.

Once McCloskey becomes the target of the posse after a bloody and vicious rage driven rampage then the emotional side of hunting a friend becomes a major issue of the story and you can never be sure which way the tale will go next when it comes to who will kill who if the opportunity arises and how much the bond of friendship will dictate the state of play.

Honthaner's writing is a pure joy to read and his background in writing for TV is very evident in how easily this story paints visual imagery in the mind-eye. Character development is excellent and the action scenes brutal and graphic. What happens to McCloskey to make him go on a killing spree comes as a complete surprise. After that the story is a straight chase tale that may not end how you think it will.

Steve Myall

THE LONESOME DOVE SAGA

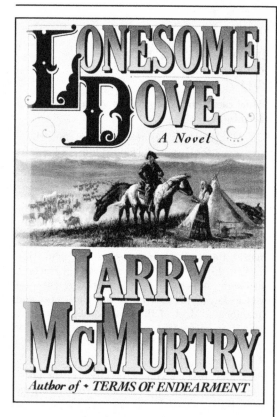

"MATILDA JANE ROBERTS was naked as the air. Known throughout south Texas as the Great Western, she came walking up from the muddy Rio Grande holding a big snapping turtle by the tail. Matilda was almost as large as the skinny Mexican mustang Gus McCrea and Woodrow Call were trying to saddle-break. Call had the mare by the ears, waiting for Gus to pitch the saddle on her narrow back, but the pitch was slow in coming. When Call glanced towards the river and saw the Great Western in all her plump nakedness he knew why: young Gus McCrea was by nature distractible; the sight of a naked, two-hundred-pound whore carrying a full-grown snapping turtle had captured his complete attention."

That opening sequence from Larry McMurtry's **Dead Man's Walk**, chronologically the first book in the **Lonesome Dove** saga, gives us our first glance of Gus and Call, the characters readers would fall so madly in love with. Only it doesn't – actually our first look at the characters was courtesy of 1985's **Lonesome Dove**. By this

point Gus and Call were a pair of down on their heels aging cowboys, an entire life, thus far untold, behind them. The events depicted in **Dead Man's Walk** took place many years earlier and offered eager readers the chance to live the events that shaped many of the beloved characters that make up the remarkable **Lonesome Dove** saga. The first published book was the Pulitzer Prize winning **Lonesome Dove**, and this was followed in 1993 by the **Streets of Laredo** which was a true sequel and told of Woodrow Call's twilight years. That was meant to be an end to the story, but readers couldn't get enough of McMurtry's vivid creation. And bowing to the public demand, and perhaps driven by the needs of his characters, the author rounded out the saga of Woodrow and Call by giving us two prequel novels with **Dead Man's Walk** (1995) and **Comanche Moon** (1997).

If we take the books in chronological order, and I would recommend new readers do so, then the sequence is **Dead Man's Walk**, **Comanche Moon**, **Lonesome Dove** and **Streets of Laredo**.

Opening in 1842 and set in the Republic of Texas, **Dead Man's Walk** presents us to a young Gus and Call with both men joining the Texas Rangers; rashly signing on with the prospect of seeking adventure in West Texas. Although a lot of the characters that skirt the two protagonists are stock B-western – the prostitute with a heart of gold, the mournful black cook, the wily old mountain man – they are all built upon so that in the author's skilled hands they become real and no less compelling that Gus and Call themselves. The story although first and foremost an enthralling western adventure is as much a character study, as anything else and the world building that McMurtry has engineered here is nothing short of spellbinding.

It's a dark story with much cruelty played out within the pages, but none of this seems gratuitous nor forced. There are scalpings, mutilations and death by disease, and it is all presented in a raw matter-of-fact way. It's very much rough and ready though the author's writing is anything but.

The story told here becomes very real within the mind of the reader. We witness the first time Gus and Call meet the Comanche war chief Buffalo Hump, the character who had an almost mythical feel in **Lonesome Dove**. Later, our heroes witness the cruelty of the Apaches and finally the might of the Mexican Army. Towards the end of the book we are introduced to a series of interesting characters who elevate this novel to a work of true beauty, when we meet several English prisoners stuck in an El Paso leper colony. It is here that the book becomes particularly mesmerising and to my mind elevates it to one of the finest works ever written about the mythical West. And it is a mythical west, for all its realism, because although the author understands the real history of the period he also holds a love for the stories of the Wild West, and what he has done here is combine reality and myth to create a world that is truly unique in all of western fiction, a fantasy in many ways but that has a grounding in the banality of real life.

At the end of this novel Gus and Call have not yet become the hardened characters we first encountered in **Lonesome Dove**, but they have become wedded to the wild lands that will one day claim them.

Chronologically then, this brings us to **Comanche Moon** – when the novel opens, we find that Gus and Call are newly promoted captains of their ranger troop. This comes about when their superior, Inish Skull, a wonderfully eccentric Bostonian, goes off into the wilds in search of the notorious horse thief, Kicking Wolf, who has stolen his prize mount. Inish pursues the wily horse thief into Mexico where he is captured by the Mexican bandit, Ahumando.

Throughout the story the characters of Gus and Call are built upon, and the reader comes to fully understand them. On the surface of it they are complete opposites but the interplay between them is a joy to read and it is this aspect that really drives the novel. Their relationship with the Comanche, Buffalo Hump, is further built upon when he leads a raid into Austin while the rangers are away searching for Inish Skull. Though Buffalo Hump is no stock character and he is drawn as carefully as anyone in the book; we learn of his deteriorating relationship with his son, Blue Duck, and of how both men struggle to fulfil a perceived destiny. Blue Duck is used almost as a metaphor for the end of a way of life and we witness the struggles of a man uninterested in tribal customs and geared towards stepping out from his father's shadow by wiping the pestilence of the white man from the land.

Again, it is a dark book with much violence and cruelty but perversely it is the beauty of the story that remains after the final page is turned. Which, of course brings us to ground zero and that is **Lonesome Dove**, the first book written but actually the third book in this remarkable tetralogy. And it is no exaggeration to claim that this is quite likely the grandest novel ever written about the last days of the American West.

It is a bona fide masterpiece. There is no doubt about that. Named for the fictional small town of Lonesome Dove and focusing on a cattle drive to Montana, the novel on the surface seems to be about new horizons, but the engine that drives the story is very much a lament for times soon to vanish forever. Gus and Call are both facing old age at the start of the novel but neither of them seems to want to acknowledge this. Call is hard working, brutal and straight to the point while Gus is quite happy to idly sit around, a jug at his side and watch the days go by. A little whoring, a lot of drinking and telling tall tales of his glorious past is the Gus way, while by contrast Call sees these activities as wasteful and he is determined to carve out a future worth living. The town of Lonesome Dove is also on its last legs, a decaying artefact rotting in the dustbowl and it becomes as much a character in this book as Gus, Call and all the truly wonderful supporting characters.

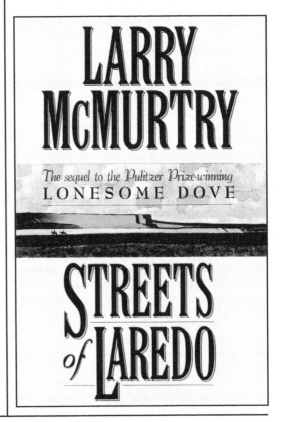

What is remarkable about this book is that it is a massive tome, more than 900 pages and yet it reads with the vibrancy of a much shorter book. It contains all of the standard western tropes but at the heart of the work there are the characters, flesh and blood creations that live and breathe, eat and shit, love and cry, hope and dream. The reader really does come to know these characters. Remember this was actually the first book in the **Dove** cycle to be published and one imagines the publisher having many sleepless nights, because there simply weren't any other books like it on the market. Westerns rarely stretched to much more than 200 pages and yet here was a doorstop of a book that was no doubt a western, a horse opera, an oater. This was a genre that was wrongly considered by most in the industry to be disposable, a harmless distraction that could never be elevated to true art and yet **Lonesome Dove** showed those prejudices for the horseshit they were. **Lonesome Dove** is a work of art, a masterpiece, perhaps the pinnacle of the genre.

Following the success of **Lonesome Dove**, McMurtry delivered a sequel (it would still be some years before he rounded out his remarkable series with the prequel novels) in **The Streets of Laredo**. And this book is without doubt the darkest, most elegiac part of the entire series. It suffers from the fact that the central pairing of Gus and Call are no more, Gus having died in the previous novel but at the same time it takes many strengths from refusing to flinch from the sheer depravity of the life that Woodrow Call lives.

Call, now an old man, makes his living as a bounty hunter and he finds himself called upon by the head of a railroad to hunt down the young outlaw Joey Garza, a kind of Billy the Kid figure. This is a McMurtry novel and there is no romance to the baby faced killer, but instead a brutal story of yet another life ruined by a harsh land. Call is joined on his quest by a railroad accountant from Brooklyn and although this pairing provides much of the beloved banter the series has become known for, this accountant really doesn't fill the very big boots left by Gus. Call also enlists old friend Pea-Eye Parker, a character who played a pivotal part in **Lonesome Dove**, and is now married to Lorena, the whore whom Gus spent many of his years lusting after. Perhaps I should give a nod here to McMurtry's female characters who are all as finely and realistically drawn as the men. Long before the woke generation waved their tedious rattles, the western genre was presenting women in a way that was far from patronising and showing that they too were every bit the equal of the men who

shaped the country. Behind every great man is a great woman, indeed.

Along the way Call finishes off Mox Mox, a truly despicable character whose speciality is burning victims alive for his own gratification, but with his arthritic fingers, failing eyesight and general malaise Call is no match for the youthful Joey Gazza. If **Lonesome Dove** was a novel that warmed the heart, then **Streets of Laredo** not only breaks it, but tramples it in the dirt afterwards.

Taken as a whole the **Lonesome Dove** saga is a remarkable feat of storytelling genius, and the only thing I can really liken it to is Tolkien's **Lord of the Rings** and whilst these works may seem a million miles apart they have many similarities, they both create entire worlds that are alien and yet at the same time familiar, they both take myths and twist them until they become believable and almost commonplace and they both give us characters that tower over their respective genres. There is more than that though and whilst Tolkien's Dark Lord seems a constant presence over Middle Earth, the Comanche Buffalo Hump has the same hold on McMurtry's landscape. I have no doubt that here McMurtry has created the western version of the epic fantasy. It's a sweeping saga of the 19th century that takes the mythology of the west and makes it seem very real indeed. Indeed, **Lonesome Dove** may be the one western to rule them all.

The **Lonesome Dove** series is something that every western reader needs to be familiar with.

Gary M Dobbs AKA Jack Martin

THE LONESOME DOVE SAGA

Dead Man's Walk (1995)

Comanche Moon (1997)

Lonesome Dove (1985)

Streets of Laredo (1993)

CONTRIBUTORS

Paul Bishop is a recognized expert in the area of western action paperback original novels and their cover art, Paul Bishop is the author of fifteen novels and has written and edited three western reference works—**52 Weeks 52 Westerns**, **52 Weeks 52 Western Movies**, and **52 Weeks 52 Western Television Shows**. He is a thirty-five year veteran of the Los Angeles Police Department, with over twenty-five years' experience in the investigation of sex crimes. Along with his writing, he is currently the acquisitions editor for Wolfpack publishing, and also conducts law enforcement related seminars for city, state, and private agencies. He has twice been honoured as LAPD's Detective of the Year.

Jim O'Brien's first western experience was seeing **The Virginian** on TV – and being too scared to carry on watching. Not an auspicious beginning for a future **Hot Lead** contributor. Things improved when his kind grandmother accidentally gifted her twelve-year old grandson a copy of **Herne the Hunter 5: Apache Squaw**. He was hooked. Soon though westerns had to shoot it out for space on Jim's shelves with NEL nasties and Wehrmacht pulps. Comics too – hence some of his odder choices here. Much more recently he discovered Elmore Leonard and reckons the author the very best western writer there's been.

Jules Burt has been a collector of vintage paperbacks, amongst other things, for over thirty years. He has written for many magazines and books in that time but now concentrates his efforts mainly on YouTube where he shares his many collections and passions with a wider audience through his videos. Check out Jules' channel on YouTube at 'Jules Burt - Collections and Unboxings', Twitter @julesburt Instagram @penguinbookaday

Steve Carroll started reading very age-inappropriate books in elementary school and by the time he was 12 could be found with a men's adventure paperback in his possession at all times and in every circumstance, usually reading 2-3 per week. Years have passed but these habits have remained. Steve now pastors a church, works in marketing and graphic design, and is deep into writing his first novel, a supernatural western. Steve is the father of 2 girls and lives with his wife, 2 cats, and a hyperactive dog in a small town outside of Atlanta, GA where he enjoys being a grandfather even more than reading.

Eric Compton lives in the most haunted city in the world, St. Augustine, Florida with his wife and two daughters. He currently serves as the more handsome half of the PaperbackWarrior.com team, writing daily reviews, features and columns on vintage fiction and crime-noir. Eric also co-hosts the Paperback Warrior podcast with colleague Tom Simon. Weekly, the duo plunge into the wild, wacky and entertaining world of men's action-adventure fiction.

Andreas Decker was born in Germany and his interest in genre fiction started early. What we today call pulps was available at every corner back then in its translated incarnations, and reading was a natural pastime for him. Horror, SF, Western, the more the better. Along the way he started to write SF reviews, which in turn led to some translating. Since the mid-nineties after other professions like the book-trade and a decade in health-care services he works as a literary translator, doing mostly Fantasy and YA, and is an occasional writer.

Chuck Dixon is the most prolific scripter in the history of comic books with well over 40,000 pages of comics in publication. His work on both **Batman** and the **Punisher** are considered seminal to those franchises. He also co-created the iconic Batman villain Bane. Characters he's created for both DC and Marvel have appeared repeatedly in movies, television, and games. He remains a major player in the growing world of independent comics with dozens of new titles produced in recent years. He continues to write entries for his series of action novels, Bad Times and Levon Cade.

Michael Hauss has written for numerous publications, including, **Weng's Chop**, **Monster!**, **Exploitation Retrospect**, **Grindhouse Purgatory** and **We Belong Dead**. He has also contributed to the books' **70s Monster Memories**, **Unsung Horrors**, and **Son of Unsung Horrors**. Author of two books on Italian westerns called Spaghetti **Westerns!: Volume One** and **Spaghetti Westerns!: Volume Two**. Editor of the soon to be released **Spaghetti Western Digest**!

Howard Andrew Jones is the author of the Ring-Sworn heroic fantasy trilogy from St. Martin's, starting with **For the Killing of Kings**, the critically acclaimed Arabian fantasy series starring Dabir and Asim, and four **Pathfinder** novels. He's the editor of the print magazine **Tales From the Magician's Skull**, among other things, and can be found lurking at

SIX GUN JUSTICE
PODCAST

WITH PAUL BISHOP AND RICHARD PROSCH

www.sixgunjustice.com

sponsored by WOLFPACK PUBLISHING
— EST 2013 —

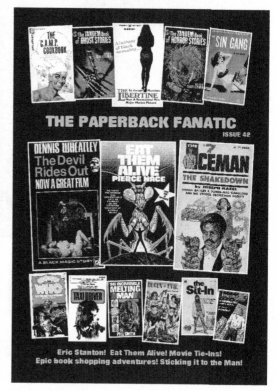

www.howardandrewjones.com, where he blogs about writing craft, gaming, fantasy and adventure fiction, and assorted nerdery.

Dave Karlen was raised by an overbearing mother and two mean sisters, this Cinderfella was the original Texas couch potato. Little Dave, also known as the albino kid, should have become an infamous serial killer, but he had the dream of becoming a professional. Afraid of girls and small dogs, the kid with prescription shoes had only one vice, living out his overprotected youth reading Westerns! As the spud grew, so did his dreams, but the only range he ever rode was a Hotpoint. Many years later discovering gold in his backyard, he applied for both Ringling Brothers Clown College and Eastern Michigan Law School. Unfortunately for us, the acceptance letter from law school came first. Now representing clowns full time in night court, "the man with no game", still dreams of action and adventure on the high plains while composing briefs on his couch in his underwear.

Scott Kime was on a fishing trip with his father and grandfather in Northern Minnesota in the early 80's and needed something to pass the time at night. There was a stack of **Carter Brown** mysteries that was read. After back in civilization, the author was sought out but another author was discovered by the name of **Nick Carter**. Through the years numerous authors and genres were read and enjoyed. Genres from the 50's, 60's, 70's and 80'. Westerns, Mysteries, and Adventures. Currently lives in Denver Colorado.

Ed McBride's vintage paperback book reviews can be found at Mostly Old Books and Rust - https://www.mostlyoldbooks.com. He is also the moderator of the American Westerns group on Goodreads.

Justin Marriott made his first fanzine at the age of 12 and four decades later is still going strong. He hated westerns as a callow youth, so is still confused about how this is the fourth edition of **Hot Lead** he has published. He self-publishes a number of fanzines devoted to collecting and reading vintage paperbacks, including **The Paperback Fanatic**, **The Sleazy Reader**, **Pulp Horror**, **Men of Violence**, **Monster Maniacs**, **Hot Lead** and the forthcoming **The Doomsday Warrior**. All available through Amazon. He pin-points his parents confiscating a Hell's Angels book from him at the age of 9 as the reason for his lifelong obsession with hoarding paperbacks. He is very proud to be able to publish such a super array of voices in this **Hot Leads All Review Special** and hopes it will become a yearly event.

Steve Myall is from the U.K. and read his first western before his age was recorded in double figures. Not long after this he began reading and collecting the books put out by the Piccadilly Cowboys. This led to him becoming an avid collector and he now owns thousands of western books, mainly paperbacks that form series. Steve also runs the popular blog Western Fiction Review, which is now in its thirteenth year. As well as book reviews you can find author and cover artist interviews there. You can find the blog here: http://westernfictionreview.blogspot.com/

Sean Nodland is a 24-year-old librarian from Southern Maryland who got his start into adult westerns and men's adventure fiction in high school after finding paperback sequels to Dollars films, notably the entry A Coffin Full of Dollars by Joe Millard. In looking up spaghetti western style books he inevitably came across the Edge series and other Piccadilly Cowboy books and with that he was hooked. Other than westerns and MA fiction, he enjoys film, history, and strategy games when he's not working or traveling with his wife.

Roy Nugen is a writer, award-winning filmmaker, a brazen book collector, actor and professional chef with a background in law enforcement and security work. He is a co-owner of America's Front Porch Film Co. whose films have played all over the United States and which can be found @afpfilms on Facebook, Instagram, Twitter and YouTube. Also, he chronicles his literary acquisitions as royiscool86 on Instagram and via book reviews on his blog Bloody, Spicy, Books.

John Peel was born in England, but brought up in the West of the imagination - TV, movies and lots and lots of books. He has since become a writer himself, with over 100 novels to his credit. Curiously enough, none has been a Western.

Jeff Popple's parents were avid readers of popular fiction and he was raised on westerns as a child. The first adult novel he can remember reading was Frank Castle's **Blood Moon**, followed by Louis L'Amour's **Last Stand at Papago Wells** and a pile of other western titles. He is also a huge fan of western movies, with the original **Stagecoach** and **The Wild Bunch** being his favourites. Nowadays Jeff mainly reviews crime novels and thrillers for a variety of publications, but has still retained his fondness for westerns. His reviews can be seen at his blog: murdermayhemandlongdogs.com.

Scott Ranalli was born 1962 in Chicago, moved to San Antonio at age 10 and been in Texas ever since (currently Houston). It all started with **Doc Savage**. The next step was when he discovered flea markets and all their riches: **Executioner**, **Destroyer**, **Butcher**, **Death Merchant**, **Sherlock Holmes**, **The Shadow**, **Spider**, **Avenger**, **G-8**, **Conan**, **Tarzan** and more. 45 years later, Pulp Heroes still top his list, along with PI mysteries, police procedurals, spy, SF, fantasy, and horror. Don't get him started on the sub-genres!! Westerns are a new item on his menu.

S. Clayton Rhodes is the Executive Director of a non-profit organization which assists citizens with developmental disabilities and an author. With over a dozen published short stories in the horror, sci-fi, adventure, and fantasy genres to his credit, his largest published work is (coincidentally enough) a western of sorts, **The Wiz of the West**. He makes his home in Marietta, Ohio with his wife, daughter, and three cats of questionable morals. For more information on some of his in-print works, please see his Amazon page: https://smile.amazon.com/S-Clayton-Rhodes/e/B0045773D6/ref=dp_byline_cont_book_2

Dan Shanahan hails from the mystical island of Ireland, and spent the majority of his twenties living and working in Japan. In this strange land, he had only his collection of men's adventure paperbacks for company. Now back in his ancestral home, he lives in constant fear that one or more ninjas may have followed him home and are now secretly sharing his house with him.

Benjamin Thomas is a retired US Air Force medic and author of several western short stories as well as an historical science fiction novel, the first in a series. His short story, "Clear Creek Bounty" has recently been selected as a contest winner and will be appearing in an upcoming western fiction anthology. He has been a lifelong voracious reader and longtime respected reviewer on both Goodreads and Amazon. A native of New Mexico, Benjamin has always been a "westerner" at heart and currently makes his home with his family in Colorado Springs at the foot of Pikes Peak.

Made in the USA
Monee, IL
04 August 2020